Foundations of Indian Ethics

With Special Reference to *Manu Smṛti*, *Jaimini Sūtras* and *Bhagavad-Gīta*

Foundations of Indian Ethics

With Special Reference to

Manu Smṛti, Jaimini Sūtras

and *Bhagavad-Gīta*

ILLA RAVI

Kaveri Books

New Delhi-110002

ISBN: 978-81-7479-047-7

Edition 2021

Published by

Kaveri Books

4832/24, Ansari Road,

New Delhi-110002 (India)

Tel: 011-23288140, 47072321

E-mail : info@kaveribooks.com

kaveribooks@gmail.com

Web : www.kaveribooks.com

Typeset at: Delta Book World, Delhi.

PRINTED IN INDIA

To My Father and First Preceptor

Sri Illa Narasimha Rao

Acknowledgements

Gurubhyōnamaḥ. I express my great sense of gratitude to my Research Supervisor, Professor A. Ramamurthy, without whose able guidance and kind help this work could not have taken shape.

I cordially thank Professor Amitabh Dasgupta, Head, Department of Philosophy, for his constant encouragement and timely help. He has been a great source of inspiration.

I owe a lot to Dr. S.G. Kulkarni who exercised great influence on my ways of thinking and analysis. He decisively moulded my career as a student, as a research scholar and as a teacher.

I am grateful to Professor Suresh Chandra who taught me how to raise questions and present arguments. I am proud to be his student.

I am extremely thankful to my teachers late Prof. Chakravarthy, Dr. Vidya Subrahmanyam, Dr. R.C. Pradhan and Dr. Chinmoy Goswamy who, with their great teaching abilities, helped me in understanding various philosophical systems in detail.

I sincerely thank Dr. Raghu Rama Raju and Dr. K.S. Prasad who never let me down when ever I sought their help. I thank Dr. Varalakshmi and Anand Wazalvar for their concern.

I cordially thank the University Grants Commission for the award of Junior Research Fellowship and Senior Research Fellowship.

I am very much thankful to our departmental office staff Mr. Murthy, Ms. Bhargavi and Mr. Sattaiah for all their help.

I also thank Prof. Haragopal, and Prof. Reddanna for their support.

I am indebted to my senior colleague Sri I. Parthasarathi for those long academic discussions and valuable insights. He helped me in many ways and exerted great pressure to complete my work. I am also grateful to Sri D.V.S. Murthy, Sri L. Subha Prasad for their support. I am thankful to Sri V. Joshi, Dr. Chand Basha, Sri N. Lakshmana Rao, Sri E. Pratapa Reddy and others who are of great help.

I have great regard for Sri K.G.C. Hari Vittal, Regional Joint Director, Department of Higher Education, who helped me in pursuing my academic interests.

I am obliged to Sri V. Natarajeswara Rao, Principal, S.R.R. & C.V.R. Govt. College, Vijayawada, for his constant encouragement and help in completing my research work.

I thank my friendly students Narendra, Arava Ramesh and Linguistics Sreenu.

I can not forget my friends in the Department: Hussain, Radha, Anjoom, Kesva Kumar, Tomy, Shyama Sundari, Aseema, Koshy, Reddayya, T.Sreenivas, Ananda Sagar, Naidu, Katta Ravi, Moid, Anil and others. They helped me in many ways. I thank them for their affection.

I love my friends: kow M.D., Bhas, Lambadi, Lambu, Ramesh, Balaram, Kid, Som, Bheri, Boulder, Dr. J., Softy,

Babai, Babu, Krupa, Laddu Ramesh, Arul, Santosh, Brahmam, Nalla Sinu and others who made my stay in the hostel pleasant and funfilled.

My special thanks to Dad Charles, Pulihora Bava, Matthew Anna, K.V.N. Raju for their boundless love.

My friend Harsha, Soft-ware professional, deserves my immence gratitude for his help in correcting the thesis. I thank Thota Seshagiri for not disturbing me while I am Working.

I am grateful to my pals Muralidhara Reddy and Rama Krishna for their great help in getting the print outs. I can not forget their timely help.

Thanks to my loving friend Srinivas, who carried out the tidious job of typing and correcting the thesis even at odd times. His help is of great significance in completing this thesis work.

I have no words to express my gratitude to Vijay, Bhatti and Aunt Prabhavathi who gave a new direction to my life.

I am so lucky to have such lovely present who stand behind me in all my endeavours. I thank God for this peerless boon. My brothers Chinnari and Kumar, and my sister Lakshmi kept me in comfort throughout. Their love for me makes my place lovely.

The innocent smiles of my kids Rachana and Srujana brought me out of depressing moments many a time. Kisses to their soothing tender hands.

Last but not the least, my wife Uma deserves a great share in all my afforts. I thank her for rejunevating love.

Dr. Illa Ravi

Contents

1

Introduction

The object of the study is to analyse some of the foundational concepts of Indian ethics, in their evolution, with special reference to *Manu Smṛti, Jaimini Sūtras* and *Bhagavad-Gīta*. Before further explanation of the object, it is incumbent on us to counter an important view which cuts at the root of our objective. It is concerning the very possibility of Indian ethics. Our object i.e., to examine the foundations of Indian ethics presupposes that there is something ostensively called Indian ethics. However, there are some western scholars who seriously doubt whether there is anything worth named 'ethics' in Indian thought. According to them, there is a conspicuous absence of systematic ethical theory in Indian philosophy. They claim that Indian thought itself is non-moral in the sense that its essential features are not congenial to the development of a proper ethical system. This claim is not altogether groundless. However, on a closer examination, we find that the claim is infested with a considerable degree of astigmatism concerning the nature of Indian philosophy.

The so called ethical lacuna is often attributed to the very nature of Indian modes of thinking. Critics of Indian thought claim that Indian speculations are non-moral, and sometimes anti-moral, in character. To quote a few, Professor A.B. Keith observes that "... it is beyond possibility of doubt in India from the first philosophy is intellectual, not moral, in interest and outlook".[1] Karl Potter says that "... for better or worse, the ultimate value recognized by classical Hinduism in its most sophisticated sources is not morality but freedom, not rational self-control in the interests of the community's welfare but complete control over one's own environment..."[2] According to Max Weber, "the social theory of Hinduism, however, furnished no principles for ethical universalism which would raise general demands for life in the world".[3] The above views of the celebrated western scholars pertain to the general features of Indian thought which, according to them, defy the possibility of systematic ethics.

Following the Indian philosophical tradition, let us take up the case of the *Pūrvapakṣin* (the opponent) first. Indian ethics is impossible because Indian thought in general is extremely spiritualistic. *Mokṣa* or absolute liberation, the ultimate ideal in all Indian systems, is a spiritualistic ideal which seeks freedom from the world. It suggests not only withdrawal from the world but also denies substantial reality to the world. Hence, Indian thought in general is world-denying. Further, human life is viewed as a suffering and this view lead to pessimistic attitude towards the material world. In India the place of morality is occupied by ritualism or atleast Indian moral practices are thoroughly ritualistic.

Further, reason as such is denied a place in ethical inquiries. The law-books which decisively moulded the Indian moral conscience refuse to accept reason as a source of morality. The Vedas are accepted by all the systems as manuals for ethical conduct from which the law-books derive their authority. Again, the morality is extremely individualistic and Indian philosophy hardly recognizes, morality as a social value. Mokṣa is an individualistic ideal which does not suggest any social appeal. There are no universal principles of morality with wider application except the individualistic morality with a limited field of moral exertion. Lastly, morality is not viewed as independent of religion and metaphysics and no Indian thinker has attempted to assert his moral ideas independent of his metaphysics or religion. Hence, ethics has not acquired an independent character. The *Pūrvapakṣin* argues that the above mentioned grounds are more than enough to show that there cannot be Indian ethics in the real sense of the word.

On the face of it, the above argument brings out some of the important features of Indian thought, and these features seem to resist the development of systematic ethics. However, the argument is unwarranted for it involves extreme generalisation of Indian philosophy and thus neglects its rich variety and diversity. The reasons adduced by the *Pūrvapakṣin* do not apply to all the systems of Indian thought, but each criticism applies to a specific system or a limited number of systems. For example, extreme spiritualism and denial of the material world cannot be shown as the general characteristic of Indian philosophy, because majority of Indian systems are in fact materialistic or realistic.

Except Advaita Vēdānta and Yogāchāra Buddhism, all the Indian philosophical schools accept reality of the material world. Carvaka theory of material elements *(Bhūtavāda)*, Sāmkhya theory of primordial matter *(Pradhānavāda)*, atomism *(Aṇuvāda)* of Nyaya, Jaina theory of material substance *(Puḍgala* or *Ajīva)* are some of the most impressive alternatives for explaining the physical world. Vaiśeṣikas dedicate themselves chiefly to explaining the physical manifestations in terms of material categories *(Viśeṣa)*. The orthodox Mīmāmsakas ardently argue for the reality of the material world and Kumarila Bhatta advances some of the strongest anti-idealistic arguments in his *Ślokavārttika*. Sautrantika Buddhists expressly admit the reality of the world. Even the Advaintins cannot right away make the so palpable empirical reality wither away. So, they ascribe some pragmatic truth *(Vyāvahārikasatya)* to it. How consistent the theory of two realities i.e., *Pāramārthika* and *Vyāvahārika* is another issue.

It is true that all the Indian systems except Carvaka and Buddhism accept the reality of soul or spirit. But a simple acceptance of soul does not make them thorough-going idealists. So, the attribution of extreme idealism as a general character to the Indian thought as such involves the fallacies of over simplification and unwarranted generalization.

Again, Advaita Vēdānta, Sāmkhya and Buddhism portray human life as a fact of suffering. The pessimism is more than apparent. However, this pessimism is not common to all the systems. Indian philosophy in general does not undermine the value of worldly life. Human life is no where said to be an evil in itself. Rather, it is man and man alone can strive for better values and can attain freedom. Even the so called pessimistic schools are not altogether pessimistic, as liberation from suffering is always considered as teleologically certain and as potentially achievable. Again, the apparent pessimism did not deny ethical possibilities, but emphasized on them as necessary preconditions for freedom.

It is Buddhism which preached that liberation is not individual but collective. Through its concept of *Mahākaruṇa* or universal compassion, it showed that liberation of the other people as a necessary condition for one's own freedom. Again, Advaita Vēdānta, irrespective of its mysticism and orthodoxy, aims at liberation of all human beings and spread the message of freedom throughout the country. This is vouched by the fact that even the people in remote parts of the country are aware of *Mokṣa* as the final liberation. To speak more positively, Buddhism and Advaita constructively insist on the evil of excessive indulgence in material pleasures. In fact this is a positive ground for moral consciousness because strict hedonism or clinging on to worldly pleasures mars or limits the moral vision of an individual. Moral vision has to be expanded beyond the material interests, and only such a vision can be truly human.

Again the ritualistic morality seems to be an impediment in the development of theoretical ethics independent of religion. The ritualism bears a strong mark of religious fervour and sometimes is devoid of any moral justification. This is true to an extent as most of the moral activity is intricately interwoven into collective religious practices. But if we pay a little more attention to go into the depth of ritualism, we find that it is not totally devoid of ethical prudency or rationale. The problem with most of the western scholars is that they limit themselves to a superficial understanding of the ritual, and therefore regard it as barren activity meant to serve the interests of priestly class and continuation of orthodoxy. It is true that priestly class plays an important role in promulgation of ritualism and is in turn materially benefited. This fact cannot be denied. However, this is not the end of the tunnel. An unprejudiced philosopher has a responsibility to dig into the sub layers of the crest of ritualism in order to estimate their moral worth. This is not to say that orthodoxy and ritualism are absolutely impeccable. The suggestion is only that they should not be disposed off as barren, without a proper examination.

As to the theism and its influence on the Indian way of ethical cognition, we cannot claim that theism had an overwhelming support from all systems. Most of the systems are not-theistic. Cārvaka, Sāmkhya, Mīmāmsa, original Nyāya-Viśeṣika, Buddhistic philosophy (contrary to the later religion) are certainly non-theistic. Theism was smacked into Nyāya mainly for non-ethical reasons. The primary objective in admitting the idea of god by the later Naiyayikas was to explain the primordial conjunction of atoms. The ethical views of Nyāya are least affected by this epigonal god in the system. Again, one can question - what is wrong with religion as far as the moral worth of a principle is concerned? A moral idea cannot be rejected outright because of its religious origin or justification. What one had to find out, on the other hand, is whether there is any rationale or ethical character in a precept in question beyond its reference to the authority of god.

This brings us to an important problem of the place of reason in ethical inquiry. Ethics as a branch of philosophy is certainly a rational discipline and it differs from sophistry precisely in its being so. Our *Pūrvapakṣin* may argue that Indian moral principles are more or less authoritarian in as much as they fall back on the Vēda or on idea of god for justification. He often shows the negative attitude of Indian law givers towards reason as a proof for his argument. He further shows how śabda or testimony, one of the valid sources of knowledge (*pramāṇa*), has come to mean the *Vēda* exclusively.

This argument of the *Pūrvapakṣin* has real significance concerning the evolution of Indian philosophy in general and ethics in particular. It is true, Manu's denial of reason as a source of morality had far-reaching impact or influence on the intellectual atmosphere in India. Manu's censure on application of reason to the Vēda or critical analysis of its doctrines curbed free thinking to a great extent. No philosopher, except Cārvākas, had ever attempted to condemn the vedic doctrines and the Cārvākas were treated as vulgar hedonists. Manu's distinction between āstika, and nāstika in terms of reverence for the *Vēda,* made the so called orthodox systems to express their veneration for the *Vēda,* even though it is not necessary for the coherence of their systems. Due to their superficial acceptance of the *Vēda*, Nyāya, Viśeṣika and Sāmkhya are considered as orthodox systems even though they oppose some of the prominent vedic doctrines. Their philosophy is hardly affected even if they give up acceptance of the *Vēda* as a *pramāṇa.* The acceptance of the Veda by some philosophical schools was, as Debi Prasad Chattopadhyaya puts it, a technique of *'evading censure'*.

On the other hand, those Indian systems were not really supporters of the vedic authority. Sāmkhya explicitly states that vedic rituals are fruitless concerning the ultimate emancipation. Nyāya ascribes the validity of the *Vēda* to the trustworthy character of its authors and thus denies its absolute authority. Buddhism and Jainism openly criticise the vedic orthodoxy and oppose its doctrines. Even Advaita, if not explicitly, treats the vedic rituals as irrelevant to the ultimate goal of liberation. The rituals are assigned a nominal value in as much as they are said to be serving the purpose of preparatory purification of mind to attain liberation. The real emancipation comes only through knowledge of the soul. Still Advaita half heartedly supports the vedic rituals only for the reason that the *Upaniṣads* are a part of the Vēda which enjoins those rituals.

Again, we find no system of Indian philosophy denying the validity of reason. Reason is said to be the light which guides the human activity as a whole. Except Cārvākas, who claim that reason is included in perception, all other systems accept reason as a distinct mode of cognition and accord to it its deserved place in their epistemologies. Even Advaita accepts it as an independent *pramāṇa* but says that the knowledge of the soul is not available to it. No system blindly accepts the vedic authority as given. Even Mīmāmsakas, whose fundamental interest was to establish absolute authority of the *Vēda* and through it the ritual practice, try to do so on rational grounds. Kumarila Bhatta, one of the gaints among Indian philosophers, puts forward astonishingly rational arguments in support of his thesis. Further, no system presupposes the Vedic authority in its treatment of moral reality. However, all the Indian systems including the heterodox systems like Buddhism and Jainism are thoroughly influenced by the vedic tradition. Getting influenced by a tradition does not make a system subservient to the tradition. We cannot say that Berkley is not a philosopher because his thought was thoroughly influenced by Christianity.

The above description of deep commitment of Indian systems to reason or inference and their nominal acceptance of the vedic anthoritarianism proves contrary to the argument that Indian ethics is not rational. Indian systems, which are rational, defend their ethical thought in the light of their epistemological commitment to reason and other *pramāṇas* rather than on the basis of external authority.

Even Manu, despite his explicit commitment to the authority of the Vēda, attempts to put his legal maxims on a rational footing. He tries to explain the efficacy of the vedic *yajña* in terms of its natural consequences rather than simply imposing it as given by the Vēda. Manu arranges his legal precepts within a comprehensive perspective or framework which is amazingly coherent. He presents his code with a proper metaphysical and epistemological frame work. Though he accepts idealism, he does not deny the reality of the world in favour of it. We shall see more of this in the fourth chapter of this work.

It may not be out of place here to say a few words concerning rationality in general and its place in ethics in particular. Most of the scholars, whenever they analyse a system, are prone to pass a quick judgement concerning its rationality. In most of the cases the idea of rationality, which they apply as a paradigm to the system in hand, is mostly a product of the modern scientific world-view. They think of rationality as a standard with which we can measure and judge whether a system is valid or not. If it falls short of the standard, it is superstitious and if it comes near to our standard, it is acceptable. Therefore when we look at any system, especially an ancient one, with this attitude, we make a fundamental mistake. We forget that rationality is a social product and that it depends for its validity on the cultural backdrop in which we operate. Again, reason is not a free floating phenomenon but relative to a system. It is not absolutely system-free so that we can have a universal standard of rationality. It is conditioned by the social epoch. This position should not be mistaken as denying any fundamental value for reason. The point intended, however, is that a system should not be out rightly rejected, by branding it irrational, without judging its intrinsic merit in terms of its own coherence.

Coming to Indian ethics we find that the *smṛti* literature and the *Mīmāṃsa Sūtras* are made victims of such indiscriminate use of modern paradigm of rationality. Their study is neglected even by the Indian scholars as irrelevant orthodox literature. So is also the case with *Bhagavad-Gītā*. Most of the modern works on Indian ethics hardly allocate a few pages to these texts. Thus modern scholarship makes us feel that *smṛti* literature and orthodox systems like Mīmāmsa are philosophically irrelevant.

Now, going back to the problem of the possibility of Indian ethics, our *Pūrvapakṣin* blames that Indian philosophers indulge excessively in metaphysical speculations that they did not care to develop systematic ethical theories. Here, we have to accept our friend that as far as independent systematic ethical theories are concerned we have a lacuna. At the same time we have to remind him that the whole Indian philosophy is concerned with the problem of life and freedom. The fundamental objective of philosophical inquiry in India was not exclusively abstract theoretisation but to find out how best human life can be lived.

Buddha's silence over abstract metaphysical questions is the prime example of the concern of Indian thinkers for problem of life and freedom rather than for intellectual gratification. All the Indian systems which indulge in theoretical endeavours recognize the real problems of life as the object of their philosophical activity. Precisely for this reason, the idea of liberation, with its different appellations, looms large in all the systems.

For Indian philosophers problem of life is not merely a material problem but a spiritual one too. Ancient India with its rich natural and human resources, was not troubled by material living and therefore could afford a dedicated intellegentsia which could speculate on the deeper problems of life. Indians developed Mathematics, Astronomy, Temple Architecture, Nature Cure Medicine to name a few positive sciences. The people of India are more concerned about their religious and spiritual life through enrichment of culture and morality. They prefer to lead a moral life by limiting their desires than for gratifying their desires by exploiting or mending the ways of Nature.

Since the whole intellectual activity in India is aimed at problem of worthy human life, it is essentially ethical. Thus we often find moral concepts are entangled with metaphysical and epistemological concerns of a system. As the intellectual enterprise itself is essentially ethical, Indian thinkers hardly felt any need for separate or distinct ethical theories. For an ancient thinker this could be as funny as asking for a tumbler full of water when we are standing in a lake. So, independence of ethics is nothing short of a misnomer in Indian intellectual activity which itself is essentially ethical. Want of the so called systematisation thus cannot be shown as impossibility of ethics.

If our opponent means by ethics a linguistic analysis of the words 'goods', 'bad', 'right' etc., we certainly do not have Indian ethics in this sense. The classical systems of Indian philosophy are not concerned with superfluous semantic analysis of words but are concerned more with practical purpose of ethical ideas. Though Indian philosophy has developed theories of language, it was not indulged in mere verbal trifles. On the other hand, it is concerned more with practical insights into moral conduct. This is the strength of Indian ethics in contrast to the western tradition which stops at the level of theoretical explanation of concepts. In India, Philosophy is not merely a "view of life" but a "way of life". In Indian tradition, a philosopher is expected to guide the people with his moral insights. The society looks at sages and philosophers not for theoretical excellence but for practical moral guidance.

Even the so called mystical idea of liberation, whether it is called *Mokṣa, Nirvāṇa, Kaivalya* or *Apavarga,* has a moral significance for the people. We find all the systems of Indian philosophy enunciate their own theories of liberation in their peculiar ways, but all of them recognize the ethical aspect of it. Indian classical systems are unanimous in their recognition of good conduct as the necessary condition for liberation. There is no short cut to human freedom except through proper moral exertion and observance of moral virtues like compassion, non-violence, equality etc.

It is true that there are certain theoretical lapses in adopting liberation as the *summum bonum* by the Indian systems. Some of the Indian systems risk theoretical inconsistency in adopting the idea of final liberation. But they have not given it up for the sake of theoretical rigour. The reason for this is the fact that the urge behind the idea of liberation is ethical rather than theoretical.

In the light of the above discussion, it is clear that the arguments of those who undermine Indian ethics for reasons of systematization etc. are loosely grounded, if not groundless. The Indian moral vision is so comprehensive that a grand encompassing system of ethics is embedded in it for modern scholarship to work on. However, except a few distinguished scholars, most of the writers on Indian ethics are content with the description of moral principles and categorising them. The object of the present work, however, is not to enumerate the moral principles but to look into the fundamental considerations which justify those principles. The work is not concerned with the description of morality but with finding out the ethical foundations of the moral vision. It therefore brings into relief the social and cultural precedents which reflect the moral precepts. It thus involves a study of the fundamental ethical concepts in their origin and development.

In this context, two questions arise. The first, what is meant by foundations of Indian ethics? Then, why special reference to the *Manusmṛti, Mīmāṃsa Sūtras* and *Bhagavad-gītā?* In answering these questions, an attempt is made to further elucidate the theme of the work.

As to the first question, by 'foundations' we mean the fundamental considerations, philosophical, religious, economic or simply prudential, which have gone into the origin of the dominant ethical concepts and influenced their development. In this sense, the work is partially a historical study of Indian ethics. A proper historical understanding of ethical concepts is necessary for an effective systematisation of Indian ethics. Hence, this study may pave way for a systematic understanding of Indian ethics.

One major problem with this objective is to identify the fundamental ethical concepts common to the Indian philosophical systems. Given the rich variety of ethical ideas available and the widely differed treatment of those ideas, it is really difficult to identify the common features of Indian ethics among the classical systems. However, viewed from the seminal importance of certain ideas in all the systems, irrespective of their differences in treatment, we can distinguish a few ethical motifs as the nucleus of the Indian ethical vision. A brief note on these motifs is presented below.

Any study on Indian ethics should start with the *Ṛg-vēdic* concept of *ṛta*, the vedic notion of 'order', both cosmic and moral. The study of *ṛta* is indispensable for it is in this concept we find the earliest traces of Indian ethical thought. Viewed from the comprehensive character of this concept, probably *ṛta* is the most wholistic ethical paradigm which influenced the Indian ethical thinking. In the first chapter, a detailed discussion is undertaken dealing with the antiquity of *ṛta*, its relation to vedic gods and *yajña,* the chief moral features of the vedic society in the light of *ṛta* and finally the conditions which caused withering away of the grand ethical order entailed by *ṛta*. In the final chapter, an account of the relevance of ancient *ṛta* to the modern problem of ecological conservation is given.

The chapter on *Dharma* briefly records the ethical transition from *ṛta* to *Dharma*. The origin of Monotheism, the doctrine of the theory of human action *(karma)* and the speculations on the nature of soul which moulded the concept of *Dharma* in its history are dealt with. It is also shown how these concepts are structurally interdependent. The notion of *Dharma* which is common to both orthodox and heterodox systems is the chief general feature of Indian ethics. Despite the differed treatment in various schools, the idea of *Dharma* constitutes the soul of Indian ethics. It is such a comprehensive or all absorbing ethical concept that it includes even *Mokṣa* or liberation in its fold in the sense that it is man's duty to strive for liberation. It is the chief among human pursuits *(puruṣārtha)*.

What is really surprising is to see that the idea of metempsychosis enters all the philosophical systems, both orthodox and heterodox, without distinction. The theory of transmigration is adopted by even Buddhism which does not accept the existence of soul as a distinct reality. The supernaturalism involved in transmigration is invariably connected with the concepts of bondage and liberation which are again common to all the systems. Though Indian schools of thought uncompromisingly differ as to the nature of bondage and liberation, they are unanimous in realising the study of those two as an important theme of intellectual activity. There are only two exceptions to this. The Cārvākas and Mīmāmsakas. The Cārvākas never recognise liberation as a human end while the Mīmāmsakas emphasize more on *Dharma* as religious duty and hardly care for *Mokṣa,* though they do not deny it.

Given these general features or central concepts of Indian ethics, an attempt is made to see what are the considerations which lead to these concepts and how the contemporary social conditions influenced their conception. An allusion to the possible social factors is made wherever there is such an occasion but the analysis of the ethical concepts is not carried out solely in terms of those conditions. It is, in fact, not possible always to do so. For we cannot trace one to one correspondence between social facts and moral ideas. So, within the reasonable limits, an attempt is made to take into account the historical social reality in relation to the ethical speculations.

Now, as to the special reference to the three ancient texts, there are sound reasons in selecting the three texts for a detailed study. *Dharma,* the nucleus of Indian ethics is a multifaceted concept. It has a social aspect, a religious aspect and spiritual aspect. *Dharma* as duty is dealt by Manu in its social realm, in its religious sphere by Jaimini in his *Mīmāṃsa Sūtras* and the *Bhagavad-gīta* shows how *Dharma* is connected with the spiritual end of human life. These three texts together offer us a comprehensive and complete picture of *Dharma*, as the three aspects are mutually complementary to each other. Again, each text by itself is a complete 'system in itself'.

There are certain common features among these three texts. First of all, the reality of world which is a basic condition for moral operation : these three texts equally put forth the reality of the physical world in unambiguous terms. The efficacy of human action is the second major foundation for ethics, and the three texts insist on the importance and value of human action in their respective fields. They also commonly accept the theory of transmigration to explain their respective subjects. Further they are the most resourceful texts in terms of their practical ethical purport. It is in these texts that we find a central place for moral action and a direct insistence on practical life than the philosophical systems which go for them in an indirect way. As our object is to understand the central ethical concepts in their origin and development, we have to take recourse to these texts primarily because it is in these texts that we find the fundamental ethical concepts in their basic form. Again, it is these texts that throw a focal light on the concepts.

Besides the aforesaid reasons for preferring these texts, there is another equally important reason. While law-books and *Bhagavad-gīta* are more or less neglected as *smṛti* literature, Mīmāmsa is denied a proper place in Indian philosophical systems which it deserves. The modern scholars have not evinced much interest on this system because of its obvious connection with vedic rituals. The Mīmāmsa is generally viewed as nothing more than a quasi-philosophical attempt to account for or justify vedic orthodoxy. This is unwarranted. We should not forget that it is the Mīmāmsakas who took up *Svataḥprāmāṇyavāda* or theory of inherent validity as a sound alternative for Nyāya epistemology. The anti-theistic arguments of Kumarila Bhatta against God and creation are show pieces of excellent scholarship. The unfortunate disregard for these texts results in losing their valuable contribution to Indian thought in general and ethics in particular. Further, while *Manu Dharma Śāstra* represents *smṛti* literature, *Mīmāmsa Sūtras* represents *darśanas, the Gītā* is a part of an *itihāsa*. Thus the work incidentally deals with the three categories of literature which enriched the Indian tradition.

The work ends with a discussion on how to understand and evaluate the key concepts of Indian philosophy in the light of analysis undertaken in the work. Here, an attempt is made to show that Indian ethics has a great scope for further development through creative understanding of our modern problems.

References

1. The Religion and Philosophy of the Vēda and *Upaniṣads,* p. 434.

2. The Presuppositions of India's Philosophies, p. 3.

3. The Religion of India, p. 147.

2

Ṛta and the Ethics of Antiquity

Our search for the foundations of Indian ethics has to begin with the study of the *Vēdas,* not only because of their being the earliest available records of Indian antiquity, but also because they contain some of the fundamental ethical concepts on which the whole edifice of Indian ethical thought is founded. *Ṛta* is one such foundational ethical concept which entails a profound ethical theory.

The *Vēdas* come to us in a fourfold division i.e., *Ṛg-Vēda, Yajur-vēda Sāma-vēda and Atharvaṇa-vēda.* The *Rg-vēda* contains hymns in praise of *nature-gods.* These hymns are called *Ṛks,* from which this division derives its name. The *Yajur-Vēda* borrows many hymns from the *Ṛg-vēda* in addition to its own characteristic liturgic formulate in prose called *yajus,* which are concerned with procedure of ritual practices. The *Sāma-Vēda* borrows a lot from the *Ṛg-Vēda* and puts those *riks* to music by slightly modifying them to suit the purpose. The *Atharvaṇa-Vēda* contains charms and spells which refer to the superstitions, folklore and primitive forms of magic. These four *Vēdas* put together form the great compendium of Aryan thought with the generic name *'Vēda'*, which means 'to know' or 'knowledge'.

The *Vēda* consists of *Samhitas, Brāhmaṇas* and *Araṇyakas*. The *Samhitas* are collections of verses in praise of nature-gods, which are used in *yajña,* — the vedic rituals. The *Brāhmaṇas* contain rules and discussions pertaining to the application of hymns in *yajña*. The *Araṇyakas* primarily comprise of theosophical speculations, the germs of which can be found in the *Brāhmaṇas*. These speculations reach their zenith in the *Upaniṣads* which are appended to the *Araṇyakas*. The *Samhitas, Brāhmaṇas* and *Upaniṣads* betray a continuity in evolution of thought. The *Brāhmaṇas* and *Upaniṣads* are of later origin and presuppose the existence of the *Samhitas*.

Ṛg-vēda

Among the *Samhitas, Ṛg-vēda Samhita* is the oldest and serves as basis for rest of the vedic literature. The *Ṛg-vēda Samhita* contains the basic and original hymns which are incorporated by the other three *Vēdas* to a large extent. As a compilation, it is the oldest and offers us the genuine primitive structure of social and religious thought of the vedic Aryans. As Wilson rightly states, "from the extensive manner in which the hymns of *Ṛg-vēda* enter into the composition of the other three, we should naturally, infer its priority to them and its greater importance to the history of Hindu religion. In truth, it is to the *Ṛg-vēda* that we must have recourse, principally, if not exclusively, for correct notions of the institutions, religions or civil, of the Hindus".[1]

Ṛg-vēda Samhita consists of 1,028 hymns with more than 10,000 stanzas. These hymns or Sūktas of the *Samhita* are attributed to specific *Rishis,* i.e., poet-seers or to families of those seers, traditionally. Katyayana's *Vedānukramaṇi* (Index to the *Vēda*) specifies the name of the seer or of his family, the deity addressed, the number of stanzas and the meter or composition of each *Sūkta*. The hymns of *Ṛg-vēda* are doubtless composed over a very long period of time and the *Ṛg-vēda* itself vouches for this fact. The oldest strata of the hymns are separated from the latest by some centuries. The hymns are preserved by an uninterrupted oral tradition, even to this day. Despite of conflicting opinions of the scholars, we can safely presume the period between 2000 B.C.- 1000 B.C. as the *Ṛg*-vedic age.

Ṛta is the most dominant ethical concept in the *Ṛg-vēda*. Before we embark on a philosophical understanding of *ṛta,* a few remarks on the general character of the *Ṛg-vēda Samhita* are in the order. It is generally viewed as a collection of primitive poetry in praise of the nature-gods, expressing wishes which are mostly materialistic, and connected with the performance of rituals. It is also probable that only those hymns which are useful in the practice of *yajña* found a place in the compilation of the *Samhita*. Though these hymns are primarily liturgic in purpose, they, nevertheless, incidentally describe the primitive form of life and the institutions thereof. As poetry, these hymns are of high literary value and it is really astonishing to see such high standards of creativity in such a remote antiquity.

Ṛta, the Cosmic and Moral Order

The word *ṛta* stands for the unerring order found in the course of natural phenomena, which are defied in the *Vēda,* and also, more importantly, it is the moral order in obeyance to which gods and men are to conduct themselves. The concept of *ṛta* is not a speculative abstraction but a concrete reality which is apprehended directly in the course of natural phenomena. Further, it is not a mythical concept, for nowhere do we find deification or anthropomorphication of *ṛta.* It is rather discussed in man's relation with Nature and with fellow men. The vedic idea of Nature is not disconnected with man's social and personal experiences and thus we have a complex idea of Cosmic-Moral order. This may not be intelligible for a positivist for whom the world is made up of facts and ethics is devoid of cognitive value. But it is not so with Vedic man for whom Nature and society have a unitary order.

In its cosmic aspect, it is due to *ṛta* that the sun travels, the sky and the earth are firm, dawns arise, waters flow, cows yield milk. Simply, everything is what it is and how it is due to the working of *ṛta*. It is the regulative law in the universe. In its moral aspect, *ṛta* is the order because of which gods and men live in harmony. *Ṛta* constitutes the ethical standard which had a direct impact on the lives of the Vedic people. According to Bloomfield, "*ṛta* is unquestionably the best conception that has been elaborated by Aryans... we have in connection with the *ṛta* a pretty complete system of Ethics, a kind of counsel of perfection".[2]

Though *ṛta* is first found in the *Vēda,* its origin, however, can be traced back to much earlier prehistoric age called Indo-Iranian period. This is the period prior to the advent of Aryans into North-Western provinces of India from the Iranian highlands. The concept of *ṛta* is inherited from the age when Indian and Iranian Aryans were still one people.

The conjecture about the prehistoric origin of *ṛta* is based upon the conceptual and linguistic similarities between Persian *Zend Avesta* and the *Vēda* which inherited much in common from the Indo-Iranian period. The pioneering studies of Indologists in comparative mythology and philology established these similarities. The *ṛta* in the *Vēda* corresponds to *asha* or *areta* of the *Avesta* which too means the cosmic order. In the *Avesta,* we find parallel gods to some of those in the *Vēda,* and this fact suggests the prehistoric origin of those gods. Among such gods, *Dyaus, Agni, Indra, Varuṇa, Yama, Āryamān, Sōma, Mitra, Vivasvant, Trita* are some. The discoveries in the field of comparative mythology and ethnology suggest that Aryans had migrated in the pre-vedic times, for reasons unknown, to the plains of Indus from Iranian highlands with some traditional ritual practices, ethical notions and prehistoric gods. They later developed their own isolated culture and religion, which acquired an independent character. However, the relics of past were not totally lost sight of, and some of the vedic poets look at their antiquity with nostalgic exuberance.

According to Bloomfield, the idea of *ṛta* might have existed a long time before 1600 B.C.[3] The cuneiform tablets discovered at Tel-el-Amaran of Egypt mention the Persian name *Artashuvara* and *Artatama*. The prefix in those names i.e., the stem *arta* is identical with *arta* of Western Iranian and Acamendian inscriptions, *asha* of *Avesta* and *ṛta* of the *Vēda*. Hence Bloomfield argues that the idea of *ṛta,* with its parallels in *Avesta* and Acamendian inscriptions, is older than the cuneiform tablets which date back to 1600 B.C. This evidence suggests a much earlier date for the beginning of Vedic literary activity too.

Ṛta and the Vedic Gods

Before we see how the vedic gods and *ṛta* are connected, let us briefly recall the character of the vedic gods in general. The scholars are mostly unanimous in accepting the view that the vedic gods are deified natural phenomena. The *Vēda* considers god as luminous, benevolent and right minded divine entities. The Sanskrit word for gods *devas, with* its root *div* or *dyu, suggests* that gods are personified luminous manifestations of Nature. In the *Vēda*, most of the gods represent ostensible natural phenomena. Though some of the gods are thoroughly anthropomorphised in course of time, yet there are some gods who are still not deprived of their obvious natural characters. Among such gods, *Dyaus* (sky), *Agni* (fire), *Vāyu* (air), *Prithvi* (earth), *Usha* (dawn), *Sōma* (*Sōma* plant), *Sūrya* (sun) are some. There are, however, some gods whose correspondence to natural phenomena is obscure. In the *Vēda*, we find even the articles employed in the ritual also defined - the sacrificial post, the vessels of *Sōma,* the *Sōma* pressing stones being the examples for such deification. There are some abstract qualities and actions deified too - *Śraddha* (faith), *Dakṣina* (sacrificial fee) are the examples. However, the most important vedic gods are representatives of natural objects and phenomena. Nature as a whole, every natural object between the sky and earth found a place in the vedic pantheon. In fact Father sky *(Dyaus pitar)* and Mother Earth are said to be the parents of all the gods.[4]

It is true, gods are also spoken of as progency of *Aditi,* which literally means 'limitless' or 'boundless'. According to Giffrith, one of the translators of the *Ṛg*-vedic hymns, *Aditi* is the boundless, infinite Nature. Hence, all the gods owe their origin to Nature. In other words, they are Nature-gods. However, the idea of Father sky appears to be much archaic, having its corresponding words in Greek *Zeus Pater* and Roman *Diespiter* or *Jupiter.*

The Nature-worship is common to all the primitive peoples of the world. This lead to the deification of Nature in its various aspects. Such deification found expression in the stupendous mythology of the *Vēda.* In fact, the *Vēda* stands as the paradigm for understanding how natural phenomena acquire the status of deities through the primitive art of deification and myth-making. "Deprived of hymns of the *Ṛg-vēda,* we should hardly know to this day that mythology is the first and fundamental adjustment of the individual human life to the outer active, interfering, dynamic world, which surrounds and influences man from the moment when he opens his eyes upon the wonders of its unexplained phenomena. In this sense, vedic mythology in its day what empirical science is in our day".[5]

Further, the studies in primitive mythology show that while the primitive people draw from Nature the basic materials for myth-making, they also express their own patterns of life in the mythology. This explains why the mythologies of different peoples vary, though they deify the same Nature: "A certain amount of the complications and entanglements of human life must be imported into mythology before it becomes mythology".[6] Again as Thomson asserts, "...man's consciousness of the world around him is a social image or a product of society".[7] Hence an analytical study of a mythology provides us with, if not a detailed description, the broad outlines of the social reality.

Given the naturalistic origin of gods, *ṛta* as the order in the universe must also guide the gods. Precisely this is what the *Ṛg-vēda* speaks of gods in relation in *ṛta*. Gods are intimately connected with *ṛta* throughout the *Samhita*. The epithets like *Ṛtajata* (born of *ṛta*), *Ṛtajña* (knowers of *ṛta*), *Ṛtavṛdh* (promoter of *ṛta*), etc., are frequently given to gods. What is more remarkable is that nowhere gods are viewed as controllers of *ṛta* rather than followers or upholders of *ṛta*. The *ṛta* on the other hand is viewed as regulating order according to which gods conduct themselves.

Generally, all the gods, at one place or the other, are related to *ṛta* as its followers or upholders. Heaven *(Dyaus)* and Earth are regarded as the mother of *ṛta*.[8] At a few places, Dawn and Night are called 'mothers of *ṛta*'.[9] The sky and the wide expanse was held to be the domain of *ṛta*.[10] Again it is frequently called as the offspring of *ṛta*.[11] Goddess Dawn is said to be arising according to *ṛta*.[12] At one place *ṛta* is likened to the wheel of time, a year with twelve spokes (months) and six hundred and twenty sons (days and nights) paired together.[13]

Mitra and *Varuṇa*, especially the latter, stand in a special relation to *ṛta*. The dual gods, the most important among *Ādityas*, are the guardians of *ṛta*. The *Ṛg-vēda* poets usually address these two together. However, a few hymns, mostly deprecatory or expiatory, are addressed to *Varuṇa* in isolation.[14]

Mitra and *Varuṇa* are said to have attained their mighty power through *ṛta* and by being lovers and cherishers of *ṛta.*[15] They are the gods who by *ṛta,* uphold *ṛta* and are the lords of shining light of *ṛta.*[16] They are true to *ṛta,* born in *ṛta* and the strengtheners of *ṛta.*[17] The supremacy of these gods is established by X. 36.12 of the *Samhita,* according to which *Mitra* and *Varuṇa* govern all the gods through *ṛta.*

As guardians of *ṛta,* they are said to have established heaven and earth firmly. They caused the cows to stream, the plants to flourish and by scattering the swift drops, sent down the rain.[18] All the workings of *ṛta* are ascribed to *Mitra* and *Varuṇa* in general.

Varuṇa, though usually is accompanied by *Mitra,* is the chief guardian of *ṛta.* While *Varuṇa* is addressed by a few hymns in solitude, *Mitra* was hardly so addressed except by III. 59 of the *Samihta.* Again, *Varuṇa* is regarded as the moral chastiser and is prayed for moral condonation but *Mitra* is generally viewed as mere moral exhorter. This shows the relatively greater significance of *Varuṇa* over his partner.

Ṛta is the very form of *Varuṇa.*[19] He is the principal guide of *ṛta.*[20] He is the very alert observer of *ṛta* among men. He is an omniscient god who knows every act of men.[21] *Atharvaṇa-Vēda* speaks of *Varuṇa* as the god from whom no one can conceal one's thoughts and whenever two people sit together and scheme, *Varuṇa* will be there as the third man and knows it. He is omnipresent and is hidden even in a pretty drop of water. Even winkings of men are counted by him.[22] *Varuṇa* knows the path of birds, ships on sea and even the path of wind.[23] *Ādityas* are said to be the spies of *Varuṇa* who observe the moral conduct of men.[24] The character of these *Ādityas* serves as an important clue for the moral description of Aryan social organisation. We shall deal with it in a later part of this chapter.

Varuṇa establishes his unsurpassable supremacy as the guardian of moral order and as the omnicient chastiser.

Varuṇa's refuse is sought by transgressers of *ṛta* in an interesting way. Those hymns vouch for moral probity and conscious rectitude of the vedic people. Much of it will be seen a little later. Presently, let us look into the prehistory of *Varuṇa,* which throws light on our analysis of *ṛta* in a very important aspect.

Varuṇa and Prehistory

As mentioned earlier, *Varuṇa* is one of the prehistoric gods inherited by the Vedic people from their hoary Indo-Iranian past. *Varuṇa* has his counterpart in *Avesta* known as *Ahura Mazda* or *Ormezd.* The epithet *Ahura* which means 'lord' is also found in the *Vēda* in the form of *Asura.* This word in its original sense means 'lord' in the *Vēda* also. However, surprisingly enough, *Asura* in the later parts of the *Vēda* came to mean evil spirits distinct from *Rākṣasas* and demons. The *Asuras* are perennial foe-men of god *Indra,* one of whose popular Vedic names is *'Asura*-slayer'.[25] However, the *Vēda* still retains the original sense of the word to mean 'the lord or chief of gods'. *Asura* in the later sense became an appellation of non-Aryan aborigines, the dark-skinned Dasyus. The epithet in its former sense of 'lord' is given to *Varuṇa* specifically.[26]

Ahura Mazda, like *Varuṇa* is chiefly connected with *asha*, the corresponding concept of *ṛta,* in the *Avesta.* However, unlike *Varuṇa, Ahura Mazda* is the creator of the divine order. In the *Vēda, Varuṇa* is nowhere said to have created *ṛta.* He is rather a guardian of it. In this sense, *Mazda* has a somewhat different stature than that of *Varuṇa.* In the *Vēda, Varuṇa* is vested with magical powers *(māya).*[27] But this does not certainly suggest that he created *ṛta.* Except this particular feature, Varuṇa and *Mazda* are almost identical.

As far as the moral preservation is concerned, they have a striking similarity. *Mazda,* like *Varuṇa,* cannot be deceived and knows all the thoughts and needs of men.[28] Again, *Varuṇa* and *Ahura Mazda* are ascribed certain identical celestial exploits- like paving paths for sun and stars, causing moon to wax and wane, governing waters and plants etc.,- in the *Vēda* and *Avesta*. *Ahura* also has his partner called *Mithra*, phonetically almost identical with the Vedic *Mitra*. Notwithstanding minor differences, *Varuṇa* and *Ahura* can be described as two images of the same diety, in two mirrors.

The identity of *Varuṇa* and *Ahura*, with their cosmic and moral responsibility of guarding the order, reveals two important facts: first, the antiquity of *Varuṇa* beyond the Vedic period; secondly, the symbiotic origin of *Varuṇa* and *ṛta*. The second point is very important for it amply explains the fading away of *ṛta* and *Varuṇa* together in the later Vedic period. This is the significant theoretical purpose served by our digression into the prehistory of *Varuṇa*.

Ṛta and *Yajña*

The two distinguishing characteristic features of the *Ṛg*-Vedic religion, unanimously accepted by the scholars, are the naturalistic polytheism and the cherished practice of *yajña*. Without these two, the *Ṛg*-Vedic religion is simply inconceivable. We have already noted how the naturalistic polytheism of the *Ṛg*-Vedic period is related to *ṛta*. Now, let us try to discern the relation between *yajña* and *ṛta*. Our interest here is not to somehow account for the primitive ritual practice or to accommodate it in the bossom of *ṛta*. On the other hand, our primary concern is to see what light the fostered ritual heritage, in its origin and development, can throw on our understanding of *ṛta*.

To start with, let us take up the popular opinions of two renouned western Indologists - Maurice Bloomfield and A. A. Macdonell - regarding the general estimate of the vedic literature and religion. This is essential for our study, because the question of ethical relevance of the ritual obligates a clear understanding of the nature and purpose of the ritual itself.

Let us first see what Bloomfield has to say. In his famous book, *The Religion of the Vēda,* Bloomfield observes:

"The Vedic religion is a hieratic or priestly religion. As regards its mechanism, or its external practices, it is unmistakably liturgic or ritualistic. As regards its purpose, or its economic aspect, it is thoroughly utilitarian and practical. Its purpose is to secure happiness and success, health and long life for man, notably the rich man, while living upon the earth; to secure a very talented and thrifty class of priest-poets abundant rewards in return for their services in procuring for men this happiness, success and so on; to satisfy the divine powers visible and invisible, beneficent and noxious, gods and demons, that is, to establish liveable relations between gods and men; and finally to secure after death the right to share the paradise of gods in the company of pious fathers that have gone there before".[29]

The problem with the foregoing analysis and understanding of the vedic ritual by Bloomfield is that, despite of his brilliant work in comparative mythology, philology and ethnology, he completely missed the ethical aspect of *yajña* and confined himself to the trivial formal characterization of it. He, unfortunately and unduly, restricted his characterization of ritual to the overt and immediately economic aspect of it, without probing for any fundamental considerations beneath the origin of the institution.

In his opinion, the ritual is primarily a hieratic or priestly practice. He arrives at this by looking at the trivial liturgic discussions of the *Yajur-Vēda* and *Brāhmaṇas;* the way *Dakshina* (sacrificial fee for the priests) is deified; the presence of *dāna-stuti* or munificence hymns in the *Ṛg-Vēda,*[30] and the way liberality is eulogised by the priests. These evidences certainly show the formal character of the ritual practice. However, this is a later development in the practice of *yajña,* which gave rise to excessive formalism. The *Ṛg-Vēda,* on the other hand, certainly points to a time when *yajña* was not strictly a priestly activity rather than a collective activity. The hieratic culture was without doubt a later offshoot and the *Ṛg-Vēda* contains some hymns which unmistakably defy the existence of specialized priests as the principal partakers in the ritual performance. They show the existence of *yajña* much prior to the rise of priestly class. The hymns should not be neglected while defining the purpose of *yajña*.

The primary assumption or hieratic for characterization of the ritual is the distinction between the priest and *yajamana*, the rich patron. The *Ṛg-Vēda* contain some hymns where the poet himself is the *yajamana*. Again, there are numerous hymns which speak of not a solitary *yajamana* but a number of *yajamanas* sacrificing together and offering hymns.[31] Most of the hymns address the deities with a self-referential we. Again, wealth, progeny, long life are desired, in most of the hymns, for not a particular patron but for the tribes men as a whole. Sometimes, wishes are advanced in favour of the ancient five tribes of Aryans of the Aryan race as such.[32] The hymns in their origin were not production of priests for the sake of rich patrons. In I.114.9, we find a herdsman praying *Rudra* for the welfare of his cattle. All these hymns, along with similar hymns abundantly found in the *samhita*, show the pre-hieratic practice of *yajña*. So, one can neither evince priestly interest as the motive for sacrifice in general nor can claim that the entire vedic religion is principally hieratic.

Further, Bloomfield suggests 'satisfying gods' as one of the primary motive behind the rituals. On the face of it, yes! It is true. But why should the gods be satisfied at all? And how does the sacrifice satisfy gods? The clue lies in the fact, well stated by Giffrith, that 'the preservation of the whole world rests, according to the Vedic view, on the scarifies offered by men, as these give the gods strength and enable them to perform their duties'.[33] As gods perform their duties according to *ṛta*, *yajña* is nothing but the process of strengthening *ṛta*. It is not meant for, as Bloomfield contended, merely satisfying gods but for rejuvenating them. Sacrifice is the process of revitalizing the deified forces of Nature, through whom *ṛta* will be strengthened. But what exactly is the mechanism through which a sacrifice can revitalize gods? To know this, we have to examine the material features of sacrifice in general.

First, how does anyone, forget about gods for the moment, gain strength? The answer is simple - food! As our practical experience reveals, food is the cause of strength in any organism. For the primitive people, gods are no exception to this rule. Even the gods have to be fed in order that they gain strength to discharge their functions in accordance with *ṛta*. If gods get weakened, as men do after continuous work, then *ṛta* is also weakened in the sense that its operation becomes difficult. If *ṛta* is weakened, the natural course of happenings would get disturbed. For the people who were still in the secure lap of Nature, who derive their sustenance from Nature, it is disastrous. As mentioned earlier, rain is due to *ṛta*. Due to rain, pastures grow; through pastures cows will be fed; well-fed cows multiply and the multiplied cows are the wealth for the nomadic Aryan tribes. They liken every important thing to cows. Clouds are cows, the sun is a cow, sacrifice is a cow and remember, cows yield milk due to *ṛta*. Hence, proper course of *ṛta* i.e., efficient working of gods is directly and ostensibly linked with their food, subsistence, wealth, longlife, progeny and everything good in their lives. Rain and food are the most immediate benefits of strengthening *ṛta*.

Rain is so closely connected with *ṛta,* that the word itself acquired the sense of waters. God *Varuṇa* is the god of rain and waters. Even in the later mythology, *Varuṇa* retained this image. *Varuṇa* and *Mitra* are frequently urged for rain and food:

From you, *Mitra* and *Varuṇa*, may we gain fully food for our sustenance.[34]

Send us from heaven, O *Varuṇa* and *Mitra*, rain and sweet food, ye who pour down your bounties.[35]

May we be thine *Varuṇa* and with our princes, *Mitra*, thine:

Food and heaven's light will we obtain.[36]

Eternal Law hath varied food that strengthens: thought of eternal law removes transgressions.

By holy law long lasting food they bring us; by holy law have cows for our worship.

... To law belong the vast deep Earth and Heaven. Milch-Kine supreme, to law their milk they render.[37]

These hymns show how materialistically relevant strengthening gods and *ṛta* is for those people. Now, strengthening gods being the aim of sacrifice, it is the process, by implication, of feeding the gods. There are three important features of the vedic sacrifice. They are - fire kindled, the oblations poured into the fire and the hymns offered to gods. All other materials used in the sacrifice are incidental or subservient to these three main features.

Sōma drink, clarified butter and barley are the most general oblations. Among these, *Sōma* is doubtless the most important that it acquired by itself the status of diety. It is said to be surprisingly revitalizing drink. Clarified butter and barley are the staple food of the early vedic people. Hence these oblations are offered to gods in order that they gain strength and perform their functions well, under *ṛta*, with renewed strength.

Direct allusion to this idea is repeatedly found in the samhita:

"He who with dainty food hath won you, *Indra* and *Varuṇa*, won gods as his allies to friendship ... when they, as friends inclined to friendship, honoured with dainty food, delight in flouring *Soma*".[38]

Again, *Sōma* is addressed thus:

"Stream to us food and vigour, kine and horses; give us broad lights and *fill the gods with rapture*."[39]

Indra, the warrior god is the most fond drinker of *Sōma*. The anthromorphic description of *Indra* includes big belly, rugged jaws, big mouth, broad shoulders, big lips etc., to suit the image of a heavy consumer of *Sōma*. He is said to have drunk three lakes-full of *Sōma*. As a warrior god, he needs greater quantities of revitalizing *Sōma* than anybody else. Hence it is clear that oblations are offered primarily as the food for gods.

Now, coming to the hymns offered to gods, they serve two important purpose. First, to address each god with his specific share of oblation and secondly to express wishes or the materialistic desires to the gods. The first purpose is closely connected with oblation, the food of gods. So, prayers, in the first place, serve the purpose of offering each god with his share of food. In the samhita, even prayers are likened to food:

"O *Asuras,* O *Varuṇa* and *Mitra,* this hymn to you like food, anew I offer."[40]

"Sing forth to lofty *Dyaus* a strength - bestowing song ...[41]

At one place, a holy song is directly said to be strengthening *ṛta:*

"O *Indra,* hear him that hath produced for thee a new and lovely song, with comprehending mind a pious *song such as of yore has strengthened the divine order of the universe*."[42]

Hence, the fundamental purpose of hymns is to address gods their due shares of food. The expression of desires is, however, secondary. The eulogies, of the gods and their exploits, are also aimed at strengthening gods by inspiring their zeal.[43] The idea of pleasing gods through well decked songs is also frequent in the *Vēda*. But it cannot be taken as the primary purpose because it does not explain why hymns should be a part of *yajña* alone. The simultaneous acts of offering hymns and oblations prove otherwise. The hymns are thus intricately linked with the process of offering food i.e., oblations to gods.

This understanding of hymns appears to be naive and an oversimplification. However, this is not to undermine the aesthetic aspect of hymns. In fact, it is their poetic beauty that elevates the otherwise monotonous hymns to a respectable place in the world literature. Our point here is that as far as the fundamental relation of hymns to *yajña* is concerned, the hymns are essentially, if not solely, connected with offering oblations to gods. So, our view is not one sided or incomplete and does not undermine the other important aspects of the hymns. Nor do we evaluate hymns only in terms of their function in the *yajña*. In fact, there are some beautiful hymns e.g., the hymn on dice[44]. the hymn of frogs[45] and many other verses describing things external to the ritual which are more of literary interest than of any liturgic value. The hymns on Dawn stand apart as some of the most excellent pieces of poetry ever produced by *man kind*. However, our generalisation does not preclude the appreciation of these better aspects of the holy hymns.

Sacrificial fire, another chief feature of *yajña,* is also closely related to offering food or oblations to the gods. *Agni*, as the sacrificial fire, is viewed as the envoy or herald to gods. The oblations are carried by *Agni* to gods.[46] He is the deity whose importance in the vedic ritual lies in the conception that gods receive their shares oblation through him. He is called the messenger and courier between the two worlds (Heaven and Earth).[47] Numerous hymns in the *Vēda* eulogise this sacerdotal aspect of *Agni*.

Now, it is clear that the three chief features of *yajña* are closely connected with invigorating gods. The mechanism in the sacrifice through which this intention is carried out is also clear, the oblations poured into fire are carried by it to gods and the oblations are apportioned by the hymns as they address the gods. *Agni* is said to be 'the mouth of gods' into which oblations are poured. The gods are also called 'fire tongued' in the sense that it is through *Agni* they taste their food. Again, *Bṛhaspati* or *Brahmaṇaspati,* the deified prayer is supposed to be the celestial apportioner of shares among gods. These views concerning the mechanism of the vedic rite amply supports our thesis that the primary purpose of *yajña* is to invigorate gods and through them *ṛta.*

In this sense, the vedic sacrifice, as far as its original intention is concerned, is more an ethical act than any thing else. If it were, as Bloomfield suggested, a mere instrument of priestly interest, it hardly explains how *yajña* is cherished by people for ages even to this day. A practice cannot survive through such a long history if it were just a product of parasitic interest of a particular class. On the other hand, *yajña* acquired so much of emotional significance due to ethical considerations beneath it. Hence, the survival value of *yajña* lies precisely in its ethical character. It is true that the later tradition lost sight of the original intentions of poet-seers and priests replaced gods in *yajña*. However, the ethical significance of *yajña* was never questioned in Hindu tradition on the basis of priestly interest. Carvakas are of course an exception to this.

The conception of the sacrificial mechanism to bring out the desired ends has undergone thorough transformation in the later *Brāhmaṇas* period. But the ethical grounds for the sacrifice are not entirely lost sight of. *Yajña,* even in the smriti period, is viewed as a debt *(ṛṇa)* to gods.

The early vedic idea of strengthening gods through sacrificial offering, nevertheless, involves a certain amount of primitive belief in magic. This is quite apparent and obvious. However, the magical element in the sacrifice does not invalidate the ethical purpose beneath it. We may not, in terms of modern science, be able to explain completely the efficacy of *yajña*. But we cannot question, on the basis of our modern reasoning, the ethical presuppositions of a grand tradition and the great peoples of antiquity. Nor can we consider them as lesser rational beings. If we do so, we are committing ourselves to 'Judicial Blindness'. Afterall, *reason* or *rationality* is a social product and thus cannot be evaluated independent of the specific social conditions. *Reason* is not an extrasystemic value but is an immenent category peculiar to a system. Then what is the object of the so called rational studies of antiquity? The answer is simple - understanding! Better understanding!! Still better understanding!!! This understanding of our past helps us in moulding ourselves towards better objects of thought and action. This precisely is the relevance of studying the conceptions and lives of our own forefathers. Man makes himself through his history!

Coming back to our original topic, let us see what Macdonell observes in relation to the vedic literature: "It *(Ṛg-vēda)* is rather a body of skilfully composed hymns produced by a sacerdotal class and meant to accompany the *Sōma* oblation and the fire sacrifice of melted butter which were offered according to a ritual by no means so simple as was at one time supposed, though undoubtedly so much simpler than the elaborate system of the Brahmana period."[48]

What concerns us much here is Macdonell's view of the priestly origin of the *Ṛg*-Vedic hymns. But, as we have seen, the formation of priests as a class is epigonic to the long tradition of pre-class ritual practice. Many of the hymns certainly speak of priests, but it does not mean that priests alone are the authors of hymns. Our point here is that the *Ṛg*-Vedic allusions to the priests cannot be taken as an evidence to characterize the whole

Ṛg-Vēda as a product of priestly class. Such undue generalisation hampers our understanding of *ṛta* and *yajña* in their original ethical significance.

Fortunately, we have certain internal evidence in the *Ṛg-Vēda* which show that all composers of hymns are not priests and vice versa. One of the poets of the *Ṛg-Vēda* in III.43 asks *Indra* to make him a ruler, *priest* or a richman. If every composer of hymns were a priest by himself, then it is funny that he is asking *Indra* to make him what he already is. So, this hymn shows that all composers are not priests. Further the *apri* hymns, which the *yagamana* has to recite, composed by his forefathers, show that hymns used to be composed by all their families long back. The hymn on frogs VII. 103, which is a satire in priests, exhibits that it was no work of a priest. Again, IX. 112 of the *Ṛg-Vēda* is a popular old song[49] incorporated with a refrain at the end of each stanza vouches for this fact.

Our argument, further, is substantiated by the popular character of the magical charms in the *Atharva-Vēda*. Though *Atharva-Vēda,* as a compilation, is later to the *Ṛg-Vēda,* some of the hymns of the former are, if not older, as archaic as those in the *Ṛg-Vēda*. Even the *Ṛg-Vēda* contains charms and spells which betray a popular character.[50] The tradition referred to by *Gṛhya Sūtras* also is popular in practice entailing household practices. So, Macdonell's observation regarding priestly origin of the *Ṛg*-Vedic hymns is partially true. Our point, on the other hand, is that the Vedic religion, in its entirely, is not a hieratic religion solely supported by rich patrons but is also has a popular aspect of it which is much earlier to the rise of priestly class.

Again, Macdonell, commenting on *ṛta,* says that "the unvarying regularity of the sun and moon, and the unfailing recurrence of dawn, however suggested to the ancient singers the idea of unchanging order that prevails in Nature. The notion of this general law, recognized under the name *Ṛta* (properly the 'course' of things), we find in the *Ṛg-Vēda* extended first to the fixed rules of the sacrifice (rite), and then to those of morality (right).[51]

This observation of Macdonell implies that the procedural rules are the first outcome of *ṛta* and that the moral rectitude is rather a secondary application of *ṛta*. However, it is not convincing to make the formalism in the sacrifice, insistence on which is found in the later vedic literature, the first and foremost relevance of *ṛta*. It is true, order in the rite is alluded. But it certainly is not the principal application of *ṛta,* atleast in the older portions of the vedic literature. Macdonell's view fails to understand the organic ethical relationship between *ṛta* and the sacrifice. It relates them only on the surface of formalism involved in the sacrifice. It does not explain why ritual has to be practised and the ethical relevance of *ṛta* to the question. The problem with Macdonell's view, precisely, is that a prehistoric conception of moral order and a prehistoric practice of ritual are connected in terms of formalism, the magnification of which is clearly tracable to the later vedic period. This is not to say that the prehistoric and early vedic practice of *yajña* is totally devoid of any procedural norms. The point, however, is that the formalism should not be the basis of understanding *ṛta* and its essentially ethical relation to *yajña*. *Ṛta* as an ethical order entails *yajña* itself and not merely the formalism followed in it.

What is really remarkable about the *Ṛg*-Vedic conception of the relation between *ṛta* and *yajña* is that *yajña,* as a practice to strengthen *ṛta,* is not an external stimulus to *ṛta* but an integral part of the order of the universe. *Yajña,* in this sense, is not like the modern artificial respiratory equipment which stimulates the process being external to the organism. It is rather like lungs which promote the process as an internal organ. This is the precise reason why *ṛta* acquired the sense of *yajña*. The word *ṛta* is frequently found to mean *yajña* in the *Ṛg-Vēda*. Hence, the relation between *ṛta* and *yajña* is almost that of an identity. In fact, the *Ṛg-Vēda* uses the word *ṛta* so often to mean *yajña* that the translators of the samhita are frequently confounded as to the appropriate use of it in a given stanza. Giffrith and Wilson differ in their rendering of the word very often. Giffrith mostly translates it as 'the law' while Wilson favours the other rendering.

Hence, in the course of examining the views of the most renouned scholars - Bloomfield and Macdonell - we arrived to the conclusion that *ṛta* is primarily the ethical order which entails *yajña* as an ethical practice. The ritualistic religion, atleast in its origin, was not entirely a hieratic practice rather than a collective activity. This popular dimension of *yajña* will be further elucidated in our next section. With this, let us set ourselves to see how *ṛta* serves as a moral standard in the social interaction of the *Ṛg*-Vedic people.

Ṛta, the Grand Moral Order

The ethical gravity of *ṛta* can be understood from various hymns of the *Ṛg-vēda,* which ostentate a high degree of moral rectitude. *Ṛta* provided moral security and an impetus for moral exertion. *Ṛta* offers stability through harmonious co-existence and collective social life:

"I laud you, O ye guileless gods, here where we meet to render the praise.

None, *Varuṇa* and *Mitra*, harms the mortal who honours and obeys your laws.

He makes his house endure, he gathers plenteous food who pays obedience to your will.

Born in his sons a new, he spreads as law commands, and prospers every way unharmed.

Even without war he gathers wealth, and goes his way on pleasant paths".[52]

Ṛta beyond doubt was the grand moral order which offered moral solace to the early vedic people. It entails not only *yajña* as an ethical practice but also a set of values cherished by Aryans. One poet distinguishes *yajña* from witchcraft or foul magic in terms of *ṛta*.[53] While sacrifice invokes gods in accordance with *ṛta,* foul magic is contrary to *ṛta.* So, *ṛta* not only characterises the moral aspect of *yajña* but also, by itself, stand as a principle of rectitude.

Ṛta is not a mere ideal set for human beings but it is a grand order adhered to be gods also. *Ṛta* is a conception which has its roots in a particular form of life as reflected in the cosmos. In order to work-out its details, we have to see what exactly it suggests in the realm of gods.

The most immediate moral principle observed among gods, the followers and upholders of *ṛta,* is harmony. As all of them work under the eternal law, they are unanimous or one-minded. The order in the universe is revealed through the harmonious working of the gods. They stand as a model for harmonious collective life. In fact, the idea of harmony among gods itself is a cosmic reflection of the primitive collective life.

The unanimity among gods is due to *ṛta* they follow. Day and Night are said be working harmoniously by following *ṛta.* The gods in general are one minded in their celestial operations:

"All gods are of one accord, with one intention, more unobstructed to a single purpose".[54]

"Fair formed, of different bues and yet one minded, Night and Dawn clash not, neither do they tarry".[55]

"Gods are one minded and they restored *Agni* together".[56]

"With *Agni* and with *Indra, Viṣṇu, Varuṇa,* with the *Adityas, Rudras, Vasus,* closely leagued;

Accordant, of one mind with *Sūrya* and with Dawn, O *Aśvins,* drink the *Sōma* juice".[57] This fundamental harmony and unanimity constitutes the gist of *ṛta,* the normal order of the early vedic people. The vedic seers fondly remembered the unanimity existed among their ancient fathers:

"Meeting together in the same enclosure, they strive not, one mind, one with another".[58]

They wished that they could foster such unanimity among themselves. The *Atharva-Vēda* tries to engender unanimity in the tribal assembly through a charm.[59] The poet of X.191 appeals for the restoration of unanimity through the hymn:

> "Assembly, speak together: let your minds be all of one accord,
>
> As ancient Gods unanimous sit down to their appointed share."[60]

Hence, unanimity constitutes one of the chief features of the ancient vedic society. This unanimity is followed from genuine conception of *ṛta* which entails harmonious conduct among gods and men. For our further analysis of chief features of the ancient social organization, we have to examine the character of *Ādityas,* the observers of *ṛta.*

While *Varuṇa* and *Mitra* are the principal guardians of *ṛta, Ādityas* in general are regarded as the moral observers. *Ādityas* are the spies of *Varuṇa,* who constantly watch men in their behaviour and thought.[61] *Ādityas* are the sons of Aditi, the infinite Nature. They are luminous celestial beings. *Mitra* and *Varuṇa* belong to this class of deities. They are the chief *Ādityas.* The *Ṛg-Vēda* gives varied number of these *Ādityas.* Sometimes they are said to be six, sometimes seven, at a few places they are eight. The later vedic literature fixes their member, at last, as twelve. But the original number of these *Ādityas* is six to which varied additions are made. The six original *Ādityas* are *Varuṇa, Mitra, Āryamaān, Dakṣa, Bhāga* and *Aṇśa.*[62]

The *Ādityas* as moral observers are of special interest for a simple reason. One can be a moral observer only if one does not lack the moral quality one is observing. A drunkard cannot be a moral observer over another drunkard. To put it more positively, the character of a moral observer, for which he is known, reveals the moral feature over which he is an observer. So, a probe into the specific character of these *Ādityas* disclose is the structure of the social morality over which these dieties are observers.

Varuṇa is the most important Āditya who is not only a moral observer but also a chastiser. The other *Ādityas* are at his disposal as his spies. As far as social organization is concerned, he is the most important diety. He is said to be "the founder of society united by common practices".[63] He is thus called "the eldest brother". So, *Varuṇa* suggests the brotherhood of primitive collective community. Trita Aptya is another prehistoric diety who also preaches brotherhood of men.[64] *Mitra,* on the other hand, is frequently called 'a friend', as his name itself suggests, who guides men in their endeavours.

Āryamān is a prehistoric god who has *Airyama* as his counterpart in the *Avesta*. This Indo-Iranian god is remembered as 'the ancient kinsman' in the *Ṛg-Vēda*. Along with *Varuṇa* and *Mitra*, he appears in many hymns as a moral observer. One hymn calls these three as the caretakers of *ṛta.*[65] He figures as a groomsman in the vedic marriage rites and appears as a share seeker or share distributor in the tribal assembly. Macdonell, Bloomfield, Muir and Bergaine unanimously suggest that *'Āryamān'* means 'comrade' or 'comradeship'. At one place, *Āryamān* is equated to a share in the assembly (VII.69.12). Hence, this specific character of *Āryamān* suggests that equality, comradeship or kinsmanship is one of the features of early vedic society.

Dasksa is another Aditya, the creative power associated with Aditi. Though he started his *Ṛg*-Vedic career as an Āditya, he later assumed very important role of the progenitor. He became a prajāpati. Gods have sprung from *Dakṣa*.[66] *Varuṇa, Mitra* and *Indra* are called 'sons of *Dakṣa*'.[67] What is really astonishing is that even Aditi is said to be his daughter (X.72.4). Sayana takes *Dakṣa* as 'the lord of vigour or strength' and Bloomfield says that this diety is an abstraction of 'Dexterity' or 'cleverness'. However, it is clear that *Dakṣa* progressively assumed a new role as the progenitor because he is the diety of skilfulness which is needed in the act of creation. As also evident from the story of Tvastru, who is elevated to the position of gods due to his dexterity, we can understand that creative skill is regarded high in the vedic society.

Bhāga and *Aṇśa*, the other two *Ādityas,* have a special significance. These two prehistoric deities show a determinate and explanatory moral features of *ṛta* and the early Aryan society. *Bhāga* has a hoary antiquity and his name is frozen in Indo-European cultures as a general term for 'spender of goods or blessing'[68] The slovic *bogu,* old Persian *baga* and *Avestan bagha* are counterparts of the vedic *Bhāga*. The deity *Bhāga* is not a general abstraction of wealth or splendour but, most remarkably, 'shared wealth'. *Bhāga,* even in the later Sanskrit refers to a part *(Bhāgam)*. *Bhāga* as a deity is 'dispenser or distributor of wealth'. *Bhāga* stands for wealth in general because in the primitive tribal communities all wealth is distributed. Wealth, for them, is what is apportioned. *Aṇsa,* the last in the list of *Ādityas,* is an abstraction which means *'a portion'* in general. Hence, *Bhāga* and *Aṇsa* are synonymous as far as the aspect of sharing is concerned. But *Bhāga* refers to 'wealth or fortune' while *Aṇśa* is just 'a portion' without any specification.

This sharing of wealth refers to a closed communal life in which people have equal claims to the wealth, which was mostly in the form of cattle. The ancient Angirasas are said to have common cattle. Distribution of cows in the assemblies is often alluded to. This aspect of *Bhāga* is unequivocally betrayed in some hymns:

Now, must *Bhāga* be invoked by mortals, lord of great riches who distributes treasures (VII.38.1).

The mighty calls on *Bhāga* for protection, on *Bhāga* calls the weak to give him riches (VII.38.6)

Thinking of whom, the poor, yea, even the mighty, even the king says give me *Bhāga* (VII.41.2).

These verses show that everyone had a claim to a share in the wealth. *Bhāga* in many hymns appears not as a deity but as a mere share of wealth distributed among men. *Agni, Savitar, Indra* and many other gods are described as apportioners of 'shares of wealth' *(Bhāga)*. At one place, *Indra* is said to be the sole distributor of shares of treasures (VII.26.4). *Agni* is called on to give shares of wealth (III.1.9.). *Savitar* is asked to send riches in earnest shares (V.82.3). Another class of deities called *Vājins* are considered as good apportioners and excellent arbiters of claims for shares, in the tribal assembly:

"Deep skilled in *ṛta,* deathless singers, O *Vājins,* help us in each fray for booty"[69]

This sharing of wealth and food is, interestingly, a feature not only among mortals but is a principle among gods too:

"For of one spirit are the gods with mortal men, co-sharers all of gracious gifts".[70]

Even the gods have claims for their shares in the oblations and libations offered by men in the sacrifice. *Agni* is viewed as 'the tongue of gods'. He carries the gifts of men to gods. *Brahmaṇaspati,* the deified prayer, is the distributor of shares among gods.[71] Remember, the primary function of prayer, in relation to the sacrifice, is to advance specific shares of oblation to gods. *Varuṇa, Mitra* and *Āryamaān* are said to be sharing the gifts of men equitably (VIII.27.17).

So, the specific characters of the *Ādityas* show that brotherhood, common religious practices, friendship, equality, comradeship, distribution of wealth and collective social life are the ethical features of the early vedic society. This collective form of life was due to simple mode of economic production and the homogeneity of the Aryan race. However, the confrontation of Aryans with non-Aryan aborigines brought sweeping changes in the economic and social aspects of Aryan life. The simple collective mode of living was ruined. The conditions for this shall be discussed in a later section. The idea of *ṛta*, the ancient law was replaced by new ideas which owe their origin to the transformed state of social affairs. However, *Ṛta* remained as a nostalgic ancient form of social concordance and its influence lasted long even after the break of primitive collective social institutions. Much of this will be discussed later. For now, let us look into the deprecatory and expiatory hymns of *Ṛg-Vēda* to estimate the moral commitment of the people to *ṛta*.

Ṛta and Moral Rectitude

In the *Ṛg-Vēda,* we find numerous verses condemning certain actions as morally wrong and some hymns seek condonation of gods for the moral misconduct. These deprecatory and expiatory hymns illumine the magnitude of moral consciousness among the vedic people. *Ṛta* as the moral order enjoins a set of moral principles to be followed by men in their social conduct. Among such principles, truth *(Satya)* is the foremost.

Ṛta, as the true path of gods and men, entails *Satya* as a moral value to be followed in thought, speech and action. *Satya* in its divine aspect, represents 'the unvarying conduct of gods'. Gods are true to *ṛta* in the sense that their adherence to the law is without variation. A thought or speech or deed is true only if it does not vary in any condition. *Satya* here is a moral character, of speech in particular. It is yet to acquire an ontological significance of *reality* as found in the later theosophical and speculative texts of the *Vēda*. *Satya* and *ṛta* are identified on the grounds that they are unvarying. *Satya* is the unvarying conduct of gods and men, while *ṛta* is the order followed by them. In this sense, *Satya* and *ṛta* hardly refer to an abstract ontological category of *sat* or reality. *Asatya* and *Anṛta,* the negatives of *satya* and *ṛta* respectively, represent variation in speech or conduct and variation in the proper order. *Ṛta* is straight-*ṛju* and whatever crooked is called *aṛjina*. Hence, falsehood, double-tongue, double dealing, false swearing, false accusation, failing to fulfil the agreement are deprecated as *asatya* and *anṛta*. They are viewed as sins against gods and men.[72] The unbinding variation of thought and action is thus transgression of *ṛta* and is subject to deprecation or condemnation.

Among the positive moral values, in addition to truth, health, strength, peace, non-injury, harmony, liberality and friendship are often praised. The hymn on gregarious liberality, which highlights helping the distressed and giving food to the hungry, is one of the most beautiful and morally significant hymn of the *Ṛg-Vēda*.[73] Probably it is the best piece of morally exhorting poetry even outside the *Vēda*. Offering food to a hungry man is emphatically called *nriyajña* or sacrifice to man.[74]

The idea of sin first appears in the *Ṛg-Vēda* in relation to *ṛta*. It is primarily viewed as transgression of *ṛta* and guile against gods and fellow men. It is considered as objective and often likened to fetters or bonds from which release is sought.[75] Sin is not only objective but, amazingly, also transferable or inflective. Some poets urge the gods not to punish them for the sins of their parents, forefathers and fellow men.[76] Sin is not just individual but is also collective and is prone to inflict the other members of the society. This idea, significantly, shows the way the early vedic people felt a collective responsibility towards the evils of fellow men.

Sin can accrue from both intentional and unintentional transgressions. Refuse of gods is sought for both committed and uncommitted sins.[77] The idea of retribution is also found in connection with sin. While *ṛta* fosters and preserves life, *anṛta* or transgression of the law, it is believed, leads to decay and death which is called *nirriti.* The transgression of law causes wrath of the gods which in turn leads to *nirriti*:

"Whatever law of thine, O god, Varuṇa, as we are men, day after day we violate give us not as a prey to death *(nirriti)*, to be destroyed by thee in wrath,

To thy fierce anger when displeased.

Far from us, far away those Destruction *(nirriti)*. Put away from us even the sin we have committed".[78]

Though the idea of divine wrath and retribution occurred in the *Ṛg-Vēda,* the idea of *hell* as a place of punishment, however, does not seem to be clear on the minds of the *Ṛg*-Vedic people. Except a few vague allusions, we hardly find any substantial description of hell in the *Samhita.*[79]

The concepts of sin and divine wrath lead the poets to seek refuge of the gods and expiatory efficacy of the sacrifice elaborated in the *Brāhmaṇas* and smriti literature:

" If we have sinned against the man who loves us, have ever wronged a brother, friend or comrade.

The neighbours ever with us or a stranger, O *Varuṇa,* remove from us the trespass.

If we, as gamesters cheat at play, have cheated, done wrong unwittingly or sinned of purpose.

Cast all these sins away like loosened fetters, and *Varuṇa,* let us be thine own beloved."[80]

As god *Varuṇa* is connected with waters, water is viewed as an instrument in expiation. This idea prevails, even today, that waters are capable of cleansing sins. The holy rivers are revered for this. The following verses appears twice in the *Samhita:*

"Whatever sin is found in me, whatever evil I have wrought, if I have lied or falsely sworn, waters, remove it far from me".[81]

The idea of expiation vouches for the moral commitment *ṛta* has been demanding even in the later vedic period. A poet urges gods to restore perfect innocence to him.[82] *Ṛta,* beyond doubt, exerted great moral influence on those people. However, the Aryan society had undergone changes, over the long period of the *Ṛg*-Vedic age, structurally and thus morally too. *Ṛta* and *Varuṇa* could not reign supreme in the altered conditions and at the end had to fade away. Some of the hymns mark this economic and ethical transition. Let us now see what those conditions were, which brought about thorough transformation in the material and ethical spheres of the Aryan society.

Loss of Ṛta and Downfall of Varuṇa

Ṛta, even in the oldest hymns of the *Ṛg-Vēda,* is referred to as the ancient law followed by the *Angirasas,* founding fathers of Aryan society. So, the antiquity of *ṛta* is confirmed by the vedic poets themselves. *Ṛta,* thus, is the traditional moral standard, the inheritance of which is fondly and proudly proclaimed by the vedic seers. This ancient law of social morality influenced the moral consciousness of the vedic society for quiet a long time. *Ṛta* occurs throughout the *Samhita* as the guiding law of men and gods. It is not an exaggeration to say that there are hardly a few hymns in which the word *ṛta* does not occur. God *Varuṇa* is the most imposing god in the early hymns of the *Vēda,* revered for his relation to *ṛta.*

However, *ṛta* and *Varuṇa* could not wield their peaks all through the *Vēda* and finally they were forced to oblivion. Loss of *ṛta* and the waning importance of *Varuṇa* found grave concern in some of the *Ṛg*-vedic hymns. As *ṛta* and *Varuṇa* had symbiotic origin in the prehistoric times and as they were closely connected throughout, it is quiet natural that the loss of one results in the fall of the other. But what were the conditions which caused withering away of *ṛta* and *Varuṇa* together?

The Aryan tribes were homogenous flocks which had a long prehistoric tradition rooted in the Indo-Iranian age. Their social life, as shown by our analysis of *ṛta,* was founded on equality, fraternity, collective wealth and communal life. The *Angirasas,* who came down through the lanes of memory as 'the ancient fathers', were recollected to have unanimous, strife-free, collective life.[83] So, the traditional Aryan society was a simple collective communal form of life.

These Aryan nomadic tribes, whose wealth chiefly consisted in cattle, entered the North-Western plains of India with rich culture and tradition different from that of the aborigines. As the Aryans started spreading towards east, they confronted the aborigines. Their confrontation with aborigines brought in a new economic dimension to their life marked by robber wars. The frequent occurrence of these robber wars is clear from innumerable hymns, especially those addressed to *Indra.*

The intensified robber wars had two fold impact on the Aryan society. Firstly, it has an economic impact which gave raise to warrior class and priestly class. The battles naturally result in a strengthened military class, over a period of time. It is not that the warrior element did not exist in the Aryan society till then. In fact, *kṣatriya vairya* is one of the *Amesha Sepents* or 'the Immortal Holy Ones' enlisted in *Avesta*. It speaks for the prehistory of this warrior element in the Aryan society.

However, this element was strengthened to form *a class* with the rise of inter racial robber wars.

The robber wars also marked the raise of priestly class over a period of time. The precondition for an intellectual or a military parasitic class is economic surplus to support that class. A primitive community cannot produce an intellectual class for it cannot produce surplus. This is true of all the primitive communities. However, due to the robber wars, the required surplus flowed into Aryan society through plunder or booty. Composing hymns and conducting sacrifices, which at one time was a collective activity, became the specialized occupation of a few. These neo-religious class was rewarded by the princes of warrior class through the plundered cattle and wealth. This resulted in composition of Munificence hymns which praise the liberal warrior donors.[84]

So, the homogenous cattle raisers (viś) were stratified into vaisya, the cattle breeders and agriculturists, *Kṣatriya,* the warriors and *Brāhmaṇa,* the priestly class. These classes further crystalized after a long time when the aborigines were totally conquered and included in Aryan society as *Śūdras*. The original Aryan classes i.e., *Vaiśyas, Kṣatriyas* and *Brāhmaṇas* wielded power over the *Śūdras* and surplus produced by them. Hence, the germs of division in the Aryan society are sown by robber wars. With introduction of this division, the original united collective community disintegrated. So was *ṛta* which supported the pre-class Aryan society.

The second impact of the robber wars was religious. The robber wars formed the condition for ascendency of *Indra* to supremacy. *Indra,* the warrior god came to forefront with the rise of military element in the society. *Indra* is closely connected with the robber wars throughout the *Vēda*. He is the chief of Aryan armies. He became the slayer of Dasyus, *Asuras* (demons) and the dark skinned. He is the inspirer of warriors. The spoil or plunder of these wars were distributed in sacrificial assemblies. So, *Indra* became a god of treasures too. He is the supporter of Aryan warriors in all the robber wars. His exploits are mostly his victories in robber wars:

Indra, indeed, is found a seeker of spoil (plunder), spoil seeker for his allies (I.132.3).

Indra that man when fighting shall obtain the spoil, whose strong defender thou will be (VII.32.11).

To the Tritsus (Aryan tribe) came the Arya's comrade *(Indra)*, through love of spoil and heroes' war, to lead them.

The foemen, measuring exceeding closely, abandoned to Sudas (Chief of Tritsus) all their provisions (VIII.18.15).

Hero, rejoicing in thy might, in combat give us a portion of the stall of cattle plundered (VII.27.1).

Indra is often invoked for victory in battles and for the wealth thereof. This made *Indra* to rise to the status of a national hero. He became tutelary god of Aryans. The clash between the old lord of order and the new chief of warriors is depicted in IV. 42 of the *Ṛg-Vēda*. The claims of each god to supremacy are alluded and the poet, at the end, strikes an equivocal compromise between the two gods. However, in X.124, *Indra* clearly supersedes *Varuṇa*. *Agni* decides to leave *Varuṇa* and seeks *Indra* as his new lord. *Indra's* supremacy is established in clear terms here. The wanning power of *Asura Varuṇa* as a god is thus simultaneous to the withering away of *ṛta*, the ancient moral order. The seer of VII.84, seeks the refuse of *Indra* from the wrath of *Varuṇa*. This shows the transition of moral consciousness of the Aryan people and their adjustment to the new order and new lord.

The deep concern and anguish over the loss of *ṛta* and fall of *Varuṇa* finds expression in I.105 of the *Samhita*. Kutsa, the seer of the hymn passionately questions:

"Where is the ancient law divine? Who is its new didffuser now? Mark this my woe, ye Earth and Heaven.

Ye gods who yander have your home in the three lucid realms of heaven.

What count ye truth and what untruth? Where is mine ancient call on you?

What is your firm support of Law? What *Varuṇa's* observant eye?

How may we pass the wicked on the path of mighty *Āryamān?* Mark this my woe, ye Earth and Heaven"

"What hath become of those our ancient friendships, when we without enmity walked together?

After a few centuries the new order was thoroughly established with fourfold division of society into stratified classes. The society could produce enough surplus to support the military and priestly classes. So, the age witnessed the origin of speculative theosophy and philosophy. By this time the Aryans stopped collecting hymns and turned their attention to elaboration of ritual norms which were preserved in the *Brāhmaṇas*.

Even *Indra* had to fade away along with other gods at a later time. When the inter racial wars were over, resulting in stabilized fourfold society, *Indra* as a warrior gods was no more necessary. His very existence was doubted in VIII.89.3 and eventually he receded to back drop. The Brahminical speculations, which ended in monotheistic conception of one great Brahman, held sway over the ancient nature-gods. With spiritualistic speculations in *Upaniṣads* concerning the nature of the Brahman, even the vedic rituals went out of vogue.

The Monotheism, reality of transmigrating souls and theory of Karma which were products of theosophical speculations, laid foundations for Dharma in social sphere,

Bhakti in religious sphere and Moksa in the spiritual sphere. We shall deal with them in the next chapter.

With the foregoing analysis, it was clear that *ṛta* was the moral order of the primitive collective homogenous communal living which founded on fraternity, kinship and unanimity. One ancient poet says: never may we enjoy another's solemn feast, ourselves, oursons or our progeny.[85] Compare him to the later spoil seeker. What a transformation! While *ṛta* explain and enforces equality, Dharma, as we will see, explains and enforce difference and division.

The ideas of primitive society with all its egalitarian features broke down due to the new order in which the society is stratified with conflicting interests. The unanimity of ancient fathers was looked upon with reverence and nostalgic fervour by later vedic poets. The last verse of the *Ṛg-Vēda* is a fitting epitaph on the tomb of *ṛta:*

"One and the same by your resolve, and be your minds of one accord.

United be the thoughts of all that all may happily agree".[86]

References

1. Wilson, H.H., *The Ṛg-vēda Samhita,* Introduction, p.IX.
2. Maurice Bloomfield, *The Religion of the Vēda,* p. 126.
3. Maurice Bloomfield, *The Religion of the Vēda,* p. 12.
4. The *Ṛg-Vēda* L 159.1; L. 185.4; VL. 17.7 etc.
5. Maurice Bloomfield, *The Religion of the Vēda,* p.82.
6. Maurice Bloomfield, *The Religion of the Vēda,* p.95.
7. G. Thomson, *Studies in Ancient Greek Society,* ill 46, cited by D.P. Chattopadhyaya in *Lokāyata,* p. 632.
8. The *Ṛg-vēda.* III,54.3; VL.17.7; X.59.8.
9. The *Ṛg-vēda.* I.142.7; V.5.6.

10. The *Ṛg-vēda* III.54.6; X.65.8; X.92.4.
11. The *Ṛg-vēda* I.144.7; I.189.6; VI.48.5 etc.
12. The *Ṛg-vēda* IV.2.19; IV.51.7-8; VII.75.1, etc.
13. The *Ṛg-vēda* I.164.11.
14. The *Ṛg-vēda* I.25.28; V.85; VIII.45, 86-89.
15. The *Ṛg-vēda* I.2.8.
16. The *Ṛg-vēda* I.23.5.
17. The *Ṛg-vēda*. VIII. 66.13.
18. The *Ṛg-vēda*. V.62.3.
19. The *Ṛg-vēda*. V.66.1.
20. The *Ṛg-vēda*. VII.40.4.
21. The *Ṛg-vēda*. I.25.11.
22. The *Atharvaṇa-Vēda*. IV.16.
23. The *Ṛg-Vēda* I.25.7-9.
24. The *Ṛg-Vēda* I.25.13; VII.87.3.
25. Cf. Giffrith's note on X.54.4.
26. The *Ṛg-Vēda*, II.24.14; V.63.7 etc.
27. The *Ṛg-vēda* V.63.7.
28. Yasna 31.13; 43.6; 45.4.
29. Maurice Bloomfield, *The Religion of the Vēda*, p. 60.
30. The *Ṛg-Vēda* I.125, 126; V.27; VIII.18; X.33.
31. e.§. I.127.2; III.35.6; X.46.2; X.150.2
32. The *Ṛg-Vēda* I.7.9; I.176.3; VI.46.7; VII.15.2 etc.
33. Giffrith's note on I.36.5.
34. The *Ṛg-Vēda* V.70.2.
35. The *Ṛg-Vēda* VIII.64.2.
36. The *Ṛg-Vēda* VII.66.9.
37. The *Ṛg-Vēda* IV.23.8-10.
38. The *Ṛg-Vēda* IV.41.2-3.

39. The *Ṛg-Vēda* IX.94.5.
40. The *Ṛg-Vēda* VII.36.2.
41. The *Ṛg-Vēda* I.54.3.
42. The *Ṛg-Vēda* VIII.84.5 cited by Bloomfield.
43. Cf. The *Ṛg-Vēda* III.34.2.
44. X.34.
45. VII.103.
46. Cf. The *Ṛg-Vēda* IV.7.7.
47. Cf. The *Ṛg-Vēda* IV.7.11.
48. Macdonell, A.A., *A History of Sanskrit Literature,* p. 64.
49. Cf. Giffrith's note on this hymn.
50. Cf. The *Ṛg-Vēda* X.161-184.
51. Macdonell, A.A., *A History of Sanskrit Literature,* p. 66.
52. The *Ṛg-Vēda* VIII.27.15-17.
53. The *Ṛg-Vēda* VII.34.8.
54. The *Ṛg-Vēda* VI.9.5.
55. The *Ṛg-Vēda* I.113.3
56. The *Ṛg-Vēda* I.65.1.
57. The *Ṛg-Vēda* VIII.35.1.
58. The *Ṛg-Vēda* VII.76.5.
59. Cf. *Atharva-Vēda* VI.64.
60. The *Ṛg-Vēda* X.191.2.
61. The *Ṛg-Vēda* I.25.13; II.27.3 and 9.
62. The RV II.27.1
63. Giffrith's note on X. 11.2.
64. The *Ṛg-Vēda* I.105.9.
65. Cf. The *Ṛg-Vēda* VII.69.13; VII.64.1; V.67.1 and VII.69.12.
66. The *Ṛg-Vēda* VI.50.2. Cf. Giffrith's note on it.
67. The *Ṛg-Vēda* VII.66.2; VIII.25.6; VIII.52.10.

68. Cf. Bloomfield, *The Religion of the Vēda*, p.109.
69. The *Ṛg-Vēda* VII.38.8.
70. The *Ṛg-Vēda* VIII.27.14.
71. The *Ṛg-Vēda* II.23.2; II.24.14.
72. The *Ṛg-Vēda* I.23.22; I.147.4-5; V.12.4-5; X.9.8.; X.89.9 etc.
73. The *Ṛg-Vēda* X.117.
74. The *Ṛg-Vēda* I.31.15.
75. The *Ṛg-Vēda* I.24.9; V.85.8; VII.86.5 etc.
76. The *Ṛg-Vēda* V.86.5; VI.51.7.
77. The *Ṛg-Vēda* X.63.8.
78. The *Ṛg-Vēda* I.25.1-2; I.24.9.
79. The *Ṛg-Vēda* IV.5.5; VII.104.3.
80. The *Ṛg-Vēda* V.85.7-8.
81. I.23.23; X.9.8
82. The *Ṛg-Vēda* X.37.11.
83. The *Ṛg-Vēda* VII.76.4-5.
84. Cf. The *Ṛg-Vēda* V.27; I.25; VII.18; X.33 etc.
85. The *Ṛg-Vēda* V.70.4.
86. The *Ṛg-Vēda* X.191.4.

3

Transition to *Dharma*

Dharma is the central ethical concept in the post-*Ṛig*-vedic Indian thought. It is the comprehensive ethical category in the light of which alone rest of the ethical ideals can be understood. It is both a definitional and a critical concept of seminal importance in all the systems of Indian philosophy, save the Carvakas. In Indian classical thought, we find the word *dharma* used in so many ways that Cromwell Crawford fittingly says '... to know India, try grasping the myriad forms of *dharma*, for in the depths of this single word lies an entire civilization.'[1]

Though *dharma* can be traced back to the Rig-vēda, it no doubt acquired the status of an ethical category only in the *Brāhmaṇas* and further gained definite structure in the *Upaniṣads*. The word occurs only once in the *Ṛg-vēda*[2] and there too it appears as a deity addressed in a group. In the *Ṛg-vēda*, it was yet to be developed as a fulfledged ethical concept. Though in the later parts of the *Ṛg-vēda* we find a gradual disappearance of ṛta, its place was not occupied by *dharma*. One reason for this is the fact that *dharma* owes its origin to a transition the Aryan society has undergone both in economic and intellectual spheres. Its origin is not independent but a part of the speculative scheme unfolded in the Brāhmaṇas and the *Upaniṣads*. Hence the development of *dharma* is simultaneous with that of some important speculative concepts the latent impressions of which can be found in the *Ṛg-vēda*. A proper understanding of *dharma* thus necessitates an analysis of its symbiotic corollaries. Before we undertake the evolution of *dharma* and analyze its structural relationship with other philosophical concepts, a note on the general uses of the word is in order.

Dharma and its Meaning

Dharma is a very comprehensive ethical concept which signifies differently in different contexts. It acquired, in the long history of Indian ethical thought, various senses and we always have to examine the context carefully before determining the sense in which the word is used. Again, the stipulated usage of the word differs with each philosophical system. However, there are certain common ways in which the word is generally used. The various uses of the word are not altogether disconnected but are complementary to each other and widened the scope of the concept. *Dharma* retained its essential ethical character all through the seemingly incompatible usages. Precisely this is what makes *dharma* a comprehensive ethical category which incorporates a wide range of ethical ideals.

In addition to the popular usage to mean Justice and Morality, the word *dharma* is used technically in six important ways signifying: 1. the law of a thing's being 2. the ethical order 3. scriptural duties 4. object of human pursuit 5. religion and 6. righteousness. A brief explanation of the various denotations of *dharma* would help us, by the way, in understanding the concept in its entirety. In fact, they are rather six important aspects of the comprehensive notion of *dharma*.

Law of Thing's Being

Dharma in this primary sense refers to the essential nature of a thing without which it cannot exist. *Dharma* is the principle which defines, preserves, underlies and regulates a thing's being. For example, fluidity is the *dharma* of water and if water loses fluidity, it will either become vapour or ice. Similarly, heat is the *dharma* of fire so that if it does not produce heat, it is not called fire. So, *dharma* is the basis for the existence of any thing: *dharaṇat dharmam ityahuḥ*[3]. The notion of *dharma* is of moral significance here when we understand what the essential nature, i.e. *dharma*, of man is. Man's *dharma* is the fundamental idea from which all other moral concepts derive their meaning. All the Indian systems build their systems of morality on their notion of the essential nature of man. The Materialists who construe man in terms of material elements end up in a morality which seeks sensuous pleasure as the highest principle. On the other hand, Advaita Vedanta which identifies individual with the absolute principle of consciousness *(Brahman)* places the realization of it as the ultimate aim of human existence. For most of the Indian schools understanding one's own nature and being at it is the highest good. This is precisely why Indian ethics is inseparable from metaphysics. What is *moral* is always determined by what is *real*. What is morally good for man depends on what man essentially is. This is the most important methodological contribution of Indian ethics to the world.

The Indian systems differ as to what is morally good for they differ as to what the true nature of man is. Despite metaphysical differences, all the Indian systems are almost unanimous on the methodological principle: *man's being and his morality cannot be conceived independent of each other.* In other words, *real is moral. Dharma* thus denotes both *real* and *moral. Dharma* in its metaphysical aspect is the basis for *dharma* in its moral aspect and the latter is the extension of the former. This conception of *dharma* is accepted by both the orthodox and heterodox schools alike. This is one of the surest foundations of Indian ethics. Even in Buddhism, we find *dharma* signifying entity.

Moral Order

Dharma in another important sense denotes the moral order. In Indian thought morality is never a matter of arbitrary adoption but always presupposes a moral order from which every moral principle derives its significance. Morality is not a sphere where blind forces hold their sway but an ordered universe having its own laws. Right from the *Ṛg-vēdic* age, Indian thinkers conceived a well established order both in the cosmos and in the moral world. The Cosmic Order when manifests in man becomes the Moral Order. The *Ṛg-vēdic* conception of the *ṛta* influenced and found continuation in *dharma*. *Dharma* inherited the sense of Moral Order from *ṛta* and expresses the fundamental ethical commitment of Indian thought to the notion of a unitary order in physical and moral aspects of the reality.

However, *dharma* differs from *ṛta in* certain respects. While *ṛta* is invariably connected with gods who uphold and execute the Cosmic Order, *dharma* acquired independence from gods in the later speculative scheme. *Dharma* has become an autonomous ethical order which hardly needed any divine support or intervention. This is an important development in the evolution of Indian ethics and marks the transition from theological world-view to the philosophical world-view.

The independent moral order is universally binding and follows its own course devoid of any divine arbitration. Even the most atheistic schools of India, for this reason, had no hesitation to incorporating *dharma* into their metaphysical and ethical systems. Man has to confirm to the higher order of universal *dharma* in order to preserve oneself. Such conformity leads to ones own welfare along with that of others. Hence *dharma* is viewed as basically of the form of welfare. Sabara in his commentary on *Mīmāmsa Sūtras,* defines thus: *Śreyaskara ēva dharmah.* This idea of *dharma* underlies further treatment of *dharma* in all the schools. It is worth noting here that in

Indian thought, welfare does not always mean mere hedonistic pleasures though it includes them. *Dharma* as the independent moral order, when truly conformed to, would help one to keep one's own *dharma* and thus gains him welfare.

Scriptural Duty

Dharma in another important sense means moral duty in general and scriptural duty in particular. *Dharma* acquired this sense in the *Brāhmaṇas,* the *Smṛti* literature and the ritualistic school of *Pūrva Mīmamsa.* The *Vēdas* were considered by the brahmanical tradition as the repositories of highest ethical wisdom and conceived as of absolute authority. According to the *Pūrva Mīmāmsakas,* the *Vedic* injunctions are the solitary source of *dharma.* This notion of *dharma* laid foundations for ritualistic morality on one hand and authority of the social codes on the other. While *Pūrva Mīmamsa* deals with religious morality in terms of the *Vēdic* ritualism, the codes of Manu and other law-givers derive the legitimacy of their codes from the authority of the Veda. However, there is one difference between Mimamsa and the *Smṛtis:* while Mimamsa puts forth philosophical arguments for the authority of the *Vēda,* the social codes presuppose it. But the notion that *dharma* consists in what is enjoined by the *Vēda* is common to both of them. Hence, in the later brahmanical tradition, *dharma* came to mean the traditional morality supported by the *Vēda.*

As we progress in our analysis of *dharma,* we find how the tradition is sought to be preserved in the *Smṛtis* and how the *Vēdic* ideas and notions influenced the later theories of *dharma* along with the moral practice in India. The social and political life in India was thoroughly moulded by the *Vēdic* notions of morality and we find a continuity of the tradition in one form or other throughout the history of India. The survival value of the tradition owes, among other things, to the rational appeal it makes to the Indian mind.

Object of Pursuit

Dharma also denotes the moral pursuit of man. It is one of the four objects of human pursuit *(puruṣārtha),* the other three being *artha* (wealth), *kāma* (desired pleasures) and *mokṣa* (spiritual liberation). These *puruṣārthas* also suggest the individual attitudes towards the world of objects. *Dharma* is considered as the most important of all the *puruṣārthas*. *Dharma* has to be followed in all the human endeavours and thus it underlies all the other *puruṣārthas*. Even *mokṣa* cannot be attained by being indifferent to *dharma*. A morally degraded individual is not fit for *mokṣa* and cannot realize the ultimate truth. There is no short cut to *mokṣa* without attaining moral purity. *Artha* and *Kāma* if pursued without *dharma* are not commendable. Despite theoretical differences, this fourfold division of *puruṣārthas* is mostly accepted in Indian philosophical schools.

Religion

Dharma in its loser sense refers to religion in general. We often find appellations like *Bouddha dharma, Jaina dharma etc.*, where *dharma* means religion. In India, the philosophical wisdom finds expression in religious practice. This is how Indian philosophy is of real practical significance. *Dharma* as religion paves way for moral development and one experiences the religious life at its best through philosophical understanding of *dharma* as expressed in the religion. Religion imbibes moral principles and instigates their practice. Religion when practised with a moral attitude becomes truly human.

Some of the major philosophical systems like Buddhism and Jainism are also popular religions known for their moral insights and practice. In India, religion and philosophy go hand in hand because of their common ethical interest and practicability. In Indian tradition, knowledge without practice has no value. Knowing is practising: *jñatva anuṣṭayet*. This amply speaks of the unity of theory and practice in Indian systems.

Now, let us have a close look at the way the various senses of *dharma* are connected organically to form a grand ethical system. *Dharma* as the justice or righteousness which has to be adhered by every individual necessarily brings into picture the very nature of his being. What is good for man obviously follows from what he is. Further, man's nature is not independent but a part and parcel of the greater order in the universe and thus involves a study of the nature of the universe and man's place in it. *Dharma* when denotes moral order brings this notion to relief. There is a greater moral order in which man's righteousness is a dependent part, and in this sense, morality transcends the realm of mere individual reference. The objectivity of the morality is emphasized here, and though man is the centre of the universe, he is not the defining principle in the universe. Man as a moral being has to confirm to the higher moral order which encloses the outer world as well. This notion of *dharma* as the order has twofold significance: first, it is holistic and secondly it emphasizes moral necessity. The objectivity of the ethical order which is beyond individual tastes is a greater insight offered by Indian ethics which is often attacked for its seemingly individualistic morality.

In the process of conforming oneself to the universe at large and the society in which one lives, one is bound to interact with the nature and fellow men in an ethical way. Man is related to the nature and fellow beings not just physically or materially but also morally. The essential relationship between man and the outer world necessitates man to adopt a moral view in all his pursuits or achieving objects. Here, *dharma* takes the form of a necessary attitude or an object of pursuit which must underlie all his activities.

The soul of religion consists in man's recognition of the essential ethical relationship between himself and his surroundings. Religion as a collective mode of adherence to the basic ethical values propels the ethical impulses of the people towards a spiritual unity. In the history of mankind this is the noblest role played by religion. Religion inculcates the fundamental values through external sacred practices. In some cases, the religious practices continue to exist while their ethical presuppositions are comfortably lost. Still religion plays an important role in propagation of basic virtues and moral practices among people. It is true, religion supports certain social institutions and particular forms of society for the sake of its own survival. It also generates certain power circles and is often used by them as a weapon for wielding power over masses. Here, religion and politics play a complementary roles. Nevertheless, religion still decisively moulds the moral attitude of its adherents.

Religion as a collective mode of life, necessarily involves an ethical vision and a code of conduct. It is here, the religious scriptures are of moral significance. All the major religions have their own scriptures which embody the moral preaching of their founders and these scriptures offer moral guidance to the adherents. As far as Hinduism is concerned, the *Vēdas* stand as the revered sources of morality, both social and religious. As mentioned earlier, the social codes derive, atleast theoretically, the major tenets of social justice and righteousness from the *Vēdas*. On the other hand, Mīmāmsakas establish and define religious duties in terms of the absolute authority of the *Vēdas*. Thus *dharma,* in both its social and religious aspects, corresponds to the teaching of the *Vēdas*.

The above analysis shows that the various denotations of *dharma* are not arbitrary adoptions but are organically connected as the grand classical ethical vision fostered in ancient India. With this understanding of *dharma,* let us now see the conditions which mark the transition from *ṛta* to *dharma*.

Transition

As noted earlier, the transition was both social and intellectual. The hitherto homogenous Aryan society had taken the subjugated aborigines, who were referred to as dasyus in the *Ṛg-Vēda,* into its fold forming the forth caste by name Sūdra. The fusion of Āryans and non-Āryans was the greatest event in the social history of Hindu society. This event gave rise to new dimensions in religion, philosophy, economy and most importantly ethics. The Sūdras who entered the Hindu society as the servile class provided it with necessary material surplus to support its warriors and the intellegentia. The new fourfold social order emerged on the ruins of the original close communal life of the *Ṛg-vēdic* age. *Ṛta,* the ancient ethical order was dispensed along with the primitive homogenous close communal life. The new order demanded a different theoretical explanation for its establishment. This is precisely the purpose served by the *Vēdic* theories of Creation which mark the beginning of the *Vēdic* speculations.

The observations made by Prof. Keith in this regard have to be mentioned here. Unfortunately, he does not see any point in analysing the *Vēdic* theories of creation and claims that they are of no ethical significance. In his own words, "the details of these stupid myths are wholly unimportant: it is enough to note that he (Prajapati) is constantly the creator, the ruler, and the preserver of the world and accepted by every Brāhmaṇa of the period as being the lord of the world: he is, it may be added, without any ethical importance. The conception of him is purely intellectual, that of the unity of the universe, and choosing of Prajapati as the symbol of this unity is one of the striking proofs of the *Rig Vēda* upon the period of *Brāhmaṇas.* '[4] Here, Keith has completely missed the immense significance of myths in understanding the value commitments of a community. Myths are not detached from real life and its social content. For that matter, even the wildest speculations, however abstract they are, can not be totally autonomous from the real life. The reason for this is the inevitability or non-disposability of the real world for man. Man's thought is neither autonomous nor is devoid of social purpose.

To render the above made point clearer, let us consider whether myths and primitive speculations have any ethical relevance. To do so, we have to pose a naive question to ourselves: why do primitive people generate myths at all? There appear two primary motives for their creating myths. First, they want to explain or answer some riddles of the reality for which they do not have an empirically satisfying answer in hand. Secondly they want to record the most significant events in their social history, the deeds of their celebreties, to perpetuate certain institutions or to admire and cherish certain values. While doing so they nevertheless apply their creative faculties embellishing or adorning the basic theme. A major part of their social life with institutional values finds expression in the myths in an intricate form. Myths are thus expressions of their fundamental adjustment to reality, both social and physical, and a means of passing on their value commitments to the following generations. Thus myths have an important sociological function. Myths provide us with important clues as to the modes and development of thought of a community. Hence they come very handy in our understanding the conditions through which sociological and intellectual development takes shape.

Coming to our main analysis, the *Ṛg-vēdic* hymns of creation serve, in addition to the poets' zeal to address the riddle of cosmic origin, the important sociological function of explaining contemporary form of society. We find for the first time an allusion to the fourfold caste system in the *Puruṣa Sūkta* of Tenth Mandala. Again, the conception of the primeval principle of the cosmic origin has a definite influence on the later speculations of the Aryan mind. In what follows, let us have a look at the way the *Ṛg-vēdic* sages conceive the origin of the world and its influence on the further ontological and ethical speculations in Indian Philosophy.

Unitary Diety of Creation

The *Ṛg-vēdic* hymns of creation mark the beginning of theoretical speculations and contain the earliest germs of philosophy. These hymns belong to the latest strata of the *Ṛg-vēdic* hymns.[5] The most important feature of these hymns is their search for a unitary principle responsible for the whole world. Dhīrgatamas, the seer of I.164, is probably the first poet-philosopher who properly arranged the ontological question:

"I ask, unknowing, those who know, the sages, as one all ignorant for the sake of knowledge. What was the *One* who in the unborn's image hath established and fixed firm these worlds' six regions?"[6]

The peculiarity of the question is that it already presupposes a unitary principle of creation. The view is further confirmed thus in the oftquoted verse:

"They call him *Indra, Mitra, Varuṇa, Agni*, and he is heavenly nobly-winged Garutman. To what is One, sages give many title: they call it *Agni, Yama, Matarisvan*"[7]

This verse recognizes the One behind all the gods and considers the different gods as nothing but mere names for the One. It asserts the unitary cause of the world on one hand and relegates the gods to mere appellations of the supreme underlying principle on the other hand. The gods are stripped of their peculiar individual divinity. This is a very important development for Hindu religion and philosophy as well. The monastic bend culminated in monotheism in the religion and lead to monistic idealism in the philosophy.

The fundamental assertion of monism by Dhīrgatamas was complemented by some stray guesses at the universal cause attributing it to various gods before the monism reached its zenith in the famous *Puruṣa Sūkta*. We find *Indra,*[8] *Viśvakarman,*[9] *Agni,*[10] *Varuṇa,*[11] *Brahmaṇaspati,*[12] Dhatar[13] etc. being alluded as the creators. These verses are not of much significance except for that they show an increasing fascination for the idea of creation in the *Vēdic* seers.

The idea of originator of the world is further elucidated in the hymns X.121 and X.130. Here are given some imaginative accounts of the process of creation but the question of the creator-God and His identity was left open. While the former hymns is addressed to *Ka* which literally means *'who'* or 'the unknown God', the latter hymn ends in a sceptical note as to the identity of the creator. It is worth noting that they nevertheless bear a strong theistic bent and mark the development of monotheism.

For a fulfledged account of creation we have to turn to the *Puruṣa Sūkta*[14] which is far developed in content and form. This hymn presents the most developed theory of creation and names the creator 'Puruṣa' whence it got its title. This hymn is more interesting for it is here we find first ever allusion to the four-fold caste system. The hymn conceives Puruṣa as the omnipresent creator with thousand head, eyes and feet. He is the creator of all that is. He produced Viraj and in turn born to Viraj. Gods and Rishis made the primeval sacrifice with Puruṣa as the victim. They divided Him into four portions and His mouth became Brāhmana, arms Rājanya, thighs Vaisya and His feet became Sūdra.[15] Manu and other law-givers borrow this idea of divine origin of the four castes from Puruṣa Sūkta and legitimize their codes for the stratified society.

This hymn also established monotheism in its fullness. Thus this important hymn laid foundation for Hindu social ethics and religion simultaneously. Hence it has far-reaching implications for Hindu thought. The major philosophical contribution of the hymn is its shift in explanation of the universe. While the earlier *Vēdic* thought explains the physical world in terms of the working of *ṛta* through various deities, the cosomogonic hymn explains it in terms of unitary all-pervading deity. However, it is not yet free from theism in as much as Puruṣa is still a deity. In the *Brāhmaṇas,* Prajapati is most often mentioned as the progenitor of the mankind and the creation is attributed to him. The real shift to non-individualistic and non-theistic principle occurs in the Upanisadic speculations where the cosmic individual i.e. Puruṣa is replaced by Brahman, the universal spirit. Nevertheless, the conception of Puruṣa is important as it is the first step towards monism.

Individual Soul

For the development of any ethical theory the conception of the moral agent or the acting individual is central. The idea of moral responsibility and retribution presupposes as individual to whom they are attributed. In Indian philosophy it is *ātman* or the individual soul which stands as the moral agent. There are two exceptions to this generality: Buddhist and Carvakas. Buddhists do not accept the existence of an individual soul and are widely criticized for this. Buddhists, due to the absence of *ātman,* could not develop a proper theory of moral reprisal. For them, thus morality or *dharma* is only a disposition of mind which takes the place of *ātman* in their system. Though this disposition has an impact on the future actions of the man, the idea of moral retribution does nor occur in Buddhism. Carvakas, on the other hand, deny the existence of a soul other than the body. Soul is a myth for them. The conscious material body stands for individuality in their philosophy. It is for this reason, they do not entertain the idea of moral vindictiveness. Individual is more a hedonistic entity than a moral agent and hence they define good and bad in terms of pleasure or otherwise a thing produces. Human action does not entail any supersensuous moral responsibility except resulting in happiness or its opposite or a mixture of the both.

Though Carvakas stop at physical pleasures, Buddhists however recognize certain positive virtues and ethical dispositions to be developed.

Again, the theory of transmigrations which is the most important component in Indian ethics presupposes the concept of individual soul. It is the individual soul that undergoes different births as a result of its own previous deeds and enjoys the fruits of those acts. Without a transmigrating soul, it is very difficult to explain metempsychosis. Buddhism undertakes this difficult task of explaining transmigration without an enduring self. The peculiarity of the Buddhist thesis will be discussed when we deal with its theory of *dharma*. Further, the Indian theories of liberation and bondage also presuppose the existence of an enduring self. Here too, Buddhism is the sole exception. The Carvakas, along with *ātman,* do not approve the notions of bondage and liberation. Thus Buddhism and Carvakas stand out as 'soul-less' systems with their own peculiarities.

The usage of the word *ātman* points back to the *Ṛg-vēda* where it is used in its primary sense of 'wind' and in a modified sense of 'breath'.[16] The *Ṛg-vēda* X.92.13 mentions wind as the breath of all and X.168.4 calls Vayu, the wind-god, as the *ātman* of all the deities. So *ātman* is conceived as the cause of life or mark of life because body organism without breath is lifeless and devoid of consciousness. Another *Ṛg-vēdic* word for life breath is *asu*[17] which is rarely used. What is peculiar about the *Ṛg-vēdic* conception of *ātman* is that it is very much corporeal. Consider the belief that after death, *ātman* or the breath goes to wind:

"The Sun receive thine eye, the wind thy spirit; go, as thy merit is, to earth or heaven. Go if it be thy lot, unto the waters; go, make thine home in plants with all thy members".[18] Again, the spirit of a pious man is supposed to reach the heavenly abode of Yama where it enjoys all material pleasures like food and drink and even conjugal bliss. *Ātman* acquired the definite sense of 'soul' or 'self' in the *Brāhmaṇas* and distinguished from the vital airs called *praṇa.*[19] We can see somewhat similar usage in the *Atharva-Vēda* which too distinguishes *ātman* from breath and other organs of body.[20] In the later portions of the *Brāhmaṇas,* the concept of *ātman* is found in a well defined form and clearly made autonomous from its other earlier connotations to mean exclusively the 'spirit' or 'self' with a reflective insinuation. Here, rudimentary attempts are made to characterise *ātman* either as mind[21] or consciousness[22] awaiting dedicated speculations on the nature of *ātman* in the *Upaniṣads.*

In the *Upaniṣads, Ātman* is deprived of all material qualities and made exactly the opposite to material body in all aspects. It is devoid of form and dimensions and all the qualities of body and is made a real spiritual entity.[23] It is said to be devoid of size, length, shadow, wind, fat, tangibility, taste, smell, organs or parts, name or identity, age and all the material qualities. It appears, the *Upaniṣadic* negative description of *ātman* is arrived at by merely denying the soul all the qualities of a material body. In their anxiety to distinguish spirit from all the material manifestations, they made path-breaking speculations about the nature of *ātman,* mostly of negative character. However, *ātman* is positively characterised for once as eternal *akṣara* and as the only conscious principle. Here too, it appears they attributed those qualities which they thought matter does not possess. From this they proceeded to the conception of *the absolute* which determined the development of the *Upaniṣadic* philosophy in its entirety. We will come to this point a little later. We shall also see its impact on *dharma* in its formation.

Transmigration

As mentioned earlier, the theory of transmigration presupposes an individual soul which undergoes it. Though the idea of *ātman* was developed more in the *Brāhmaṇas*, the notion of transmigration in its naive form could be traced back to the eschatological béliefs recorded in the *Ṛg-vēda*. What happens to man after death is a fundamental question which gave rise to varied eschatological systems in all the primitive cultures of the world. Different answers were attempted in the *Ṛg-vēda* for this question leading to the detailed theory of transmigration in the later speculative thought.

For the *Ṛg-vēdic* people, life on the earth is so precious and enjoyable that they repeatedly asked for longer lives on earth and even immortality:

A hundred autumns may we see that bright Eye *Sūrya*, God-ordained arise:

A hundred autumns may we live[24]

May this rite save me till my hundredth autumn. Preserve us ye Gods, with blessings[25]

Here I erect this rampart for the living; let none of those reach this limit

May they survive hundred autumns, may they bury Death beneath the mountain.[26]

Live your full lives and find oldage delightful, all of you striving one behind the other[27]

Correspondingly, death *(Mrityu)* and disintegration *(nirriti)* are feared as evident from various hymns in which death is wished away. Here are a few quoteworthy:

Give us not up as a prey to death, O *Soma*: still let us look upon sun arising

Let our oldage with passing days be kindly. Let Nirriti depart to distant places!

O *Asuniti,* keep the breath with us, and make the days we have to live yet longer. Grant that we still look upon the sunlight: strengthen the body with the oil we bring thee[28].

The beginnings of eschatology in the *Ṛg-vēdic* period are connected with *Yama*, the later God of Death. In the *Ṛg-vēda*, *Yama* is regarded as the first mortal died who found a place in the Heaven for the pious mortals. The Fathers of antiquity are supposed to be in the enjoyable company of *Yama* who hosts them. *Yama* is thus revered as the King of the Dead:

Yama first found for us a place to do well in: this pasture never can be taken from us

Men born on earth tread their own paths that lead them where our ancient Fathers have departed[29]

The abode of *Yama* was described as the most delightful place where *Yama* constantly puts the dead in comfort with food and drink. The priestly imagination about the Heaven culminated in detailed description of it in the *Brāhmaṇas*, and further taken to its height in the Pauraṇic literature. In the *Ṛg-vēda*, the poets wish to attain immortality in the realm of *Yama*:

O Pavamana, place me in that deathless, undecaying world wherein the light of heaven is set, and everlasting lusture shines. Flow, Indu, flow for Indra's sake.

Make me immortal in that realm where dwells the King, Vivasvan's son,

Where is the secret shrine of heaven, where are those waters young and fresh. Flow, Indu, flow for *Indra's* sake.

Make me immortal in that realm of eager wish and strong desire, the region of the radiant Moon, where food and full delight are found. Flow, Indu, flow for *Indra's* sake.

Make me immortal in that realm where happiness transports, where

Joys and felicities combine, and longingwishes are fulfilled. Flow, Indu, flow for *Indra's* sake.[30]

Spirit of the Dead

The spirit of the dead is addressed to reach the abode of *Yama* safely and to enjoy the pleasurable company of *Yama* and the forefathers who had already been there:

"Meet *Yama,* meet the Fathers, meet the merit of free or ordained acts, in highest heaven. Leave sin or evil, seek a new thy dwelling, and bright with glory wear another body".[31]

Here emerges an important question: can everyone dead go to heaven? This is a crucial question because an answer to it has far reaching echoes in the future ethical thought of India.

The answer is 'well, not everyone but only the pious dead can reach heaven'. This seemingly simple answer decisively influenced the formation of the Indian theories of transmigration, *Karma* and *Dharma*. Let us see how.

The path to heaven is not easy to tread. It is guarded by twin *Suramas,* the four-eyed ferocious dogs (cf. The *Ṛg-vēda* X.14.11). *Yama* was prayed to help the pious spirits with the favour of escaping the two dogs in their journey to heaven.

The idea that only the pious ones, who have done good works on earth, are capable of attaining heaven goes long way. What else are the good works for the *Ṛg-vēdic* Āryans except *yajñas*? This notion of good works i.e., *yajña* leading one to heaven gained strength in the *Brāhmaṇas* and the ultimate aim of *yajña* is conceived as attainment of heaven. Here we find a shift of ends. Earlier, the primary purpose of *yajña* was to uphold *Ṛta* and please gods and now it is to attain heaven.

The crucial point to note here is that the element of retribution has entered for good as the most influencing precept into Indian moral thought. Heaven as a retribution for good works has on one hand enhanced performance of *yajña* and on the other hand lead to the notion that every act has its retribute.

Not only attaining heaven but Sojourn there is also conceived as an effect of good acts. The continuance of the pious spirits in heaven depends on their good acts on the earth.

The departed one meets with 'the merit of ordained or free acts' in the heaven which helps one continue there. *Yajñas* and gifts to priests (iṣta-pūrta) and gods prolong one's stay in heaven:

"Offer*Yama* holy gifts enriched with butter, and draw near:

So may be grant that we may live long days of life among fathers".[32]

As the stay in heaven is a result of good acts, it is natural that is lasts as long as the merit lasts. The balance of merit diminishes as one's stay gets longer just as our vanity bag becomes lighter with our continued stay in a star hotel. As actions have temporal conditioning, so do their results. Longer stay in the heaven exhausts one's accumulated merit. (cf. *Taittariya Samhita*, ii.6.10.2).

What happens once the merit is exhausted? The stay ceases... it means death there. This is called re-death or *punar-mṛtyu*. *Yajñas* performed for the favour of ancestors by their progeny are supposed to help the dead continue their heavenly sojourn:

"Thou, *Jatavēdas,* knowest well the number of Fathers who are here and who are absent, of fathers who we know and whom we know not: accept the sacrifice well prepared with portions".[33]

In the *Brāhmaṇas,* detailed *yajñas* are prescribed to avert *punarmrityu.*[34] However, even these acts cannot ensure eternal stay in heaven. Hence one is bound to die in the heaven after the merit is exhausted.

Where does the soul go after the re-death? Where else but to the earth the business of which it is familiar with? - And we got transmigration! The theory of transmigration envisages re-birth, on the earth, of the soul after experiencing the fruits of its past deeds in the other world. With every re-birth, new actions and their merit accrue and the cycle goes on.

This theory of metempsychosis gains clear articulation in the *Upaniṣads*. The *Chandogya Upaniṣad* gives a curiously naive theory as to how the souls take re-birth after the end of their stay in the heaven:

"Having dwelt there till there (good) works are consumed, they return again that way as they came, to the ether, from ether to the air. Then the scarificer, having become air, becomes smoke, having become smoke, he becomes mist.

Having become mist, he becomes a cloud, he rains down. Then he is born as rice and corn, herbs and trees, sesamum and beans. From thence the escape is beset with most difficulties. For whoever the persons may be that eat the food, and beget offspring, he henceforth becomes like unto them.

Those whose conduct has been good, will quickly attain some good birth, the birth of a Brāhmaṇa, or a Kṣatriya or a Vaisya. But those whose conduct has been evil, will quickly attain an evil birth, the birth of a dog, or a hog or a Chandala".[35]

The theory of soul raining down is without a demur a naive conjecture but what is really note worthy here is that one's birth and caste are a result of one's past deeds. This is the strongest force in the theory of transmigration which entails drastic social implications.

The theory of metempsychosis along with the casual connection between acts and future conditions finds expression in almost all the *Upaniṣads* with negligible variations. *Upaniṣads* add knowledge as another determinant of future birth. One's level of consciousness and dispositions are said to affect his future life. Knowledge and deeds appear together as moulding one's future life.

"...and according to his deeds and according to his knowledge he is born again".

"Then both his knowledge and his work take hold of his and his acquaintance with former things".[36]

"And as a caterpillar, after having reached the end of a blade of grass, and after having made another approach (to another blade) draws itself together towards it, thus does this self, after having thrown off this body and dispelled all ignorance, and after making another approach (to another body) draw himself together towards it".[37]

The theory of transmigration finds place in the entire spectrum of Indian thought with a negligible exception of Carvakas. It is really wonderful to see that such primitive eschatological belief finds place in all the major systems.

The central notion in the theory of re-birth is the inevitable moral consequences of moral action. Action or *Karma* is understood as the driving force in the series of lives which constitute the moral career of an individual soul. All the systems of Indian philosophy treat the issue of moral action with utmost care and in consonance with their metaphysical and epistemological commitments. Now, let us see how the idea of *Karma* is developed in the *Vēdic* thought.

Karma

The germs of *Karma* are embedded in the eschatological belief which ensured the prolonged heavenly life, after death, as a result of good acts. The efficacy of good acts or *Iṣṭapūrta* i.e., *yajña (iṣṭa)* and gifts to priests *(pūrta)* is the forerunner for *Karma* theory. Thus *Iṣṭapūrta* can said to be the earliest form of *Karma*.

Iṣṭapūrta, the merit of good deeds, proceeds to heaven before the soul reaches there. It helps the soul to stay there according to its volume. In *Taittarīya Brāhmaṇa,* Nachiketas seeks that his store of good deeds may never decay. *(Taittarīya Brāhmaṇa, iii.11.8.5.).*

The ethical and spiritual significance of Karma is explicated in the Upaniṣads. In Bṛhadāraṇyaka Upaniṣad, a discussion as to what remains after death takes place between Yajñavalkya and Artabhaga. They confer in secret and it is said that what they conversed about was *Karma* and what they commanded was *Karma*. *(Bṛhadāraṇyaka Upaniṣad,* IV.4.2.) Yajñavalkya explains the process of *Karma* thus:

"To whatever objects a man's own mind is attached, to that he goes strenuously together with his deed; and having obtained the end (the last results) of whatever deed he does here on earth, he returns again from that world (which is the temporary reward of his deed) to this world of action". *(Bṛhadārṇyaka Upaniṣad* IV.4.6.).

"...Man becomes good by good work and bad by bad work".[38]

Karma, right from the beginning, is connected with transmigration. Sometimes it appears as if the theory of metempsychosis is a logical offshoot of the retributive theory of action.

The moral intelligibility of an action is a primary concern of any ethical reflection. Certain actions give immediate results while others bear fruit a little later. Certain actions, especially moral ones, appear to be fruitless. In such case, it is difficult to promote the moral behaviour. Moral reinforcement can be made only when moral actions are shown to have consequences, now or later, which affect the agent directly or indirectly.

The question 'why should one be moral'? Needs an answer. An action is not morally meaningful if it is futile or fruitless. Thus ethical reason necessitates certain consequences to be attached to every morally meaningful action. When an action cannot be shown as having results in this world, the results should be posited in the other world, if not in this life, in the next life.

With reference to future life, we can render meaningfulness to even those actions which hardly appear to be of any consequence here. Thus, the actions which are apparently non-consequential logically necessitate another life in which they come to fruition. Moral retribution thus entails a future life for the agent. If moral actions are deprived of consequences, the whole edifice of a moral system collapses. People would not take pains to observe moral rules or principles which are of no consequences.

Further, *Karma* explains the inequalities in human condition in a moral way. It attributes present social, economic and spiritual condition of a man to his past deeds and anticipates his future according to his present deeds. Thus the whole human situation is moralized. Fatalism is avoided and man is made a product of his own deeds. However, it presupposes an infinite series pastward and futureward. This leads to an important ethics of transcendence — the ethics of *mokṣa.*

Mokṣa — The Ultimate Ethical Ideal

Mokṣa is fundamentally the release from the series of transmigratory lives which the soul undergoes as a result of its own actions. *Mokṣa* is thus cessation of continuous mortality. It is the attainment of immortality of the soul where it rests with itself.

How to attain this freedom from unceasing process of metempsychosis? As actions are the cause of transmigration, release from it cannot be effected by actions. Rather, performance of actions with an interest in their consequences should be stopped in order to prepare oneself for the release. Then what brings out the freedom from transmigratory life? It is something qualitatively different from action and exertion ... it is wisdom...wisdom of a special kind.

What constitutes this wisdom which is supposed to save one from the multifold mortal life. It is not the knowledge of external objects which leads to action, possession, enjoyment and loss. But it is the knowledge of the innerself and its identity with the universal self. It is the knowledge of unity of being into which all duality and diversity merge. In that sense, it is not even knowledge, for it has no subject-object distinction.

The individual self *(ātman)* realizes its identity with universal self *(Brahman)*. In this awareness, the world is dispelled as an illusion with its duality and diversity.

The term *Brahman* is used in the *Ṛg-vēda* to denote prayer or spell. (cf. The *Ṛg-vēda* X.162). In the *Brāhmaṇas,* the brahminical prayer is given exaggerated eminence and *Brahman* is equated with Prajapati, the Creator. The notion that everything is a product of prayer seems to be emphasized. *Brahman* is also identified with *Brihasapti,* 'the lord of prayer'. *Brahman* is identified with speech, truth, *Ṛta* and all the dieties are said to enter into and emerge from *Brahman.* (cf. *Aitarēya Brāhmaṇa* Viii.28).

Brahman attained the status of a metaphysical principle with the conception of *Brahman* as Svayambhu.[39] The self-supporting cause of the universe.

In the *Upaniṣads, Brahman* is further given the spiritualistic treatment and He is considered as the universal soul. The *Upaniṣads* dilate a lot upon the nature of *Brahman* as the ultimate reality. The final twist in the consideration of *Brahman* comes with the proposed identity of *Brahman* with *ātman*, the individual self. The knowledge of such identity of *Brahman* and *ātman* is said to effect liberation from mundane worldly life and transmigratory existence.

Before we discuss nature of the emancipatory knowledge and the nature of freedom it affects, we need to pay attention to another important question — what is ethical about *mokṣa?*

Mokṣa hardly appears to have anything to do with ethics, far less an ethical ideal. The common place understanding of *mokṣa* is that the speculative grandeur of the *Upaniṣadic* thinkers posited a universal being underlying the whole reality and a mystical identity of individual soul with it is sought after.

This understanding of *mokṣa* is partial and misses the ethical aspect of *mokṣa*. It is true that the concept of *Brahman* is used as the ultimately reality with which identity is sought. This identity not only releases individual from transmigratory life but makes him transcend all moral considerations. Transcending world of affairs is transcending moral realm. Thus, it is claimed, *mokṣa* is not merely non-moral but a moral.

This construal of *mokṣa* is not without a basis. The *Upaniṣads* themselves time and again declare that in *mokṣa,* moral actions do not affect one:

"And he who knows me thus, by no deed of his is his life harmed, not by the murder of his mother, not by the murder of his father, not by theft, not by the killing of a *Brahman*"[40].

"...He moves about there laughing (or eating), playing, and rejoicing (in his mind), be it with women, carriages, or relatives, never minding that body into which he is born"[41]

The outspoken indifference to morality instigates even a scholar like A.B. Keith to observe: "The defect of the *Upaniṣads* is that they render morality in the ultimate issue valueless and meaningless".[42]

However, it is quite a misconstrual of the *Vēdic* ideal of *mokṣa*. One who attains *mokṣa,* it is true, is said to transcend all duality. Because all actions involve duality, the emancipated also transcends all actions moral or otherwise. Thus he raises above mundane activity which includes morality. To emphasize this transcendence, it is said that even evil deeds would not affect him. This however does not mean that a *Mukta* (the emancipated) is necessarily amoral or anti-moral. On the other hand it only means that he cannot undertake evil deeds or, to be more specific, he cannot be amoral.

Mokṣa is not an evil doer's cup of tea. One has to strictly attain moral excellence before one aims at *mokṣa*. There is not short-cut to it. Moral training of mind is a necessary condition even for receiving knowledge of *Brahman*. The secret teaching of *Brahman* is only endowed to one who is worthy (morally too) of receiving it:

"But no one should tell it to anybody else, even if he gave him the whole sea-girt earth, full of treasure, for this doctrine is worth more than that yea, it is worth more"[43].

Along with knowledge (gnosis), self-discipline (askesis) is recognized as a path to *mokṣa*[44]. Indeed, both of them are complimentary.

Self discipline as practised through observation of self-mortification, religious duties and psycho-physical discipline (yōga). This constitutes the preparatory stage in the process of seeking *mokṣa*. The moral excellence is necessary for a *Mumukṣa (mokṣa*-seeker). The *Upaniṣads* are not at all ambiguous about this. One should overcome evil in order to be fit for *mokṣa:*

"He therefore that knows it, after having become quiet, subdued, satisfied, patient and collected, sees self in self, sees all as self. Evil does not overcome him, he overcomes evil. Evil does not burn him but he burns evil. Free from evil, free from spots, free from doubt, he becomes a (true) *Brāhmaṇa;* this is the Brahma-world, O king".[45]

Mokṣa does not come along with mere apprehension of the identity of self with *Brahman*. It is rather living such a belief. Such process of believing cannot be achieved unless one raises above mundane pleasures and aims at a higher level of self-consciousness:

"The good and pleasant approach man: the wise goes round about them and distinguishes them. Yea, the wise prefers the good to the pleasant but the fool choses the pleasant through greed and avarice"[46].

Not yielding to pleasures or sacrificing certain pleasures is a primary condition for any moral exertion. If one is guided only by pleasures, one cannot achieve higher ends of morality. Pleasures often, if not always, lead one astray and distort one from one's destiny. The *Upaniṣads* emphasize this point and guides one to gain control over senses in order not to succumb to pleasures. In *Katha Upaniṣad,* this idea is brought to bear figuratively thus:

"Know the self to be sitting in the chariot, the body to be chariot, the intellect *(buddhi)* the charioteer, and the mind reins.

The senses they call the horses, the object of the senses their roads. When the (the highest self) is in union with the body, the senses, and the mind, then wise people call him 'the enjoyer'".

He who has not understanding and whose mind (the reins) is never firmly held, his senses (horses) are unmanageable, like vicious horses of a charioteer.

But he who had understanding and whose mind is always firmly held, his senses are under control, like good horses of a charioteer.

He who has no understanding, who is unmindful and always impure, never reaches that place, but enters into the round of births.

But he who has understanding, who is mindful and always pure, reaches indeed that place from whence he is not born again"[47].

The above observation made in the *Katha Upaniṣad* makes it, beyond doubt, clear that immoral person, or one who had no control over passions and urges would never attain *mokṣa*. One should purify one's thoughts and make oneself fit for the highest goal:

"For thoughts alone cause the round of births, let a man strive to purify his thoughts. What a man thinks, he is: this is the old secret".[48]

Not only the negative morality of subduing senses but even positive moral characteristics of liberaty, righteousness, kindness, truthfulness are said to be developed by one interested in *mokṣa* (cf. *Chandogya Upaniṣad*-III.17.4). *Bṛhadāraṇyaka Upaniṣad* instructs - Damyata (be subdued!), Datta (give!) and Damadam (be merciful!) - as positive virtues.

Hence, the ideal of *mokṣa* cannot be understood as value-neutral or amoral but to be taken as a process aiming at moral excellence.

Another major misconception about *mokṣa* is that it is a negative ideal. It is negative in the sense that it is freedom *from* misery... misery of real life.

Mokṣa is often described as release from the misery of transmigratory life. It is a spiritual solution to the pessimistically construed human life. The *Upaniṣadic* thinkers are accused of emphasizing the darker side of life and coming out with mystical transcendence of concrete reality. *Mokṣa* is an ideal of spiritual escape of a wandering mendicant who lost hope of all pleasures.

This view is also infested with partial incognizance. It is true that worldly pleasures are often dismissed as unworthy for one who seeks liberation. Indulgence in worldly affairs and being engrossed by immediate selfish purposes are dissuaded. At a few places, renunciation from worldly affairs is recommended.[49] The exuberance for longer life which is found in the *Ṛg-vēda* is certainly missing in the *Upaniṣads* but we should recollect that the urge for immortality is even stronger in the case of *mokṣa*. Nonetheless, there is qualitative difference. The former was a strong desire of a poet and the latter is a speculative grandeur of a philosopher.

It has to kept in mind that no *Upaniṣad* debunks the moral significance of family life and social life. Renunciation was not a rule but an exception. In the *Taittirīya Upaniṣad,* positive morality is taught to an out-going student. *(Taittirīya Upaniṣad.* I.11.1-5). He is instructed to have progeny and have a virtuous social life. The gist of *Upaniṣadic* morality is a caution not to be swerved by passions and desires.

Though human life is viewed as involving misery, disease, oldage and death, this is not absolute pessimism. People are not asked to commit suicide or run to forests. Even a mendicant is supposed to involve in social and moral life of the people by advising and helping lay man in their practical lives. It is not a coincidence that many of the *Sanyāsins* practice native medicine. Renunciation is nothing but extension of oneself. Every other being is viewed as an extension of one's own self. It is self-denial for a greater harmony, social and spiritual.

Again, *mokṣa* as freedom is not merely a negative one. It is not just freedom 'from' but also freedom 'for' positive attainment of unity, integrity and bliss.

'Unity of Being' is a major objective of ancient metaphysical systems, Indian or non-Indian. Through the unitary and non-dualistic conception of *Brahman,* the *Upaniṣadic* thinkers achieved the unification of reality in one grand principle. Deussen rightly remarks:

"Eternal philosophical truth has seldom found more decisive and striking expression than in the emancipating knowledge of the *ātman*".[50]

Any metaphysical system attempts at attaining a unitary principle capable of gratifying the fundamental urge of human beings for freedom from lower mode of existence and freedom to rise to higher levels of being. This is the central issue of any emancipating philosophy ... may it be that of plato, Hegel, Marx or Sartre.

In India, the function of philosophy is viewed not as mere analysis or explanation but as emancipation. Thus all the Indian schools of thought claim their philosophy as capable of emancipating.

The emancipation is release from finitude and freedom into infinity. Everything found around man is limited, finite and binding. The undying urge to overcome the finitude of human condition finds expression in search for infinite possibilities or possible infinity. This search for infinity makes all experience of finite miserable and posits bliss in the infinite. *Mokṣa* is fundamentally the attempt to rise above finitude:

"The infinite *(bhūman)* is bliss. There is no bliss in anything finite. Infinite only is bliss. This infinity, however, we must desire to understand.

Where one sees nothing else, hears nothing else, understands nothing else, that is infinite. Where one sees something else, hears something else, understands something else, that is finite. The infinite is immortal, the finite is mortal".[51]

The infinity has to be searched or found not in external reality which is bound by space and time but in the fathoms of inner self which shows possibility of transcending all limitations.

Further, *mokṣa* consists in elimination of false consciousness of individuality ... release from ego-centric activity. In *mokṣa,* one identifies oneself with higher universal self and looks at everything dispassionately, not as an agent or benefactor but as a witness. This is not inaction or indifference but a higher moral attitude. This is even above the enlightened self interest which is often praised in the western ethics. This is ethics of the absolute.

In the light of the above analysis, it is established that *mokṣa* is not just a spiritual ideal but has a moral dimension to it. The moral virtues of self-discipline, righteousness, kindness, liberality, truthfulness, humility are entailed by *mokṣa* which is the process of attaining ultimate unity, freedom, perfection, infinity and positive moral identity.

Dharma and its Significance

Dharma as the ethical order is intricately connected with the notions of individual soul, action, retribution, transmigratory life and freedom. *Dharma* is the autonomous order in which every action of an agent is retributed in the series of lives undergone by a soul which might attain final release in the unification with *Brahman,* the universal self.

Dharma in this sense is adopted by all the systems. Even Buddhism which denies the existence of soul as a separate entity, accepts transmigratory efficacy of moral actions.

Though different systems have varied opinion as to the nature of *Dharma* as the moral merit, all of them accept it. The reasons behind this universal acceptance of *Dharma* appears to be:

1. Its retributive character — all the systems must accept this lest they endorse moral chaos.
2. Its autonomy from external agencies — even atheistic systems accept *Dharma* for it does not require god or any external power for its operation.
3. Its opposition to fatalism — *Dharma* makes one architect of one's own destiny and thus appeals to logic of moral responsibility. It lays greater stress on voluntary moral actions.
4. Its explanatory potential — *Dharma* morally explains human condition with all its diversities and inequalities.

5. Its comprehensive character — *Dharma* more or less logically explains the social, religious and spiritual aspects of human life. Any human phenomenon can be explained in the light of this comprehensive ethical category.

6. Its popularity — the popular acceptance of *Dharma* helps it finding a place for it in every system. It is observable that many sūtras start with analysis of *Dharma*.

In what follows, we will be dealing with three important texts — *Manu Smṛti, Mīmāmsa Sūtras* and *Bhagavad-gita* which explicate the social, religious and spiritual dimensions of *Dharma* respectively.

Dharma in the sphere of social conduct forms the central thesis of *Manu Smṛti,* while *Mīmāmsa Sūtras* come out with stupendous philosophical system to justify *Dharma* as religious duty. *Gītā* gives a spiritualistic treatment to *Dharma* in its profound teaching. A proper study of these three texts enable us understand *Dharma* and its nature comprehensively.

References

1. *The Evolution of Hindu Ideals, Introduction,* p.xvi.
2. *The Ṛg-vēda,* viii.85.13
3. *Mahābharata,* xii.109.14
4. *The Religion and Philosophy of the Vēdas and the Upaniṣads,* p.443
5. cf. Macdonell, *A History of Sanscrit Literature,* p. 69
6. *The Ṛg-vēda,* I.164.6
7. *The Ṛg-vēda,* I.164.46
8. cf. the *Ṛg-vēda* VII.78.7; 85.6 etc.
9. The *Ṛg-vēda,* X.81; 82
10. The *Ṛg-vēda,* X.88.3

11. The *Ṛg-vēda,* VIII.41; 42
12. The *Ṛg-vēda,* X.72.1
13. The *Ṛg-vēda,* X.190
14. The *Ṛg-vēda,* X.90
15. *Ibid.* X.90.12
16. The *Ṛg-vēda,* I.34.7; VII.87.2 etc.
17. The *Ṛg-vēda,* I.113.16; 140.18
18. The *Ṛg-vēda,* X.16.1
19. The *Satapatha Brāhmana,* IV.23.1; XI.2.1.2
20. The *Atharva-Vēda,* V.1.7: 9.7
21. *Satapatha Brāhmana,* III.8.3.8
22. *Ibid.* X.3.5.3
23. cf. Bṛhadaraṇyaka Upaniṣad, III.viii.8.2
24. The *Ṛg-vēda,* VII.66.16
25. *Ibid.* VII.101.6
26. *Ibid.* X.18.4
27. *Ibid.* X.18.6
28. *Ibid.* X.59.4-5. *Asuniti is the god of funerals*
29. The *Ṛg-vēda,* X.14.2 cf. The *Atharva-Vēda* III.28.5
30. The *Ṛg-vēda,* IX.113.7-11
31. The *Ṛg-vēda,* X.14.8
32. The *Ṛg-vēda,* X.14.14
33. The *Ṛg-vēda,* X.15.13
34. cf. *Taittarīya Brālunaṇa* 3.11.8.5; *Kausitakīya Brāhmaṇa,* XXV. 1; and *Satapatha Brālunaṇa,* 12.9.3.12
35. Chandogya Upanisad, V. 10.5-7; cf. also *Bṛhadāraṇyaka Upaniṣad,* VI.2.26, IV.4.6, III.2.13
36. *Kaushitakīya Upaniṣad* I.2
37. *Bṛhadāraṇyaka Upaniṣad* IV. 4.2-3

38. *Bṛhadaraṇyaka Upaniṣad,* IV.4.13

39. cf. *Taittarīya Brāhmana* ii. 8.8.8; Aitareya *Brāhmaṇa*. i. 19.1; *Kausitakīya Brāhmaṇa* Viii. 4; *Satapatha Brāhmaṇa* Xi. 2.3, etc.

40. *Kausitaki Brāhmaṇa Upaniṣad,* iii.1

41. *Chandogya Upanisad,* VIII. 12.3

42. *The Religion and Philosophy of the Vēda,* p.396

43. *Chandogya Upanisad* III. 11.5

44. cf. K. Satchindananda Murthy, *Metaphysics, Man and Freedom,* Lecture II

45. *Bṛhadaraṇyaka Upaniṣad,* IV. 4.23

46. *Katha Upaniṣad,* i.2.2

47. *Katha Upaniṣad,* I.3.3-8

48. *Maitrayana Brāhmaṇa Upanisad,* VI.34.3

49. cf. *Bṛhadaraṇyaka Upaniṣad* III.5.1

50. Philosophy of Upanasids, p.38

51. *Chandogya Upaniṣad,* VII.23, VII.24.1

4

Ethics of Manu Dharma Śāstra

Introduction

The ancient Hindu law-books mark an important phase in the development of ethical thought in India. These law-books developed the rudimentary social and ethical precepts available in the *Vēdas* and certain contemporary social customs to present a coherent legal system. Among these law-books, *Manu Dharma Śāstra* is, if not the first, the most authoritative and comprehensive law-book. It is also called *Manu Smṛti* where *Smṛti* means the tradition remembered *(smārta)* as distinct from *Vēdas (Sruti)* which are supposed to be 'revealed'. The immense significance of *Manu Smṛti* lies in its comprehensive character. The fundamental objective of any law-book is to establish a legal system. But, unlike the other codes, *Manu Smṛti* considers, in addition to the legal maxims, certain religious, political, moral, economic and metaphysical principles to provide a consistent justification for its social theory. *Manu Smṛti* adopts certain philosophical views of different schools of thought, sometimes inconsistently, to project a systematic ethical theory to back its legal system. It is here, the code is of serious philosophical interest.

As a comprehensive social code, *Manu Smṛti* served as an authoritative guide for Hindu jurisprudence for a long time in Indian social history. In terms of authority and reverence, it occupies important place next only to the *Vēdas* from which it derives its authority.

Althrough the *Sruti* and *Smṛti* literature, we find references to *Manu* which furnish quite incommensurable accounts of *Manu*. Though these accounts are disconnected and inconsistent, the whole Vedic orthodoxy agrees on one point — the supreme authority of *Manu* on legal matters (of course, next to the *Vēdas*). With great reverence *Manu* is accepted as the authority on legal matters and his name appears first among the law-givers. *Taittarīya Samhita* prescribes that 'whatever *Manu* says is medicine'.[1] *Yaska Nirukta* also endorses the unquestionable authority of *Manu's* legislation. The *Bṛhaspati Smṛti* ascribes absolute authority to *Manu Dharma Sastra:*

"… the first rank (among legislators) belongs to *Manu,* because he has embodied the essence of the *Vēda* in his work; that *Smṛti* which is opposed to the tenor of laws of *Manu* is not approved".[2]

Samkaracharya, the great Vedantin, in his commentary on *Brahma Sūtras* cities *Manu* in support of his arguments and to refute those of others. He considers *Manu Smṛti* as a *pramaṇa*. This shows *Manu's* influence on philosophical issues as well. Prof. D. P. Chattopadhyaya wonders how a law-giver can have any say on matters philosophical.[3] Precisely this is the reason for which *Manu Smṛti* deserves a thorough philosophical examination.

Origin of the Law-Book

Prof. Buhler in his introduction to *Manu Dharma Śāstra* (Sacred Books of East, Vol. XXV) brings out the dominant hypothesis about the origin of the code. According to him, it belongs to the later-vedic period when "the systematic cultivation of the sacred science of Brāhmaṇas began and for a long time had its centres in the ancient *Sūtrakaraṇas,* the schools which first collected the fragmentary doctrines scattered in the old vedic works, and arranged them for the convenience of oral instruction in *sūtras* or strings of aphorisms".[4] These vedic schools collected religious, metaphysical, moral and legal ideas from the *Vēdas* and tradition. Those ideas are preserved by them in the form of aphorisms which are known as *Dharma Sūtras*. These *Dharma Sūtras* along with *Gṛhya* and *Srauta Sūtras* constitute the *Kalpa Sūtra*. The different available law-books of these *Vēdic* schools had their respective *Kalpa Sūtras* as their basis. Similarly, Buhler argues, *Manu Dharma Śāstra* is "a recast and versification of *Dharma Sūtra* of *Mānava Sūtrakaraṇa,* a subdivision of the *Maitrayanīya* School, which adheres to the redaction of *Kṛṣṇa Yajur-Vēda*".[5]

However, P.V. Kane in his *History of Dharma Śāstras* differs from Buhler regarding the existence of *Mānava Dharma Sūtras*. He thinks that though all the other *Dharma Śāstras* had their own *Dharma Sūtras,* it is extremely doubtful whether *Mānava Sūtrakaraṇa* had any *Dharma Sūtras* of its own.[6] In this regard, Jaimini, the author of *Mīmamsa Sūtras* gives us an interesting clue. In the *Mīmamsa Sūtras,* Jaimini clearly accepts the authority of *Manu Dharma Śāstra,* though interestingly, he rejects *Kalpa Sūtras* as invalid because they had other sources than the *Vēdas*.[7] If there existed any *Mānava Dharma Sūtras* of which the present code is only a versified version, then Jaimini must be contradicting himself by accepting *Manu smṛti* as authoritative and rejecting the authority of the *Dharma Sūtras* in general and as forming part of the *Kalpa Sūtras*. Jaimini, the exponent of the orthodox Mimamsa tradition, probably knew that *Manu Smṛti* is independent of *Kalpa Sūtras*. This supports the Kane's view about the non-existence of *Mānava Dharma Sūtra*.

Buhler and Kane differ on another important point. According to Buhler, *Manu Smṛti* had undergone several recasting before it acquired its present form. But Kane is of the opinion that the code might not have undergone such transformation for more than once.[8] On this point, Buhler's argument appears to be more plausible as it is evident from the fact that *Manu Smṛti* was known to the Brahminical tradition long before it was compiled in its present form.

Nārada Smṛti refers to four successive versions of *Manu's* code. The original text had 1,00,000 slokas with 1,080 chapters when it was first given to *Nārada.*[9] *Nārada* is said to have edited it before he passed it on to *Mārkandēya* with 12,000 slokas. *Mārkandēya* in turn taught it to *Sumati*, the son of sage Bhṛgu, as consisting of 8,000 slokas. *Sumati* reduced it to 4,000 slokas. But the present form of *Manu Smṛti,* as it comes to us, consists only of 2,635 slokas spread over 12 chapters. However, the authenticity of *Nārada Smṛti* is generally considered to be doubtful as it belongs to the early centuries of the Christian era. The above account of the *Nārada Smṛti* may be not reliable. Nevertheless, its suggestion that *Manu Smṛti* had different versions need not be ignored.

As to the exact date of the *Smṛti,* there are conflicting views held by different scholars. Indian chronology has been so problematic that it is difficult to ascertain the exact periods of most of the ancient Sanskrit texts and *Manu Smṛti* is not an exception. However, we can admit that the code had an oral tradition for about three centuries before it acquired present form around second century B.C.[10]

In the text of *Manu Smṛti* itself we find a mythical account about its origin: "The God *(Brahman)* having framed this system of laws himself, taught it fully to me in the beginning. I then taught it to *Marīchi* and the nine other sages, my offspring. Of these (my sons) *Bhṛgu* is deputed by me to declare the code to you *(Ṛsis)* from beginning to end, for he has learned from me to recite the whole of it".[11]

As William M.M. rightly observes, "We need hardly, however, explain that these are merely ideal personages, introduced dramatically like Krishna in *Bhagavad-gita;* or rather perhaps later additions, designed to give an air of antiquity and divine authority to the teaching of the code".[12] We find such mythical elements at many places in the code, particularly when it explains creation and origin of the four social classes.

As far as evolution of legal ideas is concerned, there are different possible reasons which might have influenced the origin and development of the low-book. The most important factor seems to be the formation of state. At the time when the inter racial struggles between Aryans and non-Aryans were intense and state organization was slowly being established on the ruins of tribal communal systems, there was a need for assimilating diverse cultural, moral and religious interests of the conflicting groups and tribes. In both *Sruti* and *Smṛti* literature these inter-racial clashes were depicted as fights between *Suras* and *Asuras*.

Efforts were made by the ruling Aryans to evolve a social system which can accommodate all the groups of society with functional differences. *Manu Dharma Śāstra* might have played a significant role in the process of bringing different races and groups into one legal fold and meet the demand for stability. *Manu Smṛti,* as part of the efforts to establish a social order based on distinct and organized economic relations between individuals and groups, carried out a functional differentiation which might have helped political, economic and moral stability.

Another important factor is religion. The efforts of the Aryan invaders to introduce their culture and religion to non-Aryan tribes, who themselves had their own culture and religious beliefs, resulted in a synthesis of cultures which gave rise to Hinduism. Though Hinduism is a blend of Aryan and non-Aryan religions, it bears a strong mark of Aryanism. The new religion and culture of Hinduism which is an admixture of different customs and cultures could gain popular approval over a long period of time and *Manu Smṛti* had its contribution in this process. Thus *Manu Smṛti* helped the process of synthesizing different cultures and bringing them into the fold of Aryan tradition.

Besides these factors viz., formation of state, demand for stability, economic relations among individuals and groups, religion, there is another important factor. It is identified by law-book as the variation in moral values. With the advent of Buddhism and other non-*Vēdic* religions, there was a change in the social situation which alarmed the adherents of Brahminical tradition. This might have resulted in executing the social code with more rigidity to counter the challenge. *Nārada Smṛti* and *Bṛhaspati Smṛti* identify moral degeneration and negligence of duty by men as the main reason for origin of moral codes.

Sources of the Code

Manu Smṛti enumerates the scriptures, the tradition, the conduct of virtuous men and self-satisfaction as the four major sources of the sacred law and morality. However, the validity and the authority of the code are mainly derived from the *Vēda* which is its primary sources:

"The whole *Vēda* is the first source of the sacred law, next the tradition and virtuous conduct of those who know the *Vēda,* further, also the customs of holy men and finally self-satisfaction. By *Sruti* (revelation) is meant the *Vēda,* and by *Smṛti* (tradition) the institutes of the sacred law; these two must not be called into question in any matter, since from these two the sacred law is shone forth".[13]

Here, one point is important. *Smṛti* or the code derives its authority from the *Vēda* and in turn it tries to legally enforce the unquestionable authority of the *Vēda.* Except this legal enforcement, the *Smṛti* does not offer any theoretical defence of the *Vēda*. Rather, the *Smṛti* presupposes intrinsic validity, and thus absolute authority, of the *Vēda*. The *Vēda,* for *Manu* does not need any justification for its validity. So, nobody can question its validity and the law takes care of those who do so with severe punishments. The task of theoretically defending the *Vēda* is, however, taken up by two orthodox *Vēdic* Schools of Mīmāmsa viz., *Pūrva Mīmāmsa* and *Uttara Mīmāmsa* while the *Smṛti* defends the *Vēda* in practice.

Manu considers the *Vēda* to be eternal and therefore the social system it prescribes is also eternal. The *Vēda*, as the eternal source of morality and religion, is never erroneous in all the matters it considers and is equally binding on all creatures, even the gods:

"The *Vēda* is the eternal eye of the manes, gods and men; the *Vēda*-ordinance is both beyond the sphere of human power, and beyond the sphere of human comprehension; that is a certain fact .... The four castes, the three worlds, the four orders, the past, the present and the future are all severally known by means of the *Vēda*".[14]

All through the code, we find extreme veneration for the *Vēda*. Even a conspicuous contradiction between two texts of the *Vēda* would not affect the supremacy and authority of the *Vēda*. In such case both the texts, *Manu* says, have to be considered as valid (II.14). Whenever a *Smṛti* text contradicts the *Vēda,* such *Smṛti* text should be ignored as invalid.

Though *Manu* accepts the *Vēda* as the primary source of his code, we do not find corresponding source for many of his legal maxims in the *Vēda*. This was explained in terms of lost texts of the *Vēda*. If we do not find any *Vēdic* text for a *Smṛti* maxim, we have to assume a *Vēdic* text, in support of the maxim, which is supposedly lost. Though all the Hindu-codes are believed to be authoritative as they are having sruti as their source, there are numerous differences, sometimes conflicting, among the codes.

In this connection, two question arise. First, if the *Manu Smṛti* is considered to be of highest authority, then what is the need for compiling other *Smṛtis?* Secondly, how can there be difference if all the codes are believed to have the same source? These questions can be answered in the light of evolutionary character of Hindu law. Though *Manu's* authority is never questioned in Hindu tradition, there was, nevertheless, a need for modifying certain rules because of changes in environment and time. Hindu law was never static. The changing social conditions over a period of time and the differences among local customs result in a need for modification of existing codes, and this explains the existence of numerous minor codes which are followed by people of different regions at different times. It is evident from the Hindu codes that even the rules concerning ritualistic orthodoxy have undergone changes keeping in view the changing circumstances and yet they retain certain continuity. In all the codes apart from the general structure of social organization, we find due importance given to local customs and contemporary beliefs. Even *Manu* acknowledges the possible changes in the social conditions and hence need for change in the rules and duties. He foresees laxity of rules depending on the ages:

"One set of duties (is prescribed) for men in the *Kṛta* age, different ones in the *Trēta* and in the *Dvāpara*, and (again) another (set) in the *Kali* in proportion as those ages decrease in length. In the *Kṛta* age the chief virtue is declared to be the performance of austerities, in the *Trēta* age divine knowledge, in the *Dvāpara* (the performance of) scarifies, in the *Kali* liberality alone".[15]

The second source of the sacred law is the tradition. By tradition, *Manu* means the institutes of the sacred law which are practised through generations. Tradition is the set of practices of the four social classes as the code depicts. The established customs of society form an important basis for social conduct:

"In this code *(Manu Smṛti)* appears the whole system of law, with definitions of good and bad actions, and the traditional practices of the four classes, which usages are held to be eternal *(sāsvataḥ)*".[16]

The tradition *Manu* talks about is the *Vēdic* tradition as it is represented by his *Smṛti*. *Manu* attaches very little importance to local customs and usages, and is rigid about the fourfold division of society and the respective duties of the four classes. So, for *Manu* tradition is not only basis of his system, but also justification for rejecting all other non-*Vēdic* traditions as defective and futile. So, for *Manu, Vēdic* tradition is not 'a tradition' but 'the only tradition' which is valid and fruitful:

"All those traditions and all those despicable systems of philosophy, which are not based on the *Vēda*, produce no reward after death; for they are declared to be founded on darkness. All those doctrines, differing from the *Vēda,* which spring up and (soon) perish, are worthless and false, because they are of modern date".[17]

Here, it is obvious that *Manu* is referring to the practices of non-*Vēdic* religions such as Jainism and Buddhism, the materialist doctrines of Cārvākas and the religious practices of aboriginals which are outside the pale of the *Vēda*. His contempt for these traditions can be easily understood from his position as a law-giver enforcing the *Vēdic* tradition.

The third source of morality is the customs and lives of virtuous men. The exemplary lives of great people and moral values they cherished have been a source of guidance to the people. The great classical Indian epic-literature has an important role of play here. The *Rāmāyaṇa* and the *Mahābhārata*, the two grand Hindu epics influenced the moral vision of the masses in their daily life. These epics depict more or less the same ideal society which the law-givers want to enforce, and highlight the moral values which are conducive to such social organization. The epics describing the lives of the holy men, who are known for their obedience to the *Vēdic* tradition and the morality.

There is an interpretation that this source of the code is secular in character and that 'virtuous men' may belong to any tradition and caste. But this interpretation may not be valid for *Manu* is very clear in defining the conduct of virtuous men as follows:

"The custom handed down in regular succession (since time immemorial) among the four chief *Varṇas* and the mixed (races) of that (Brahmavarta) country is called conduct of virtuous men".[18]

So, the above three sources of morality and law have an invariable reference to the teaching of the *Vēda* or the tradition based on the *Vēda*. The fourth source, as the code enumerates, is the satisfaction of enlightened self. Whenever the other three sources fail to guide in a moral situation, them one has to follow the verdict of one's own self. Manu, at many places, clearly emphasizes the purity of self as a preconditions for a morally commendable life:

"Neither the study of the *Vēda* nor liberality, nor any (self-imposed) restraint, nor austerities, ever procure the attainment (of rewards) to a man whose heart is contaminated (by sensuality). The soul itself is the witness of the soul, and the soul is the refuse of the soul; despise not thy own soul".[19]

This fourth source apparently has no reference to the *Vēda*. But on a close examination, we find that it is not totally independent. *Manu's* list of *Sādharaṇa dharmas* and *Nitya* and *Naimittika Karmas* is primarily aimed at the purification of self. Purity of self is a precondition for attaining all the objects of human pursuit *(Puruṣārthas)* within the frame work of *Manu's* moral system. These *Sādharaṇa Dharmas* are the values cherished by the *Vēda* as of paramount importance. Though they appear secular, they have a *Vēdic* import, however indirect it may be. Much about this would be discussed later when we deal with the chief features of *Manu's* morality.

What is rather strange about the enumeration of sources of morality is that *Reason* has no place in morality and law. *Manu* depends more on the *Vēda* for his moral system than on *Reason*. Nevertheless, *Manu* appears to be very rational in his systematic arrangement of legal maxims and in his attempt to justify them coherently with philosophical considerations. However, the question is how far does he accept *Reason* as a guide to moral behaviour and social conduct. As we have already seen, *Reason* is totally ignored while enumerating the sources of morality and is not given its due place in the field of moral cognition. *Manu* is well aware of the fact that once *Reason* is allowed to play a role in moral considerations, it certainly goes against the religious dogmas of the *Vēda* on which he founds his moral and legal system. Precisely this is the reason why he elevates the *Vēda* and his code beyond logical analysis and rational examination. Once the mythical elements in the *Vēda* and his code are questioned, the whole social scheme he proposes would simply collapse. Hence, *Manu* is very careful not to allow unrestricted use of logic and free thinking. He thinks that logic is subservient to the *Vēda* and thus to the religion and law. He is very stern against those who criticize the *Vēda* on the basis of logical reasoning, even if they belong to a higher caste :

"Every twice-born man who relying on the institutes of dialectics, treats with contempt those two sources of law (viz., the *Vēda* and the institutes of the sacred law), must be cast out by the virtuous, as an atheist and a scorner of the *Vēda*".[20]

However, *Manu* appears to recommend *Reason* and the science of dialectics. There are three grounds for such an impression. First, *Manu* recommends perception, Inference and authority as the three Pramāṇas in which one, who desires perfect knowledge of the sacred law, should be well-versed. Secondly, *Manu* prescribes logic to be taught to the king. Thirdly, he recommends the involvement of a logician *(Nyāyajña)* among the committee of judges.

Manu recommends Inference as a valid source of knowledge in the following verse: "The three kinds of evidence, Perception, Inference, and the sacred institutes which comprise the tradition of many schools, must be fully understood by him who desires perfect correctness with respect to the sacred law" (XII.105).

However, he is not at all vague about the scope of logic as a *Pramaṇa*. He does not recommend indiscriminate use of logic. For *Manu,* the ideal function of logic is to support the *Vedic* doctrines. He makes this clear in the very next verse to the above one:

"He alone, and no other man, knows the sacred law, who explores the utterances of the sages and the body of laws, by modes of reasoning, not repugnant to the *Vēda*-lore" (XII.106).

Even Samkaracharya quotes the verse of *Manu* (XII.105) as recommending *Reason*. He quotes *Manu* exactly in the same context in which he talks about the ideal function of reasoning. It is to find out the real sense or meaning of the abscure and contradictory statements of the *Vēda*.[21]

Further, in the case of passages of scriptures (apparently) contradicting each other, the ascertainment of the real sense, which depends on a preliminary refutation of the apparent sense, can be affected only by an accurate definition of meaning of the sentences, and that involves reasoning. Thus

Manu also expresses himself: 'Perception, Influence, and the sacred ... etc., *(Manu* XII. 105).

This clearly shows that *Manu* is not prescribing Inference as an independent *Pramāṇa* or source of valid knowledge. *Manu*, while including logic in educating the king, appear to identify logic as an independent branch of study:

"From those versed in the three *Vēdas* let him (the king) learn the three fold sacred science, the primeval science of government, the science of dialectics (logic) and the knowledge of the supreme soul; from the people (the theory of) the (various) trades and professions" (VII.43).

On the basis of the above passage, we cannot jump to the conclusion that *Manu* recognizes logic as an independent branch of study. As we see in the above verse, ***Manu*** recommends reasoning along with knowledge of the self *(cha ātmavidyam)*. The other three are *Trayi* (the *Vēda*), ***Danda nīti*** (science of Government) and *Varta* (science of agriculture and trade). As he prescribes logic to be taught together with *Ātma Vidya* which is a part of *Trayi* (the *Vēda*), he is not allowing logic to be taught independently but as subservient to *Ātma Vidya* of the *Vēda*. While state craft and science of trade are mentioned independently, logic is mentioned together with knowledge of the soul (the *Upanisadic* part of the *Vēda*). This is an evidence for the fact that *Manu* does not mean logic to be an independent branch of study.

This fact can further be established with a reference to *(Artha Śāstra)* of Kautilya. Kautilya, who acknowledges the independent status of logic as a branch of knowledge, considers it as 'the lamp of all the branches of learning, the aid of all activities and *the basis of all virtue*'[22] For Kautilya, logic is a distinct branch of knowledge, different from scriptures for logic deals with objects of experience. Moreover, he is keen on distinguishing his theory from that of *Manu*. He, while doing so, informs us that *Mānavas* (followers of *Manu)* consider only three branches of learning and that they include logic under the scriptures:

"Anvikṣaki, the triple *Vēda (Trayi), Varta* (agriculture, cattle breeding and trade) and *Dandanīti* (science of government) are what are called the four sciences. The school of *Manu (Mānava)* hold that there are only three sciences: the triple *Vēdas, Varta* and the science of government, in as much as the science of *Anvikṣaki* is nothing but a special branch of the *Vēdas.* But Kautilya holds that four and only four are the sciences; wherefore it is from these science that all that concerns righteousness and wealth is learnt, therefore they are so called".[23]

What is obvious from the above observation of Kautilya is that *Manu* does not accept the independent efficacy of *Reason*, either in the matters of morality or of law. On the contrary, Kautilya acknowledges logic as 'the basis of all virtue'. However, both *Manu* and Kautilya recommend logic only for the king but not to the ordinary people, being well aware of the fact that logic, if learnt by masses, would prove disastrous for their respective systems.

Again, the passage where *Manu* includes a logician in the committee of judges does not prove *Manu's* sympathy for logic or for logitians. The reason for which *Manu* does so, is not because of any consideration favouring *Reason* but because rational analysis is indispensable in understanding the merits and demerits of a case. *Manu* is very careful in including, along with a logitian, a specialist on the *Vēda,* the *Smṛti* and Mīmāṃsa in the committee:

"Three persons who each know one of the three *Vēdas,* a logician, a Mīmāmsaka, one who knows the *Nirukta,* one who recites (the Institute of) the sacred law, and three men belonging to the first three orders shall constitute a (legal) assembly consisting of at least ten members" (XII. 111).

From the above discussion, it is clear that *Manu* not only refuses *Reason* to be the basis for any moral deliberation but also ignores it as an independent branch of study. He accepts it only as an instrument in understanding the real sense of difficult scriptural passages and in so far as it does not contradict the *Vēdic* doctrines. However, *Manu* could not avoid logicians in legal assembly where a logician is important in distinguishing the rational merit of a case. Otherwise, *Manu* has little sympathy for logic or logicians. According to him a logician is not even to be entertained as a guest. This attitude of *Manu* has far-reaching consequences on the development of ethics in India.

There are two obvious reasons for which *Manu* appears to have rejected *Reason*. As we noted earlier, if *Reason* is applied to understand and analyse the *Vēdic* doctrines, it may prove unfavourable to his system. The other reason may be the assumption that *Reason* cannot be a proper guide for morality because it often leads to diversity of opinions. This view ignores agreement on majority of rational ethical judgements concerning social conduct. Another supposition which goes against *Reason* is that the social laws are immutable and any change is a degeneration. But, society as a dynamic expression of human efforts (both physical and conceptional) has never been static, though change takes place at varying degrees.

So, *Manu*, enumerates the scriptures, the tradition, conduct of virtuous men and enlightened self-satisfaction as the four major sources of morality and law, and these sources have a direct or indirect reference to the *Vēda* and its tradition. With the four sources of morality, *Manu* provides us with a comprehensive legal system touching all the aspects of social life. Before we go on to discuss *Manu's* understanding of morality, we have to deal with his theory of creation which is the bedrock of his social theory. *Manu's* theory of creation provides important clues as to what kind of society *Manu* envisages as ideal and how he tries to establish it legally. Hence, a thorough understanding of *Manu's* ideas on creation and their social implications is necessary for any endeavour to deal with his ethical theory.

Manu's Theory of Creation

Manu's theory of creation, the most significant theory of the code, forms the foundation for his metaphysics, theology, law, economics and politics. In addition to the theory of creation of the physical world, *Manu* explains the origin of the four principal social classes, which is an important feature of his ideal society, in this theory. His social theory is based on his theory of creation. *Manu* gives his theory of creation in the very first chapter of the code, and no other *Smṛti* begins with it. This led to the view that this theory could be a later addition. But *Nārada Smṛti* mentions that the original *Manu Smṛti*, which was supposed to contain one lakh of slokas, begins with the theory of creation and that the following verse is the very first verse of the code:

"The universe was wrapped up in the darkness, and nothing could be discerned. Then the holy, self-existent spirit issued forth with four faces".[24]

As the antiquity of *Nārada Smṛti* itself is questionable, it fails to provide a substantial evidence. However, it may be true that atleast some version of *Manu Smṛti* which the author of *Nārada Dharma Śāstra* knew might have began with the above verse. So, we can presume that some other version of *Manu Smṛti*, if not the oldest, also starts with the theory of creation. On the other hand, no presently available other *Smṛtis* start with the theory of creation. Both points put together, it seems probable that the theory of creation is peculiar to *Manu Smṛti* with which it begins atleast in some of its versions. As *Manu* is supposed to be father of the mankind, this theory is fit to be enunciated by *Manu* more authoritatively than other law-givers. *Manu's* theory of creation and his ethical justifications which back his legal system distinguish *Manu's* code from other *Smṛtis* and place it on top of them in importance and authority.

Manu presents his theory of creation in the first chapter from the fifth verse onwards as follows:

"The universe existed in the shape of Darkness, unperceived, destitute of distinctive marks, unattainble by reasoning, unknowable, wholly immersed, as it were, in deep sleep. Then the divine self-existent *(Svayambhu,* Himself) indiscernible (but) making (all) this, the great elements and the rest, discernible, appeared with irresistable creative power, dispelling the darkness. He who is subtile, indiscernible, and eternal, who contains all created beings and is inconceivable shone forth of his own (will). He desiring to produce beings of many kinds from his own body, first with a thought created the waters, and placed his seed in them. That seed became a golden egg, in brilliancy equal to the sun; in that egg, he himself was born as Brahman, the progenitor of the whole world. The waters are called narah, for the waters are, indeed, offspring of Nara; as they were his first residence *(ayana),* thence is named Narayana. From that first cause, which is indiscernible, eternal, both real and unreal, was produced that male *Puruṣa*, who is famed in this world (under the appellation of) *Brahman.* The devine one resided in that egg during a whole year, then he himself by his thought (alone) devided it into two halves. And out of those two halves, he formed Heaven and Earth, between them the middle sphere, and eight points of the horizon, and the eternal abode of waters. From himself *(ātmanāh)* he also drew forth the mind which is both real and unreal, likewise from the mind agoism, which possesses the function of self-consciousness and is lordly. Moreover the great one, the soul and all the products affected by the three qualities, and in their order, the five organs which perceive the objects of sensation. But joining minute particles of those six, which possess measureless power, with particles of himself, he created all being. Because those six kinds of minute particles which form the Creator's frame, enter those creatures, therefore the wise call his frame *Śarīra* (the body). But from fire, winds and the sun he drew forth the threefold *Vēda* called *Ṛk, Yajus and Sāman,* for the due performance of the sacrifice. For the sake of the prosperity of the worlds, he caused the *Brāhmaṇa,* the *Kṣatriya,* the *Vaisya* and the *Sūdra* to proceed from his mouth, his arms, his thighs and his feet".[25]

This evidently mythical theory of creation is combined version of *Ṛg-Vēdic* mythical cosmogony, Saṃkhyan description of *Pradhāna* and the *Upaniṣadic* spiritualism. As far as the mythical element in the theory is concerned, it has its *Sruti* source in the theory of creation propounded by the famous *Puruṣa Sūkta* of *Ṛg-Vēda.* In the *Puruṣa Sūkta* we find the first reference to the fourfold division of varna system. *Manu* effectively uses the mythical division of the cosmic person *(Puruṣa)* to explain and establish the functional differences among the four *Varṇas.* The *Puruṣa Sūkta* puts forth its pantheistic theory of creation with rudimentary social division as follows:

"The embodied spirit (puruṣa) has a thousand heads, a thousand eyes, a thousand feet, around on every side enveloping the earth yet filling space no longer than a span. He is himself this very universe. He is whatever is, has been, and shall be. He is the lord of immortality. All creatures are one-fourth of Him, three-fourths are that which is immortal in the sky. From Him, called Puruṣa, was born viraj, and from viraj was *puruṣa* produced, whom gods and holymen made their oblation. With *Puruṣa* as victim they performed a sacrifice. When they devided him, how did they cut him up? What was his mouth? What were his arms? And what his thighs and feet? The Brāhmaṇa was his mouth, the kingly soldier was made his arms, the husband man his thighs, the servile sūdra issued from his feet".[26]

Manu takes this *Ṛg-Vēdic* theory and enriches its rudimentary social division to include mixed castes and subcastes. He builds up his social and moral theory on this mythical śruti theory. Before we see how he does it, let us examine the philosophical aspect of *Manu's* idea of creation.

This theory is, though, substantially mythical in its form, it nevertheless expresses a metaphysical position. If we strip off the mythical aspect of the theory, we find that, for *Manu,* self-existing and ontologically independent spirit is the cause of all existence. The physical world is nothing but material manifestation of the ultimate universal self which underlies all such modifications. In the first verse of the theory *Manu* appears to assume the principle of *avyakta* as the material cause of the world. Some commentators (Medhātithi, Kullūkabhatta) tried to interpret it on Sāṃkhyan lines and read *Manu* as assuming the Sāṃkhyan principle of *Mūla Prakṛti* or Primeval principle of Matter. On the other hand, another commentator Rāghavānanda tried to interpret it on the lines of *Vēdānta* and sees it as avidya or ignorance. Whatever interpretation we take up, one thing is certain that *Manu* does not see it different from the self-existent spirit. He identifies all the modes of creation with the principle of ultimate universal soul. His idealistic outlook is explicit all through the code:

"He who scarifies to the self (alone), equally recognising the self in all created begins in the self. becomes (independent like) an autocrat and self-luminous" (XII.91).

The supreme self is defined as eternal, indiscernible, who contains all created beings. So, there is no eternal principle than the self and that is the cause of the whole creation. Thus, the self-existent supreme being is both the material and efficient cause of the creation. As the Creator or the Self-existent creates the material elements (out of his own substance) which constitute the material world, the material world is considered real, as real as the Creator. So, *Manu* admits a positive ontological status to the material world though ontological precedence is given to the spirit or soul of the universe. Here, he differs from the upanisadic Idealism which considers everything else as illusory except the unqualified spirit. *Manu,* on the contrary considers the external world as real though not eternal. It is real for it has its source of origin in the universal self. But the supreme Brahman is the only eternal principle from whom the world comes and goes to. So, the ontological status of the external world is positive but secondary as it owes its origin to the ontologically primary and independent spirit.

It is important to notice that this metaphysical position of *Manu* is supported by no outstanding ancient schools of philosophy. No school of ancient Indian thought subscribes to this ontological position. Let us see how *Manu's* metaphysical commitment is different from the ancient philosophical schools.

To start with, though *Manu* agrees with the upanisadic Idealism that supreme self is the ultimate reality, he differs from it as to its nature. For *Manu*, it is not simply pure consciousness. It is the creator of the whole universe and potentially contains within itself the whole creation. Again, the world is not illusory but real as created by the supreme being from his own substance whereas, the *Upaniṣads* preach the ultimate illusory character of the world with the analogy of phantoms of dream. The material world, including birth and death, objects of sense experience is unreal, in the final analysis. The soul in its nature is pure and uneffected by the physical world. *Manu* thus contradicts the important philosophical speculation of the *Vēda*. Quiet understandably, *Manu* cannot avoid it, for the conflict between the pre-Upaniṣadic mythical cosmogony and the speculative philosophy of *Upniṣads* is inherent in the *Vēda* itself.

Secondly, *Manu's* idea of creation appears to have a close resemblance to Sāṃkhya theory of creation, as he upholds the reality of both the spirit and the matter. But Sāṃkhya theory of evolution is different from that of *Manu*. For Sāṃkhya, *Puruṣ a* the spirit and the matter *(Prakṛti)* are two independent, though co-existing, ontological categories. Matter does not eminate from soul nor is identical with it. The primeval matter undergoes transformation in the proximity of the *Puruṣa* but that does not mean *Puruṣa* is the efficient cause of evolution. The spirit is not an active principle in the process of evolution but an indifferent spectator. Samkaracharya sees the Sāṃkhya doctrine of Kapila as opposed to the teaching of the *Vēda* and *Manu*. See how he puts it:

"*Manu* himself, where he glorifies the seeing of the one self in everything, implicitly blames the doctrine of Kapila. For Kapila, by acknowledging a plurality of selfs, does not admit there being one universal self.... All which proves that the system of Kapila contradicts the *Vēda*, and the doctrine of *Manu* who follows the *Vēda*, by its hypothesis of a plurality of selfs also, not only by the assumption of independent *Pradhāna*".[27]

Nyāya theory of Gotama goes against *Manu's* ontological position. For Naiyayikas, the world is constituted by eternal atoms which are not produced. The world of objects is an effect of atomic conjunctions. Consciousness is a product according to them and soul, is inherently unconscious substance. Soul aquires consciousness only after its contact with body, mind, external senses and objects of experience. Here consciousness, as a product of such contact, is a transitory phenomenon rather than an eternal quality of soul. Soul, as a substance like other substances, is devoid of consciousness and thus cannot deliberate any creation.

But, Kaṇāda, the founder of Vaiśēṣika philosophy, talks of creation and creator which needs a brief discussion. Kaṇāda, as the founder of Atomic theory views the world as a result of combination of atoms. Since he considers Action as external to substance, he is faced with the question as to what causes these combinations. He answers the question in terms of an unseen principle, *Adṛṣṭa,* superintended by the supreme lord. This supreme lord is the efficient cause of the combination of atoms, of which the world is an effect. The world is a bundle of effects like a jar is an effect of atoms of earth. Here, the supreme lord is like the potter who makes the jar. At the beginning of every secondary creation, the great lord desires to create and under the principle of *Adṛṣṭa,* merit and demerit, He produces action in the eternal atoms which constitute the world. Kaṇāda makes use of the theological entity, the supreme Lord, to explain dissolution also. He is the efficient cause for the disjunction of atoms which results in the dissolution. At the beginning of every secondary creation, the Lord acts as the Evolver and at the secondary dissolution, He acts as the Withdrawer. But what makes Kaṇāda to adopt the theological categories like a creator? He explains the existence of such supreme being for two reasons. He postulates the supreme Lord to account for 'names' and 'effects'.[28] How do names come to denote objects? Are they arbitrary utterances of a mad man? He answers that the Lord is the author of names. The application of names to objects is directed by the Lord. The second reason for the existence of the Lord is to explain 'effect'. When the Earth is an effect like pot, who is the efficient cause? How do these effects come into existence? Kaṇāda answers that the effect comes into existence through the efficiency of the Creator. The Creator is the author of both names and effects. Kaṇāda had to take recource in the theological being, due to his theoretical inadequacy, contrary to the scientific spirit of his atomic theory. The inadequacy is due to the view that motion is external to atoms. Precisely, this inadequacy led to Samkaracharya's criticism that neither creation nor *pralaya* could take place, if the atomic theory is adopted.[29]

The important point to be observed is that Kaṇāda is deliberately silent over primary creation. All the while he explains only the secondary creation but intentionally ignores the question of primary creation. If the supreme being is responsible for the origin of Atoms, the whole theory would be useless and inconsistent. For him, the atoms are eternal and ultimate units which make the world. They are not effected: "It is an error to suppose that ultimate atom is not eternal".[30] Kaṇāda with his silence over the primary creation, avoids a fundamental contradiction in his atomic theory which is well advanced of his times.

So, Kaṇāda's Creator is not the creator of primary creation. Moreover, unlike *Manu,* Kaṇāda does not consider Him as the ultimate material cause of creation. The only similarity between him and *Manu* is that while for Kaṇāda, the Creator assigns meaning to the 'names' and for *Manu*, the Creator draws the *Vēdas* from air, fire and the sun. So, for both of them, the Creator makes the *Vēda* intelligible. This position embarrasses the Mīmāṃsakas, and Kumārila vehemently opposes this. The orthodox school of Mīmāṃsa rests its doctrines on the assumption of eternity of the *Vēda.* Kumārila, in his *Slōkavārttika*, ridicules the theory of creation. Mīmāṃsa does not admit that the world and the *Vēda* have a beginning. So, the existence of a Creator flatly goes against the fundamental maxims of its philosophy.

The Supreme Lord, in order to be the Creator of the world, has to be an omniscient being. He must have complete knowledge of the material and instruments of such creation. The concept of creation presupposes an omniscient theological being either as the material cause or the efficient cause or as both. This position, Kumārila says, cannot be admitted into the Mīmāṃsa system.[31] Kumārila does not simply refuse to accept the theory but advances the most outstanding anti-theistic arguments in the history of Indian Philosophy.

Kumārila as a Mīmāṃsaka faces a problem here. What about the explicit references to creation in the *Vēdas?* Can Kumārila claim that the *Vēdas* do not admit creation? If they do, how to account for them? Here Kumārila adopts the technique of evasion. He explains away the *Vēdic* references to the creation as mere *Arthavāda*, which are intended to praise some sacrificial injunctions. By doing so, is he not denying the very foundation of *Manu's* social theory and opposing the authority of *Manu?* Yes, he certainly does. But this does not mean Kumārila is also opposed to the system of social organisation *Manu* tries to establish. Kumārila knows well that this is the system which is extremely conducive to the observation of *Vēdic* rituals, the *summum bonum* of his system. So, he silently accepts it. Then, why does he criticize *Manu's* theory of creation so vehemently? The obvious reason is that the theory of *Manu* contradicts some of the most crucial philosophical suppositions of his system i.e., eternity of sound and the *Vēda*. Mīmāṃsakas conceive the material world to be eternal or uncreated. This serves them to explain the eternity of the *Vēda* and validy of rituals. Though, they accept the reality of soul, it is not held to be responsible for any creation.

Mīmāṃsakas though oppose the theory of creation, they are not against the social implications of the theory. It is the ancient materialists, Cārvākas, who are the extreme opponents of both, the theory of creation and the *Varṇāśrama* system founded on it. The materialists not only ridicule the Brāhminical myths that support their social system, but also hold a view which is exactly opposite of *Manu's* view on creation.

For Cārvākas, matter does not come out of spirit. Rather, soul or self is a product of matter. They do not recognize separate existence of soul from body. The popular Cārvākas analogy for the origin of consciousness from matter is that of intoxicating quality of liquor arising out of ingrediant materials which did not possess such quality before. They do not accept the existence of universal self. Viewing consciousness as a product of a particular combination of material elements,

Cārvākas stand as the extreme opponents of *Manu's ontological* position. Cārvākas vehemently question the Brāhminical superstitions about after-death, sacrifices, heaven, transmigrations and the social system based on those superstitions which are expounded by the *Vēda* and the code.

Neither Buddhism nor Jainism contribute to the ontological position *Manu* holds. In Buddhism, the self is but five *skandas* and is not permanent. There is no universal self. Buddhism also preaches against the *Varnāsrama* system and the *Vēdic* rituals. This explains *Manu's* prejudice against Heretics. Jainism holds self to be just a category as other material categories, and that it is not responsible for any creation.

Though no ancient school of thought contributes to *Manu's* theory of creation, the theory is honoured by other law-givers and the epics. The *Mahābhārata* advocates the same theory with some changes. In *Śānti Parva* the theory of creation is attributed to sage *Bhṛgu*. It has to be noticed that Bhrigu is appointed by *Manu* to enunciate the present *Dharma Śāstra* to other sages. In *Śānti Parva, Bhṛgu* is said to have taught the theory of creation to sage Bharadwāja.[32]

In this version of the theory we find that the Absolute Spirit is called *Mānasa. Mānasa* means the will. Next come *Mahat* (the great) and *Brahman* (this time, born from Lotus). Despite of these minute differences, both the theories are similar in their substance, in so far as both hold the absolute principle of thought or spirit as responsible for and underlying all material manifestations.

Later, *Manu's* theory of creation is revived, in its chief features, by *Viśiṣta Advaita* of Rāmānuja. Rāmānuja holds a view of creation similar to that of *Manu*. Rāmānuja as an idealist, holds the supreme universal spirit as the only principle underlying all reality. But unlike an Advaitin, Rāmānuja considers the supreme soul or *Brahman* to be the real cause of all the diversity in the world. The world of plurality is the manifestation of the supreme soul. The world is a part of *Brahman's* nature and is the body of the universal self, it is not an illusion. For Saṃkara, the great Vedantin, *Brahman* is pure objectless mass of consciousness. But for both *Manu* and Rāmānuja *Brahman* is the personal Creator who from his own substance creates the world of difference. For *Manu* and Rāmānuja the world is real as part of the universal supreme soul.

Once *Manu* accepts the reality of the physical world, he is obliged to give a positive explanation of its constitution and transformation. In Indian thought, there are three distinct explanations regarding the nature and constitution of the world, offered by Lōkāyata, Sāṃkhya and Nyāya. Lokayatikas offer Bhūtavāda, the theory that the world comes out of and is constituted by material elements or *Bhūtas*. They are water, earth, fire and air. Sāṃkhya offers *Pradhānavāda,* according to which *Pradhāna*, the primeval matter is the root cause of all material transformations. Pradhana is constituted by three qualities or guṇas called *sattva, Rajas* and *Tamas*. Nyāya-Vaiśēṣika offers the most advanced theory of *Paramāṇuvāda*, which holds that the material world is constituted by ultimate atoms. *Manu,* in order to provide an explanation for the constitution and transformation of the material world, has to choose one among the above three theories.

Manu cannot adopt *Bhūtavāda* of Cārvākas, the plain speaking materialists, for the reasons obvious. The materialists are the most ardent opponents of the *Vēdic* myths, brahminical superstitions and the social order founded on such grounds. Not only that, they further see soul as a product of matter. They deny the existence of universal soul, whose existence cannot be proved by perception. Neither can *Manu* adopt *Paramāṇuvāda,* according to which the world is an effect of mechanical combination of eternal atoms devoid of production and distruction. Further, Naiyayikas also deny the existence of consciousness independent of material objects. So, *Manu* is left with no option but *Pradhānavāda* of Sāṃkhya and he conveniently adopts it. *Manu*, for this purpose, comfortably ignores his basic differences with Sāṃkhya and edits its theory of evolution to suit his purpose.

However, *Manu* cannot avoid a thorough theoretical inconsistency while adopting Sāṃkhya theory of *Pradhāna*. Sāṃkhya is famous for its *Satkāryavāda*, the causal theory that the effect must be pre-existing in the cause. The effect is not a new expression. Rather, it is realisation of the potency embedded in the cause itself. Sāṃkhya theory of evolution is also an example of Svabhāvavāda, according to which all material transformations depend on the nature of the matter. So, for Sāṃkhya, the primeval matter *(Pradhāna)* undergoes transformation independently according to its nature *(Svabhāva)*. All these transformations or modifications are latent in the primeval matter itself and thus need no external agency for the purpose. *Manu* while conceiving matter as emerging from the universal self-existent spirit, undermines the essential aspects of Sāṃkhya theory of evolution. *Manu* does not care to answer the question 'how does the universal self give rise to matter out his own substance?' *Manu's* position ignores *Satkāryavāda*. But *Manu*, on the other hand, makes use of *Svabhāvavāda* and *Satkāryavāda* while explaining further material modifications in terms of three constituent guṇas.

This contradiction in *Manu* is brought to surface by Śaṃkarāchārya in his *Vēdānta Sūtra Bhāṣya*. As we have earlier seen, Śaṃkara quotes *Manu* to show that Kapila's doctrine is opposed to the *Vēda* and that *Manu* implicitly blames Kapila's theory. Again, while refuting *Paramāṇuvāda* of Vaiśēṣika, Śaṃkara concedes that *Manu* adopts *Pradhānavāda:*

"While the theory of *Pradhāna* being accepted by some adheremts of the *Vēda*, for instance, *Manu* with a view to the doctrines of the effect existing in the cause already, and so on, the atomic theory has not been accepted by any person of authority in any of its parts, and therefore is to be disregarded entirely by all those who take their stand on the *Vēdas*".[33]

Śaṃkara quoting *Manu* as both blaming and adopting Śāṃkhya theory involves a contradiction. This contradiction is inherent not in Śaṃkara but in *Manu's* theory of creation itself. *Manu* refuses independent *Pradhāna* as a principle different from the universal self and again assumes it to explain the process of material evolution. This theoretical inconsistency apart, we cannot but admire *Manu* when we see how intelligently he makes use of Sāṃkhya ideas to substantiate his theory of social order, theory of action, its mechanism and particularly his theory of transmigrations.

Manu's Theory of Society

Manu's main aim, as a law-giver, is to prescribe a code of social conduct to enforce a particular social structure. But *Manu* is no less interested in justifying such code theoretically. As we have so far seen, he justifies it mainly on grounds of the authority of the *Vēda* and tradition. *Manu*, althrough his code, attempts to evolve a consistent theory of society which is well-founded on his mythical theory of creation.

Society, for *Manu*, is the creation and manifestation of the self-existing supreme *Brahman*. The Creator not only created the society, but also made certain rules for its conduct which *Manu* is presently offering through his code. So, for *Manu* the ideal society is one which totally corresponds to the model his code puts forth. *Manu* conceives the model society as an organic whole having the four *Varṇas* or social classes as its limbs. The four *Varṇas* are *Brāhmaṇa, Kṣatriya, Vaiśya* and *Sūdra*. Health of the society as an organic whole depends on the proper functioning of its different limbs, the four *Varṇas*.

The four *Varṇas* are said to have originated from different limbs of the Creator. This division of society is not just functional for it supposes a specific social hierarchy. The position of each *Varṇa* in the social hierarchy depends on the limb from which the *Varṇa* is said to have originated. So, the three important social implications of *Manu's* theory of creation are (1) the conception of society as an organic whole; (2) the four fold division and (3) specific social hierarchy.

By viewing society as an organic whole, *Manu Smṛti* identifies personal good with social good. Social good depends on proper discharge of duties by all the members of society. Similarly, personal good depends on the functioning of society as a whole, just like the health of body and of its limbs are identical. The body organism cannot be fully functional without all its limbs discharging their respective duties, and limbs cannot function without the general health of the whole body. The interests of different classes, seen this way, are not conflicting. Rather they are necessarily compatible, viewed from the higher level of society as a whole. Social prosperity depends on unity and mutual cooperation among the four classes. Society is explained not in terms of conflicting interests of the groups but viewed as a unity of social forces. For *Manu,* like for Plato, the ideal society is a stable society. Both *Manu* and Plato aim at stability through stratification of society into different social classes with specific social functions. As Idealists, both of them view society as an organic whole comprising of the stratified classes as its limbs. There is a little difference however, between Plato and *Manu*. For Plato the best society is a replica of the ideal society. The ideal society is a changeless society and for Plato, all change is degeneration. *Manu*, on the other hand, foresees change and for him, a stable society is not a static society. However, as he highlights the age old tradition and traditional morality *(Sanātana Dharma)*, he implicitly resists change.

Manu's view of society as an expression of unified social forces functioning for mutual benefits has immense historical significance. To understand the importance of *Manu's* view, we have to place it in the specific historical context and examine it in the light of the then existing social reality. At the time of disturbances caused by introduction of the state organization in ancient India, the immediate need of the hour was stability and peaceful co-existence of groups. Harmony or peaceful co-existence of conflicting social forces was a necessary step towards peace and stability. The importance of *Manu's* attempt towards a stable society cannot be undermined in the given historical conditions. However, while doing so, *Manu* favours the interests of Aryan community by placing it in a privileged position. This is quite natural since the invaders always dominate the invaded. Nevertheless, *Manu's* endeavour to accommodate different social classes in one systematic social spectrum has to be appreciated.

The fourfold division of society is one of the chief features of *Manu's* morality, politics and economics. *Manu Smṛti* views this division as natural and hence permanent. It is important to notice that this division is not a product of the code. Rather, the code is a product of such system. *Manu Smṛti* does not give rise to this division, but presupposes it. In the beginning of the code, the devine sages request the great *Svayambhuva* to deliver 'the code of conduct for the four *Varṇas*' (I.2). So, the division was already existing before the code is delivered. Hence, the code presupposes the *Varṇa* system. Even the *Ṛg-Vēdic Puruṣa Sūkta*, one of the most recent hymns of the *Samhita,* is a later attempt to account for the already existing division. This division can be traced back to *Ṛg-Vēdic* Aryan tribal organization. The original Aryan community was devided into holy power *(Brāhmaṇa)*, kingly or military power *(Kṣatra)* and the commonality (viś). At the time of *Ṛg-Vēda*, Aryans were slowly establishing their power over non-Aryan tribes which were later included in their scheme as *Sūdras* or *Dāsyus*. Thus evolved the simple four-fold system through the adjustment of races, with specific functional differences.

The *Ṛg-Vēdic Puruṣa Sūkta* and *Manu's* theory of creation are mere speculations to account for the social divison. Both are mythical in content. *Manu*, in his theory of creation, attempts to establish and perpetuate the social division, by describing that it is natural, universal and elternal. *Manu* extends the scope of his social division to include even foreign origins like *Yavanas* (greeks), Chinese etc. who neither belong to the Aryan community not to the native *Sūdras*. *Manu* explains these races as originally *Kṣatriyas* who later become *Sūdras* by failing to adhere to the sacredorial duties.[34]

Among the later speculations about the origin of *Varṇas*, *Gītā* attempts to furnish a rational theory about the origin of *Varṇa*. *Gītā* explains the social division in terms of temperament and moral character. Lord *Kṛṣṇa* assumes the responsibility for the creation of four *Varṇas*, which are fixed in the light of or due to character and actions of individuals *(Gītā* IV.13). This explanation is more universal in its character and application. However, the Indian caste system is hereditary. Though social esteem depends on character, one's parentage cannot be altered by one's character. It is only exceptionally accepted to consider one's caste on one's character, especially when one's parentage cannot be ascertained. King *Viśwāmitra* had to struggle and do severe penances in order to be called a *Brahmarṣi (Brāhmaṇa* sage). Such cases are very rare. As Sir Sivaswamy Iyer aptly puts it, "While we may deplore the evil effects of the institution (of caste), it is not possible to entertain the view that social classifications were determined merely by character".[35]

However, *Manu* explains the differences among the four *Varṇas* in terms of their origin from different limbs of the Creator:

"...for the sake of the worlds, He caused the *Brāhmaṇa,* the *Kṣatriya*, the *Vaisya* and the *Sūdras* to proceed from his mouth, his arms, his thiegh and his feet."(I.37)

After the creation, the Creator Himself assigned different duties, rights and privileges to the four classes. So, the differences are part of the Creator's design and thus, are natural. The specific functions of each class are fixed by *Brahman* as follows:

"In order to protect this universe, He assigned separate duties and occupations to those who sprang from his mouth, arms, thiegh, and feet. To *Brāhmaṇas,* he assigned teaching and studying *Vēda*, sacrificing for their own benefit and for others, giving and accepting alms; the *Kṣatruya,* he commanded to protect people, to bestow gifts, to offer sacrifices, to study *Vēda* and obstaining from sensual pleasures; the *Vaisya* to tend cattle, to bestow gifts, to offer sacrifices, to study *Vēda*, to trade, to lend money and to cultivate land; one occupation only the lord prescribed for *Sūdra,* to serve meekly even these other three *Varṇas,"* (I.87-91).

One's social function, as the law prescribes, is thus fixed by one's birth in a particular *Varṇa*. *Manu Smṛti* prescribes definite occupations for men of each *Varṇa*, caste and mixed caste in ordinary times and at times of distress. No *Varṇa* can follow, even at times of distress, the occupation of a higher *Varṇa*.

Apart from this, there is another important division — that of *Dvija* and *Sūdra*. The first three *Varṇas* i.e., *Brāhman, Kṣatriya* and *Vaiśya* are twice born or *Dvija*. Every *Dvija* has to undergo upanayan or the ritual of initiation, which is the most important purificatory rite and is remeniscent of Aryan tribal past. The ritual is supposed to give one a second spiritual birth. With this rite of initiation, one is introduced to the Aryan path of holy life and privileges thereof. A *Sūdra* is not supposed to undergo this rite and thus remain *ēka-jāti* or once-born. As Sir Sivaswamy Iyer observes, "while the relative estimation in which the three upper classes were held depended mainly upon the character of the occupations prescribed for and practised by them, the gulf which separated them from the *Sūdras* was due to racial considerations and the tendency to despise conquered people.[36]

Among the twice-born, *Brāhmaṇas* are the first in importance and dignity. *Brāhmaṇas* are considered gods on earth (Bhūsura). The code ascribes pre-eminence to the *Brāhmaṇas* and next come *Kṣatriya* and *Vaiśya*. The superiority of *Brāhmaṇas* is due to their origin from the mouth of *Brahman,* their possession of *Vēda* and the sacrificial thread (X.4). This supremacy is established throughout the code (IX.317, 319; XI.84 etc.).

The *Brāhmaṇas* with their dignity and supremacy earn their living by teaching *Vēda,* assisting in sacrifices and by receiving gifts. These three functions are exclusively assigned to *Brāhmaṇas* for their livelihood:

"Of the six acts (functions of the *Brāhmaṇa)*, three are the means of his subsistence viz., assisting at sacrifices, teaching the *Vēda* and receiving presents by a pious giver. These three privileges are limited to *Brāhmaṇas,* and do not extend to *Kṣatriyas* and *Vaisyas*. Hence a *Brāhmaṇa* is called 'Tri-Karman', 'One who engaged in three acts" (X.75-77).

Manu insists that a *Brāhmaṇa* should be given liberal gifts and encourages giving heavy *'Dakṣiṇa'* to him to meet his material needs. No man should undertake a sacrifice unless he has plenty of money to make liberal gifts (XI.40). One who gives wealth to the *Brāhmaṇas* would obtain heaven when one dies (XI.6). No *Brāhmaṇa* should be left starving:

"A king even though dying (far want), must not receive taxes from a *Brāhmaṇa* learned in *Vēdas*, nor must he allow such a *Brāhmaṇa* dwelling in his country to pine away with hunger. Of that king in whose kingdom a *Brāhmaṇa* learned in *Vēdas* wastes with hunger, the whole kingdom in a short time be wasted with famine" (VII.133,134).

Hence, *Manu* takes care of livelihood for the priestly class. A *Brāhmaṇa* who is not learned in *Vēdas* or one who is passing through distress can take up the occupations of a *Kṣatriya* or *Vaisya* (X.80-82).

The second in eminence is the military class which enjoys the political power. Its chief function is to protect people and maintain social order. The state with a king as its head, has to ensure peace and security to its people. The king is considered, like in many cultures all over the world, a divinity on earth:

"The Creator created a king for the protection of the whole world by drawing forth eternal particle from the essence of *Indra, Anila* (wind), *Yama* (god of justice), *Sūrya* (sun), *Agni* (fire), *Varuṇa, Chandra* (moon), and *Kubēra* (god of wealth)". (VII.3,4)

"A king even though a chiḷd, must not be treated with contempt, as if he were a mortal; he is a great divinity in human shape" (VII.8)

The king has to rule over his subjects like a father with the help of a council of *Brāhmaṇas* as ministers. He must have a *Brāhmaṇa* as his Prime Minister and has to take him into confidence. The king should be brave and never retreat in a battle. He must set an example of bravery. He has to take great care and should not indulge in sensuous pleasures. He has to divide his time properly to attend all the functions he has to discharge. (VII.154).

Though a king is powerful, *Manu* takes care that he would not become a tyrant. The king is supposed to be very obedient towards *Brāhmaṇas*. His activities are closely superintended and regulated by *Brāhmaṇas* around him. *Manu* formulates so many rules to restrict the power of the king so that he does not take away the supremacy of the *Brāhmaṇas:*

"Determination not to retreat in a battle, protection of the people, the obedience to *Brāhmaṇas* are the highest duties of a king, and secure their felicity in heaven" (VII.88)

Manu recognizes the importance of proper relations between priestly class and military class in running the state. He insists on mutual cooperation between them:

"A *Kṣatriya* cannot thrive without a *Brāhmaṇa,* nor a *Brāhmaṇa* without a *Kṣatriya, Brāhmaṇa* and the *Kṣatriya* when associated together prosper in this world and the next." (IX.322)

Vaiśyas are the agricultural traders who constitute the third eminent *Dvija* class. They are usually wealthy with rights on land and property. The state takes care to protect their property and trade from internal disturbances and external invasions. They form the tax-paying lot who finance the political and religious operations. The prosperity and stability of the state mainly depends on agricultural production and trade. So, *Vaiśyas* as very prominent class in the society. They enjoy all the privileges of being a *Dvija*.

Sūdras from the fourth *Varṇa* whose function is service to *Dvijas*. They have no access to *Vēda* and other purificatory rite which are exclusive for the *Dvijas*. As opposed to *Dvijas,* they are eka-jati or once-born:

"The service of *Brāhmaṇas* alone is declared to be an excellent occupation for a *Sūdra:* for whatever else besides this he may perform will bear no fruit for him. No collection of wealth must be made by a *Sūdra,* even though he is able to do it: for *Sūdra* who has acquired wealth, gives pain to *Brāhmaṇas*. A *Sūdra,* whether bought or unbought, may be compelled to do servile work: for he was created by the self-existent to be a slave of a *Brāhmaṇa*. A *Sūdra,* though emancipated by his master, is not released from servitude.... A *Brāhmaṇa* may confidently seize the goods of his *Sūdra* slave; for as that slave can have no property, the master may take his possessions" (X.123, 129; VIII.413, 414, 417)

In addition to the four *Varṇas, Manu* refers to many mixed castes which are the result of unlawful marriages among the four principal *Varṇas:*

"By unlawful intermarriage of classes (*vyabhicharēṇa Varṇānām*), by their marrying women who ought not be married, and by neglected of their own duties, mixed castes are produced" (X.24)

Manu refers to a number of these mixed castes such as Mahishya, Ambastha, Murdha Vasikta, Karana or Kayastha, Vaidya, Dhigvana, Ayogava, Pukkasa, Chandala, etc. These castes are assigned particular occupations.

Besides these there were some aboriginal tribes who stayed outside the *Manu's* social system, living in the hills and forests. These tribes were warrior tribes on whom probably Aryans could not establish their hold by the time of *Manu Smṛti* Mlechchas is one of such tribes which had no social distinctions, the others being Pundarikas, Odras, Dravidians, Kambhojas, Kirathas etc., mentioned in the code. Aryans could, at a later stage win over most of them and include them into their cultural fold.

As far as the social adjustment among the four *Varṇas* concerned, *Brāhmaṇas* are the most advantageously placed around whom the other classes are carefully placed to make a system.

Manu and Morality

Manu's idea of morality is comprehensive and philosophically interesting. *Manu Dharma Śāstra* deals with all the aspects of human life and comes out with a comprehensive set of duties regulating one's conduct towards oneself, towards the society, towards other creatures, towards the universe as a whole. Hence, it is very difficult to define *Manu's* view of morality unless we see what it means to him in individual, social, practical and spiritual spheres of human life.

Manu higlights the concept of *Ṛṇa* which is the most dominant moral concept of *Brāhmaṇa* part of the *Vēda*. *Ṛṇa* means indebtedness and every Aryan is born with three kinds of primary *Ṛṇa*. The first to gods which has to be fulfilled by sacrificial offering to gods. The second is towards the ancient sages which has to be discharged by studying the *Vēdas*, the repositories of ancient wisdom and cultural heritage. The third to one's ancestors which has to be observed by marrying and begetting children to continue the lineage. This idea of *Ṛṇa* finds clear expression in the code:

"By the study of *Vēda*, by vows, by burnt oblations, by the recitation of the sacred texts, by the acquisition of threefold sacred science, by offering to the gods, *Ṛṣis* and manes, by the procreation of sons, by the great sacrifices, and by *Śrauta* sacrifices this human body is made it for union with *Brahman*" (II.28).

Manu devides the holy life of an Aryan into four successive orders or stages *(Āśrama)* and preaches definite rules to follow in each stage to make the whole life morally commendable. The first stage is of religious studentship *(Brahmacharyam)*, the second is of a house holder *(Gṛhastha)*, the third is of a hermit *(Vānaprastha)* and the final stage is of a religious mendicant *Bhikṣu* or *Sanyāsin*. One who has undergone these four stages as the *Vēda* and law prescribe, will be exalted to the highest bliss.

The first *Āśrama* of Brahmachārin begins with the child going to a learned preceptor or āchārya for acquisition of knowledge in the *Vēda* and its angas. Āchārya is considered as the spiritual father of the student. The young ward has to live with his preceptor satisfying him with service and obedience. The student has to observe rigorously the rules of conduct and live a puritan life (II.177-179). He has to go around the village for receiving alms and collect food for himself and his preceptor and also fuel for the sacred fire (II.187). The student after completing his *Vēdic* education at his preceptor's place will be relieved after he offers valuable presents to his preceptor. Thus he discharges his duty towards ancient sages by studying the *Vēda* and repeating it.

The student after completion of education returns home. He, then, has to select a girl from his own class and enter *Gṛhasthāśrama* or the stage of a householder by marrying. *Manu* offers certain guidelines to chose a bride (III.8-10). *Manu* offers eight forms of marriage and prescribes definite forms for each *Varṇa* (III.21). *Gṛhasthāśrama* is the most important stage in life. *Manu* enjoins a number of daily domestic religious duties to householders which are dealt in detail by *Gṛhya Sūtras.* The most important are the morning and evening oblations, and the five *Mahāyajñas*. The five *Mahāyajñas* are:

1. *Brahma Yajña* or *Japayajña*: repition of the *Vēda;*
2. *Pitṛ Yajña*: offering *srāddha* to departed ancestors;
3. *Dēva-Yajña*: offering oblations to gods;
4. *Bhūta-Yajña*: offering rice for all creatures and spirits;
5. *Manuṣya-Yajña*: hospitality towards men.

These five *Yajñas* remind one's duty towards *Ṛṣis,* one's ancestors, gods, creatures and fellow men. Of these *Brahma Yajña* is the most efficacious. *Pitṛ-Yajña* is the key for Aryan patriarchical inheritance. The fifth *Yajña* - i.e., hospitality to men is cherished as a traditional virtue. *Manu* says that a

Brāhmaṇa who is not received well would take away all the wealth and merit of the householder.

Gṛhasthāśrama gives ample scope for the pursuit of *Puruṣārthas* or ends of life which we shall discuss a little after. A householder has to pursue a holy life with the help of his partner. *Manu* emphasizes mutual trust and love between a man and his wife (IX.45, 101; V.157). Social prosperity depends on healthy family relations, for family is the primary unit of the social nexus.

The next stage in life is that of an anchorite (*Vānaprastin*) in which one has to retire to a forest after duly fulfilling the three *Ṛṇas* and discharging all other duties towards family. *Manu* says that one has to take up *Vānaprastha* when one sees one's hair turning gray or as soon as one begets a grand child. In this *Āśrama* too, one has to fulfil the prescribed religious duties (VI.4,5,22,20,24,25). This is a preparatory stage for the final *Āśrama*. In this stage one has to practice restraint over one's sense organs and keep one's mind in control.

The fourth and final stage of an Aryan's life involves renouncing the world, suppression of passions and wandering about as a *Bhikṣu* or *Parivrājaka*. Renouncing the world does not mean that one has no obligation towards society. Indeed, this is the stage in which one can devote oneself towards the welfare of society. After suppressing passions towards worldly objects and thoroughly overcoming desire for physical pleasures, one can do disinterested *(Niṣkāma)* service to humanity and society. This stage is not free from social duties. A *Bhikṣu* or mendicant still depends on the society for his bare maintenance and in turn serves the society by going around enlightening people, showing the path of welfare and liberation. This is the reason why sanyasins are revered by people even today. This is the stage in which a man is supposed to attain the spirit of freedom through control of passions and service to society.

This is the holy life of an Aryan spread over four stages or orders closely regulated by law and tradition. One cannot but appreciate the scheme of life envisaged by *Manu* which gives due importance to all aspects of human life. It is not probable that all Aryans observed the third and fourth stages i.e., *Vānaprastha* and *Sanyāsa.* But as *Manu* says, one who undergoes these four stages, according to the prescribed *Dharma,* is said to have lived a meaningful life and would attain emancipation.

Now, let us see what morality or *Dharma* means to *Manu* in this context. For *Manu, Dharma* is not free floating. It is rather relative to one's situation in life. *Dharma* is what is demanded by one's *Varṇa* and *Āśrama* in accordance with *Vēda*, the tradition, the lives of holymen and self-satisfaction:

"So act in thy brief passage through this world that thy apparel, speech and the inner store of knowledge be adapted to thy age, thy occupation, means and parentage." (IV.18).

Manu classifies *Dharma* or one's ethical obligations into twofold: *Sadharaṇa Dharma* and *Viśiṣta Dharma.* While the former refers to the common duties of three higher castes, the latter refers to the duties relative to one's caste and particular stage in life. *Manu* enumerates steadfastness *(Dhairya)*, forgiveness (*Kṣama*), application (*Dama*), non-appropriation *(Chowryābhāva)*, cleanliness *(Soucha)* repression of senses *(Indriyanigraha)*, wisdom *(Dhī)*, learning *(Vidya)*, veracity *(Satya)* and restraint from anger *(Akrōdha)* as the tenfold virtues for the twice-born (VI.92). These are the virtues intended for individual perfection.

These common duties or virtues are often mistaken to be 'universal duties' meant for all men irrespective of caste and social position. S.K. Maitra says that "the universal duties are the duties irrespective of one's age, caste or creed i.e., duties obligatory on man as man and not as a member of a particular community or social class or as being at a particular stage or period of life."[37] However, *Manu* is not ambiguous about it. He clearly mentions that the tenfold law is meant for twice-born:

By twice-born men belonging to (any of) these four orders *(Āśramas)*, the tenfold law must be obeyed (VI.91). We can easily see that this tenfold *Sādharaṇa Dharma* is not meant for Sūdras for it consists sacred wisdom (*Dhī*) and Learning (*Vidya*) which are refused to *Sūdras*. Manu says that the purpose of the tenfold law is self-purification for the attainment of final liberation i.e., *mōkṣa* (VI.93). As Debiprasad Chattopadhyaya observes, "these general duties are meant exclusively for the members of the prīvileged class, the law-giver's *Dvija-s*. The toiling majority — known to the law giver as the *Sūdras* — being debarred from it are not entitled to salvation."[38]

However, Manu's list of *Sadharaṇa Dharma* is important for it gives us the essential virtues of the Vēdic tradition. *Viśiṣta Dharma* refers to the particular duties which depend on one's specific caste and stage of life. *Sadharaṇa Dharma* and *Viśiṣta Dharma* together from the *Manus's* moral prescription.

Viśiṣta Dharma depends on one's *Varṇa* and stage in life. General duties and specific duties with reference to one's *Varṇa* and *Āśrama* together make a comprehensive set of ethical principles. All the virtues cherished in the *Vēdic* tradition are incorporated in this set of duties.

Again, *Dharma* is regarded as the first and most important thing to be pursued or end of human life *(Puruṣārtha)*. The other three pursuits or ends are *Artha* (wealth), *Kāma* (desire) and *Mōkṣa* (liberation). *Dharma* is the underlying principle of the other three pursuits. *Artha* and *Kāma* pursued in accordance with *Dharma* would lead to *Mōkṣ a* the *summum bonum* of human life. There is no short-cut to *Mōkṣa* without observing *Dharma*.

Wealth should be acquired in a way that does not contradict one's *Dharma*. Wealth is necessary to take care of material comforts. A *Gṛhastha* should acquire wealth in a morally acceptable way to pursue *Kāma* and *Dharma*. Among the four *Puruṣārthas, Dharma* and *Artha* are means whereas *Kāma* and *Mōkṣa* are ends in themselves. *Artha* is needed for Kama and *Dharma* is essential for *Mōksa*.

Now, we shall try to understand *Manu's* conception of *Dharma*. *Dharma,* for *Manu,* is the set of moral principles, to be followed by every member of society in accordance with one's *Varṇa, Āśrama* and sex, which has the sanction of *Vēda,* tradition, holy men and one's conscience. *Dharma* is the guiding light for other pursuits of life and is higher than all human beings.

Law and Justice

Manu uses the word *Dharma* to mean not only individual and social duties, but also to mean law and justice. *Dharma* as justice is higher than king and the state. The king has to be impartial in administration of law and justice and he himself is bound by them. The king has to punish every offender whether the offender is his father, mother, wife, son, teacher, priest or a friend (VIII.335).

The interesting feature of *Manu's* justice is that the social hierarchy of classes has its influence on the administration of justice. The inequality among social classes is reflected in the matters of rights, duties, witnesses and punishments. The law and justice vary depending on one's *Varṇa* and social status. While the principle of equality is observed only within the confines of each *Varṇa*, the law discriminates between *Varṇas*. Both civil and criminal law reflect these distinctions.

The law prescribes different rates of interest to different *Varṇas*. A *Brāhmaṇa* can borrow at the rate of three or four per cent. While the other three *Varṇas* can borrow at five per cent, for a month (VIII.142).

Though a crime committed by a *Sūdra* attracts the most severe punishment, in the case of theft, it is the higher castes that deserve more punishment. A *Vaiśya* and a *kṣatriya* are liable to pay two or four times the fine payable by a *Sūdra* thief. If a *Brāhmaṇa* does it, he has to pay eight or sixteen times the fine payable by a *Sūdra* thief. If the king himself is the offender, he has to pay one thousand times the fine (VIII.337, 338). The idea behind this is that the gravity of offence increases in the case of higher castes for they are supposed to be more responsible.

Manu mentions four offences as *Mahāpātakas* or mortal sins which are considered serious. One who slays a *Brāhmaṇa*, who drinks intoxicating liquor being a *Brāhmaṇa*, who steals gold belonging to a *Brāhmaṇa* and one who violates a Guru's bed are said to have committed *Mahāpātaka* (IX.235). One who is guilty of these *Mahāpātakas* would be branded on forehead unless one undergoes prescribed penances. However, the penances save him only from branding while he is liable for other punishments.

In administration of law and justice, *Brāhmaṇas* are again the most privileged class. *Brāhmaṇas* are exempted from punishment of death. The most severe punishment for them is deportation. A *Brāhmaṇa* who finds a treasure can take all of it. *Brāhmaṇas* are exempted from paying taxes (VII.133-136).

However, *Manu* is really humanitarian when he says that whenever declaration of truth causes death of a *Sūdra, Vaisya, Kṣatruya* or *Brāhmaṇa,* it is better to speak false. Such falsehood is preferable to truth (VIII.103). Despite of the discremination between the social classes in administration of justice, *Manu's* endeavours have to be appreciated for his consistent and comprehensive view of justice. *Manu's* view of justice makes the different *Varṇa* to adhere to their respective duties and contribute to the smooth running of the state and the society.

Theory of Action and Transmigrations

In view of their philosophical content, the eleventh and twelfth chapters of *Manu Smṛti* are the most important. In these chapters, *Manu* establishes his theory of action, theory of final liberation and transmigration. His views on human action are very important for his theory of action plays a key role in understanding his views on *Mŏkṣa* and transmigration. In his theory of action, *Manu* adopts the Sāṃkhyan views to explain mechanism of action and its fruition. He extends his theory of action to explain his ideas on transmigration in a commendable way. So, it is very important to analyse his view on *Mōkṣa* and transmigration.

Contrary to the idea of renuniciation as the means to liberation, *Manu* understands the importance of desire in the mechanism of action. He sees every empirically significant action as having founded on desire. Desire for rewards is what prompts man to action:

"To act solely from a desire for rewards is not laudable, yet an exemption from that desire is not found to be in this world; for on that desire is grounded the study of *Vēda* and performance of actions prescribed by the *Vēda*. The desire for rewards, indeed, has its roots in the conception that an act can yield them, and in consequence of that conception sacrifices are performed; Vows and the laws prescribing restraints are all stated to be kept through the idea that they will bear fruit. Not a single act below here appears to be done by a man free from desire; for whatever man does, it is the result of impulse of desire." (II. 2,3,4)

Action, for *Manu*, is of three types viz., mental *(mānas)*, bodily *(śarīra)* and speech *(vāk)*. Mind is the instigator for all the three types of action. These actions, *Manu* says invariably bring out good or evil consequences:

"Action which springs from the mind, from speech and from body, produces good or evil results; by action are caused the various conditions of men, the highest, the middling and the lowest. Know that the mind is the instigator here below, even to that action which is connected with the body, (and) which is of three kinds, has three locations and falls under ten heads. In consequence of many sinful acts committed with his body, a man becomes (in the next birth) something inanimate, in consequence of sins committed by speach, a bird or a beast, and in the consequence of mental sins he is reborn in a low caste" (XII. 3,4,9).

So, *Manu's* theory of action is central to his theory of transmigrations also. As far as the mechanism of action is concerned, *Manu* gives the four fold division of the subject. The body consisting of material elements *(Bhūtātman),* the mind which knows the field of action *(Kṣētrajña),* the individual soul through which the mind experiences the world *(Jīva)* and the supreme soul which prevades the individual souls and resides in its own multiform manifestations — constitute the moral subject. In addition to these four, *Manu* considers another subtle body which undergoes the after-death experience:

"Him who impels this corporeal self to action, they call the *Kṣētrajña* (the knower of the field); but him who does the acts, the wise name the *Bhūtāṭman* (the self consisting of elements). Another internal self that is generated with all embodied *(Kṣētrajñas)* is called *Jīva*, through which the *Kṣētrajña* becomes sensible of all pleasure and pain in successive births. These two, the great one and *Kṣētrajña*, who are closely united with elements, pervade Him who resides in the multiform created beings. Another strong body, formed of particles of the five elements and destined to suffer the torments in hell, is produced after death in the case of wicked men." (XII. 12,13,14,16).

Mind, the instigator of actions, is characterized by the three qualities *(Triguṇa)* of *Sattva* (goodness), *Rajas* (Activity) and *Tamas* (Darkness). This triple characterization of mind corresponds to Sāṃkhya description of *Pradhāna* which is conveniently adopted by *Manu.* All actions are expressions of these three qualities. It is the efficacy of the actions that determines the present and future states of the agent. With this conception of action, *Manu* tries to explain his theory of transmigrations:

"Know *Sattva, Rajas* and *Tamas* to be the three qualities of the self, with which the great one always completely pervades all existences. When one of these qualities wholly predominates in a body, then it makes the embodied soul eminently distinguished for that quality. Goodness is declared to have the form of knowledge, Darkness of ignorance, Activity of love and hatred; such is the nature of these three which is all pervading and clings to everything created. When a man, having done, doing or about to do any act, feels ashamed ... all such acts bear the mark of the quality of Darkness ... when a man desires to gain by an act much fame in this world and feels no sorrow on failing, know that it bears the mark of the quality of Activity. But that bears the mark of the quality of Goodness which with his whole heart he desires to know, which he is not ashamed to perform and at which his soul rejoices. The craving after sensual pleasures is declared to be the mark of Darkness, the pursuit of wealth the mark of Activity, the desire to gain spiritual merit the mark of Goodness; each later named quality is better than the preceding one. Those endowed with goodness reach the state of gods, those endowed with Activity the state of men, and those endowed with Darkness ever sink into the condition of beasts; that is the three fold course of transmigrations. But know this three fold course of transmigrations that depends on the three qualities to be again three fold, low middling and high according to the particular nature of the acts and of the knowledge of each man. Women, also, who in like manner having committed theft, shall incur guilt; they will become the females of those same creatures which have been enumerated above." (XII. 24,25,26,35-38,40,41,49).

But *Manu* does not attempt to explain how precisely do these actions mature into effect, especially in the case transmigrations and efficacy of sacrifices. Look at how *Manu* tries to explain the way a burnt oblation brings out the intended effects:

"An oblation duly thrown into fire, reaches the sun; from the sun comes rain, from rain food, there from the living creatures derive their subsistence." (III.76).

This naturalistic explanation of the sacrificial efficacy is interesting. On the one hand, it refers to the archaic belief in the pragmatic value of sacrifice for sustenance and on the other hand, it is admirable for it does not bring in any supernatural potency into picture in terms of gods. However, in the absence of explicit explanation by *Manu* as to how actions result in consequences, we can presume that he adopts Sāṃkhya way of explaining in terms of the changes in *guṇas* brought out by an action.

Manu says that *Vēdas* prescribe two paths of action:

"The acts prescribed by the *Vēda* are of two kinds such as procure and increase in happiness and cause a continuation of mundane existence *(pravritta)* and such as ensure supreme bliss and cause cessation of mundane existence (*nivritta*). Acts which secure the fulfilment of wishes in this world or in the next are called *pravritta*; but acts performed without any desire for a reward, preceded by the acquisition of true knowledge, are declared to be *nivritta*. He who seriously performs acts leading to future births (*pravritta*) becomes equal to gods; but who is intent on the performance of those causing the cessation of existence *(nivritta)* indeed, passes beyond the reach of five elements." (XII. 88, 89, 90).

Manu prescribes *pravritta-mārga* for the attainment of intended goals *(kāma)* but always identifies *nivritta-mārga* as a better means towards the liberation, the fourth object of pursuit *(Puruṣārtha)*:

"If one man should obtain all those sensual enjoyments and another should renounce them all, the renunciation of all pleasure is far better than the attainment of them." (II.95)

But one should aim at final liberation only after duly fulfilling his empirical duties:

"A twice-born man who seeks final liberation, without having studied *Vēdas*, without having begotten sons and without having offered sacrifices, sinks downwards." (VI.37)

So, one is not supposed to aim at the final *Puruṣārtha* without discharging the three debts *(Ṛṇa)*. *Mōkṣa* or final liberation, *Manu* says, is attainable in the empirical world:

"By not injuring any creatures, by detaching the sense from objects of enjoyments, by performance of rites prescribed in the *Vēda*, and by rigorously practising austerities, men gain that state *(Mōkṣa)* even in this world." (VI.75).

Manu understands knowledge of the ultimate reality as sure guide to final liberation. Knowledge of reality leads one beyond one's actions and the attainment of this knowledge is emphasized as the most virtuous action:

"He who possesses the true insight into the nature of the world, is not fettered by his deeds; but he who is destitute of that insight, is drawn into the circle of births and rebirths. The knowledge of soul stated to be the most excellent among all of the virtuous action; for that is the first of all sciences, because immortality is gained through that. When by the disposition of his heart he becomes indifferent to all objects, he obtains eternal happiness both in this world and after death. He who has in this manner gradually given up all attachments and is freed from all the pairs of opposites reposes in *Brahman* alone. He who is not proficient in the knowledge of that which refers to the soul reaps not the full reward of the performance of rites" (VI. 74; XII. 85; VI. 80,81,82).

Finally *Manu* summarises the whole moral teaching of his law-book as follows:

Abstention from injuring creatures, veracity, abstention from unlawfully appropiating the goods of others, purity, and control of the organs, *Manu* has declared to be the summary of the law for four castes (X.63).

Manu and Other Philosophical Theories

Before we undertake a philosophical reflection of *Manu's* attitude towards other theories and his adoption of various philosophical views, we must keep one thing in mine that *Manu* is not a philosopher but a law-giver. His business is not to entertain philosophical debates but to establish a social system. Before we appreciate the philosophical commitments of *Manu*, let us see what philosophical systems he is repeller to. This gives a clue as to what kind of philosophy is acceptable to *Manu* and why.

As could be easily understood, *Manu's* attitude towards those philosophical views which do not accept *Vēda* as a *Pramāṇa* is not favourable:

"All those traditions and all those despicable systems of philosophy, which are not based on *Vēḍa*, produce no reward after death; for they are declared to be founded on Darkness. All those doctrines, differing from the *Vēda*, which spring up and perish soon, are worthless and false because they are on modern date. Every twice-born man, who relying on the institutes of dialectics, treats with contempt those two sources of the law, must be cast out by the virtuous as an atheist and scorner of *Vēda*. Let him not honour, even by a greeting, those heretics, men who follow forbidden occupations, men who live like cats, rouges, logicians (arguing against *Vēda*) and those who live like harons. Let him not dwell in a country where the rulers are *Sūdras*, nor in one which is surrounded by unrighteous men, nor in one which has become subject to heretics, nor in one swarming with men of low-castes. That kingdom where *Sūdras* are very numerous, which is infested by athiests and destitute of twice-born, soon entirely perishes by famine and disease." (II. 11; IV. 30,60; VIII.22).

So, *Manu's* attitude towards Buddhists, heretics and materialists is generally unfavourable. Heretics who vehemently question the superstitions of after-death, sacrifices, heaven and transmigrations, which is ardently propounded by *Brāhmaṇa* part of the *Vēda*, are banished from the state (IX.225).

Now let us examine the philosophical views of different schools adopted by *Manu*. *Manu* acknowledges certain views of Advaita Vēdānta especially those on final liberation. *Manu* describes supreme soul in an analogous way to Advaitins as beyond all the valid sources of knowledge:

"He who can be perceived by the internal organ alone, who is subtile, indescernible, and eternal, who contains all created beings and is inconceivable, shone forth of his own will."

So, *Manu* submits all *Pramāṇa* to mysticism which alone, according to *Manu*, is capable of knowing the supreme soul. Advaitins rest the Reality outside the field of comprehension which can be realized only through mystical experience. Thus all valid sources of knowledge are taken to be useless. So, logic which operates within the field of *Pramāṇa* or valid sources of knowledge is considered to be of no use in comprehending the Reality. Advaitins as thorough-going idealists understand the world to an illusion. This concept of world as an illusion preaches passive acceptance of the social reality and thus serves the purpose of the law -giver in a sense. The common platform for the Advaitins and *Manu* is their faith in the scriptures, rejection of logic as capable of reaching to reality and common understanding of final liberation. *Manu* like an Advaitin feels that final liberation can be attained only through the knowledge of the soul.

But *Manu* faces one important problem from an Advaitin. He cannot totally adopt the Advaitin view of the world. If the world, as Advaitins sees, is an illusion, the efficacy of sacrifices is effected. If the world is an illusion, who would like to take pains to do sacrifices for desired ends? But, for *Manu*, *Vēdic* sacrifices have effiacy to bring out the intended results and these sacrificial acts are the fundamental duties of *Brāhmaṇas* on which they live.

So, *Manu*, in order to establish the importance of sacrificial acts, has to establish the reality of the phenomenal world. This purpose of the law-giver is best served by the Pūrva-Mīmāṃsa view which strongly argues for the reality of the world. Reality of the world should be accepted not only for justifying the *Vēdic* sacrifices but also for the moral operation in society. Society has to be real for the observation of social law. Here *Manu* unconditionally accepts the reality of the world.

Manu, to a great extent, adopts the Sāṃkhya concept of Matter as constituted of three qualities, he does not share Sāṃkhya's dualistic metaphysics. The Matter is a manifestation of the supreme soul for *Manu* whereas for Sāṃkhya it is a separate ontological category. Further, for Sāṃkhya actions are empirical modifications of *Prakṛti* and thus do not entail any transcendental significance. Actions, good or bad, necessarily bind the soul. So, all actions even the sacrificial acts, have to be renounced. Liberation for Sāṃkhya is liberation from all experience because experience necessarily involves *guṇas* or qualities. As actions appertain to the empirical mode of mind, morality is just a function of mind. Sāṃkhya denies scriptural sacrifices as constituting *Dharma* for all actions lead to impermanent consequences for they have a beginning in time and the ultimate liberation comes from cessation of all actions, actions of every kind. *Manu* agrees with the materialists as far as reality of the world is concerned. But materialists differ from *Manu* in matters of after-death. It is materialists, Pūrva-Mīmāmsakas and *Manu*, however, that realize the importance and efficacy of human action.

References

1. *Taittarīya Samhita* II.2.10.2.
2. *Bṛhaspati Smṛti*, XXVII.3.
3. cf. *What is living and what is dead in Indian Philosophy*, p. 188.
4. *Manu Dharma Śastra,* SBE. Vol.25, P. XVIII.
5. *SBE*, Vol. 25, P. XIX.
6. *SBE*, Vol. 25, P. XIX.
7. *History of Dharma Sastras*. Vol. I; p.142.
8. *Ibid,* p.333.
9. *Nārada Smṛti*, Preface 1-4.
10. For a detailed discussion of the topic. cf. Buhler's preface to *Manu Dharma Śastra,* SBE, Vol. XXV.
11. *Manu Smṛti,* I. 58,59.
12. William, M.M., *Indian Wisdom*, p.207.
13. *Manu Smṛti* II. 6,10.
14. XII. 94, 97.
15. *Manu Smṛti* I. 85, 86.
16. *Manu Smṛti* I. 107, 108.
17. XII. 95, 96.
18. *Manu Smṛti* II. 18.
19. *Manu Smṛti* II. 97; VIII. 84.
20. *Manu Smṛti* II. 11.
21. Samkaracharya. *Vēdanta Sūtra Bhāṣya*, p. 315.

22. Kautilya, *Artha Śāstra i.* 2. 12.
23. *Artha Śāstra* II. 1. 1-3, 8,9.
24. *Nārada Smṛti*, Preface, p. 5.
25. *Manu Smṛti* I. 5-17, 23. 31.
26. *Ṛg-Vēda* X Mandala 90.
27. Samkaracharya, *Vēdanta Sūtra*, pp. 294, 295.
28. Kanāda, *Vaiśēsika Sūtras*, II-i.18.
29. Samkaracharya, *Vēdanta Sūtras*, pp. 386-89.
30. *Vaiśesika Sūtras*, IV. i. 5.
31. cf. *Slōkavārttika*, Sambandhakṣepa Parihāra Vāda, 44-62, p. 356.
32. *Sānti Parva*, Section 182.
33. *Vēdānta Sūtra Bhāṣya*, p. 394.
34. *Manu Smṛti* X. 43-44.
35. *Evolution of Hindu Moral Ideals*, p. 81.
36. *Evolution of Hindu Moral Ideals*, p. 92.
37. *The Ethics of Hindus*, p. 7. For a similar view Cf. S.C. Crawford, *The Evolution of Hindu Ethical Ideals*, p. 52.
38. *What is Living and What is Dead in Indian Philosophy*, p. 627.

5

Ethics of Pūrva Mīmāṃsa

Introduction

'*Mīmāṃsa*' etymologically means 'enquiry' or 'ascertainment'. *Mīmāṃsa* as a system of ancient Indian thought stands for 'determination of the meaning of the *Vēdas*'. The object of *Mīmāṃsa*, as the name suggests, is to interpret and explain the meaning of the *Vēdic* texts.

As we know, *Mantras, Brāhmaṇas* and *Araṇyakas* constitute the *Vēda*. *Mantra* or *Samhita* part contains the formulae which have to be recited at the time of sacrifices. *Brāhmaṇas* are the elaborate rules to be observed and the procedural details to be followed in the sacrifices. *Araṇyakas*, especially their end parts i.e., *Upaniṣads* contain the philosophical speculations. The former two are together called *Karmakhānda* or Action-part as they chiefly deal with the ritual activity. *Upaniṣads* are called *Jñānakhānda* or Knowledge-part, as they deal with the philosophical understanding of reality and knowledge.

In the post-*Vēdic* period, efforts were made by the orthodox *Vēdic* schools to collect the fragmentary *Vēdic* doctrines and to systematically interpret them for a unified understanding of the *Vēdas*. These efforts gave rise to the *Sūtra* style of literature. The *Sūtras* are aphorisms, cryptical in nature, to facilitate learning them by heart and easy recitation. The foundational works of all Indian philosophical systems are in the *Sūtra* form.

The *Sūtra* period is the most productive period in the ancient Indian literature. Different schools of Indian thought systematically compiled their fundamental views in *Sūtra* form. In the *Vēdic* tradition, elaborate treatises were produced, dealing with various aspects of the *Vēda. Śrauta Sūtras, Gṛhya Sūtras* and *Dharma Sūtras* were compiled in different *Vēdic* schools. In this period, Indian science and crafts have taken new dimensions. This was a period of high intellectual activity in the ancient India. Scholars on Indology place this period between 6th and 2nd centuries Before Christ.

To this period belong *Mīmāṃsa Sūtras* of Jaimini and Vēdānta *Sūtras* of Bādarāyaṇa. *Jaimini Sūtras* deal with judicial interpretation of *Brāhmaṇas* and *Vēndānta Sūtras* or *Brahman Sūtras* of Bādarāyaṇa deal with interpretation of *Upaniṣads*. Both these systems share the name *'Mīmāṃsa'* for both deal with interpretation of the *Vēda*. They together make the *Mīmāṃsa* system in full. However, as *Jaimini Sūtras* deal with the *karmakhānda*, the former part of the *Vēda*, his system is called Karma Mīmāṃsa or Pūrva Mīmāṃsa or simply Mīmāṃsa. As the *Brahma Sūtras* of Bādarayaṇa deal with the later part of the *Vēda* i.e., the *Upaniṣads*, his system is known as Uttara Mīmāṃsa or Vēndānta. Though both these systems claim their fidelity to the basic teaching of the *Vēda*, they differ on certain important metaphysical and epistemological issues. These differences make them independent schools of thought, now with standing their adherence to the *Vēda*. This is due to the inherent inconsistency in the philosophical positions presupposed by *Brāhmaṇas* and *Upaniṣads* on which Mīmāṃsa and Vēndānta are based respectively. We would undertake this issue when we deal with the philosophical foundations of Mīmāṃsa in detail.

However, Jaimini and *Bādarāyaṇa* refer to each other in their *Sūtras*. This could be taken as evidence for the view that both the works are redacted simultaneously. But Mīmāṃsa as a science of rituals might have developed much earlier than *Vēdānta* as a philosophical system. However, as Prof. Keith rightly observes, "...it is not impossible that the redaction of the two *Sūtras* was contemporaneous, despite the earlier development of Mīmāṃsa, the probability surely lies in favour of the view that the *Mīmāṃsa Sūtras* was redacted first and served as a model for other schools"[1]

Origin of Pūrva Mīmāṃsa

Mīmāṃsa discussions regarding the true meaning of the *Vēdic* texts were traditionally much prior to the actual redaction of *Jaimini Sūtras*. This fact is evident from the texts itself. Jaimini himself refers to many views of opponents concerning different interpretations of the *Vēdic* passages. Indeed, the discussions on rituals are germinal in the *Brāhmaṇas* which aim at translation of hymns of *Vēda* into ritual actions. *Brāhmaṇas* lay down details of sacrifices and explain the ceremonial procedures. In the age of *Brāhmaṇas* sacrifices are developed into a complex system. The *Upaniṣadic* period witnesses a shift of emphasis from sacrifices to speculations. The philosophical spirit found its expression in the *Upaniṣadic* literature pushing sacrifices to background. This might have caused an apparent breakdown in the ritualistic tradition.

In the post-*Upaniṣadic* times, there was a need to enliven the tradition which has already suffered degeneration. The *Smṛti* literature is the direct outcome of the situation. The *Smṛtis* are digests of old rules and regulations which are scattered in the *Vēda*. The compilers of *Smṛti* had to systematically interpret the *Vēdic* texts in all aspects. This activity was carried on in the ancient *Vēdic* schools. As part of the activity, those *Vēdic* passages are collected, studied and discussed which have bearing on *Dharma* or duty. This accounts for the origin of Mīmāṃsa system the main objective of which is to interpret and understand the *Vēdic* maxims with references to *Dharma*. Jaimini, for the first time, compiled systematically the rules of interpretation in his *Mīmāṃsa Sūtras*.

Besides, there is another important reason involved in the origin of *Pūrva Mīmāṃsa* as a distinct philosophical system. In the *Upaniṣadic* and post-*Upaniṣadic* ages, different philosophical speculations gained ground. Some of these philosophical views question the very presuppositions underlying the practice of *Vēdic* sacrifices. If these challenges are not properly met with, the practice of sacrifices would be severely endangered. So, Mīmāṃsa had to deal with those challenges and establish fundamental assumptions underlying its adherence to *Vēdic* sacrifices. This is one of the chief objective *Pūrva Mīmāṃsa* set for itself. Jaimini not only advanced philosophical arguments for the purpose but also formulated all his *Sūtras* in the form of arguments. Following Jaimini, later Mīmāṃsakas made significant contribution to the treasure of Indian thought with commendable philosophical sophistication. In the process of theoretically defending the ritual orthodoxy, Mīmāṃsa advanced certain doctrines which are extremely stunning even for a modern mind. Before we go into critical understanding of Mīmāṃsa doctrines, a brief history of Mīmāṃsa literature is in order.

Mīmāṃsa Literature

Jaimini is supposed to be the founder of Mīmāṃsa system, despite the fact that Mīmāṃsa as a tradition was there much before Jaimini. However, *Jaimini Sūtras* is the first systematic compilation of Mīmāṃsa doctrines. *Mīmāṃsa Sūtra* has twelve chapters devided into sixty padas. It contains 894 *adhikaraṇas* or discussions and 2621 *Sūtras*. The later literature of Mīmāṃsa is nothing but elaborate commentary on the doctrines propounded by Jaimini in his *Sūtra*. Nothing in certain is known about the author. *Sāma Vēda* contains *Jaiminiya Samhita* and *Jaiminiya Brāhmaṇa*. From this it is supposed that Jaimini is rather name of a clan. *Mahābhārata* recognizes Jaimini not as author of *Mīmāṃsa Sūtras* but as an ancient *Vēdic* sage. It is also probable that *Mīmāṃsa Sūtras* are compiled by a *Vēdic* school the founder of which is Jaimini. However, *Vēdānta Sūtras* and later philosophical works recognize Jaimini as a philosopher. *Pañchatantra* describes the death of Jaimini, the founder of Mīmāṃsa as caused by a wild elephant. Though the exact date of *Mīmāṃsa Sūtra* is still doubtful, we can safely suppose that *Mīmāṃsa Sūtra* was redacted in its present form somewhere around second centure B.C.

The later literature of Mīmāṃsa mentions a number of commentators on *Mīmāṃsa Sūtras*. The works of those early commentators are not available. The earliest commentary extent is that of Śabaraswāmin,[2] which is a comprehensive commentary dealing with all the aspects of *Mīmāṃsa Sūtra* in detail. This work stands as the basis for all the later works on Mīmāṃsa. Śabara refers to an early commentator *Upavarṣa* whose work is known as *Vritti*. *Upavarṣa* is known in Mīmāṃsa tradition as *'Vrittikāra'* while Śabara is refered to as *'Bhāṣyakāra'*. *Upavarṣa* is supposed to have introduced the epistemological discussion of all the means of knowledge in the Mīmāṃsa literature. It is also possible that *Vritti* of Upavarṣa also dealt with metaphysical issue involved in the *Sūtra*. However, his work is not extant in its full form, except in fragmentary references, to support the view. In addition to Upavarṣa, Mīmāṃsa literature also refers to a few other commentators. *Nyāyaratnākara* and *Kaśika* mention Bhartṛmitra while *Slōkavārttika* mentions Bhavadāsa, *Śāstradīpika* mentions another commentator by name Hari. The works of these commentators of Jaimini are not available. While there is a view that Bhavadāsa and Upavarṣa are two names of the same person, it is not admitted for *Slōkavārttika* mentions them as different individuals. *Mādhavācharya* of 14th century also commented on *Mīmāṃsa Sūtra*. But he comments on each Adhikaraṇa not on each *Sūtra* while *Śabarabhāṣya* is a full fledged commentary on each *Sūtra* of each Adhikaraṇa or discussion.

After *Śabara*, there was a bifurcation in the Mīmāṃsa tradition. Two seperate schools were founded by two commentators on *Bhāṣya, Kumārila* Bhatta and *Prabhākara Miśra. Kumārila* and *Prabhākara* slightly differ on certain issues but these differences do not affect the fundamental maxims of Mīmāṃsa. *Kumārila* exerts more freedom in his commentary on *Bhāṣya,* differing from the original at many places and substituting the original arguments. He is also known for his complex style of writing. He uses compound sentences frequently and sometimes a sentence is as big as a paragraph. He has a remarkable power of argumentation and presentation which makes him, beyond doubt, one of the most outstanding philosophers in Indian History. Kumārila is known, in the tradition, as the preceptor of Prabhākara. Prabhākara might have brought out his work on *Bhāṣya* earlier than Kumārila. We find Kumārila criticizing certain views of Prabhākara whereas Prabhākara is hardly found criticizing any views of Kumārila. Prabhākara's style of writing is lucid and simple compared to that of Kumārila.

The celebrate commentary of Kumārila on *Bhāṣya* is in three parts: *Slōkavārttika, Tantravārttika* and *Tuptika*. Kumārila is thus known as the Varttikakāra. *Ślōkavārttika* is a voluminous commentary on the first *pāda* of first chapter. *Tantravārttika* deals with remaining three *pādas* of first chapter and two more chapters. *Tuptika* is a brief commentary on the remaining nine chapters. Kumārila allotted the first two parts of his commentary to deal with the first three chapters for they are the most significant philosophically. In *Slōkavārttika* and *Tantravārttika* Kumārila establishes the Mimāṃsa polemics and attacks heterodox systems of Indian philosophy with outstanding philosophical eminence. Kumārila lived in the 7th century A.D. and a senior contemporary of Śaṃkara and Prabhākara.

Kumārila's *Slōkavārttika* is commented upon by Pārthasārathi Miśra in his *Nyayaratnākara* and by Sucharita Miśra in his *Kasika. Tantravārttika* was exposed by Somēśwara in his *Nyāya Sudha* which is otherwise known as *Rāṇaka.* Mandans Miśra,[3] also a pupil of Kumārila, was the author of *Vidhivivēka* which emphasizes the significance of *Vēdic* injunctions and he also wrote *Mīmāmsānukramaṇi*, a summary of *Bhāṣya.* Venkatēswara Dīkṣita commented on *Tuptika* in his *Varttikābharaṇa.*

Prabhākara commented on *Śabara Bhāṣya* in his *Bṛhati.* Prabhākara in his work closely follows the Bhāṣyakāra in a simple style and provides careful elucidation wherever it is necessary. *Bṛhati* was commented on by Salikanatha in his *Ṛjuvimala.* Salikanatha exposes the views of Prabhākara in another work called *Prakaraṇapanchika* which is a valuable compendium of the foundational views of Prabhākara school.

Other important works of *Mīmāṃsakas* include *Śāstradīpika* of Pārthasārathi Miśra. Samkara Bhatta commented on *Śāstradīpika* in his *Mīmāṃsa Sāra Sangraha.* Vācaspati Miśra wrote *Nyāyakaṇika* which is an exposition on *Vidhivivēka* of Mandana Miśra. Khandadēva is another *Mīmāṃsaka* of 17th century known for his *Bhāttadipika* and *Mīmāṃsa Kaustubha. Mīmāṃsanyāyavivēka* of Bhavanatha Miśra, *Subhōdini* of Ramēswara Sūri, *Bhāttacintāmaṇi* of Gaga Bhatta, *Mīmāṃsanyāyaprakāśa* of Āpadēva, *Arthasangraha* of Laugākṣi Bhāskara are of considerable importance. It is interesting to see how the concept of God alien to original

Mīmāṃsa was brought into the system by Venkatanātha, a Vēdāntin, in his work *Sēsvara Mīmāṃsa*.

To a western reader it might be surprising to know about these commentaries over commentaries. But this has an important story to tell about the Indian philosophical situation. After the crystalization of Indian thought into major philosophical systems, philosophy is studied in the Brahminical schools of each system. After the study, the students had to elaborate the doctrines of their preceptors or predecessors taking some source books. This resulted in the elaborate commentaries over other commentaries and this limited the scope of freedom for them. At a later stage, there was hardly anything for them to contribute except supplementing the original doctrines with a few innovative arguments and thus continuing the tradition. This is not to say that there was no philosophical development as such. In fact, some of the commentaries tackled the arguments from opponent schools with more vigour than their source books and sometimes the original themes are thoroughly modified to suit the new challenges. The point, however, is that Indian philosophical progress suffered certain limitations though it was never in a state of suspended animation.

Now, let us understand the foundations of Mīmāṃsa philosophy in general and of its ethics in particular. While doing so, we have to bear in mind the fact that Ethics in Indian thought was always structurally intertwined with Metaphysical and Epistemological issues. It is not possible to locate ethics outside the metaphysical and epistemological commitments of each system. We cannot understand the former without carefully examining the latter.

Foundations of Pūrva Mīmāṃsa

The central theme of *Pūrva Mīmāṃsa* is the *Vēdic* sacrifices and right interpretation of the *Vēdic* texts with reference to the sacrifices. On the face of it, it involves only exegetical analysis and as such has not got anything to do with philosophy. It is also important to note that Kautilya in his *Arthaśāstra* refers to Mīmāṃsa not as philosophical system but as included in theology (Trayi). He refers to Saṃkhya, Nyāya (with its old name 'Yōga') and Cārvāka as systems of philosophy *(Anvikṣsiki)*.[4] Further, Kautilya differentiates philosophy, as a logical investigation of the world, from the scriptures which deal with non-worldly objects too. As both systems of Mīmāṃsa are based on scriptures, they do not find place among philosophical systems. Another reason for this discrimination could be the non-secular nature of Mīmāṃsa, and Buddhism is no exception.

Even some of the western scholars also express the same attitude. William M.M., for example, refuses to recognize *Pūrva Mīmāṃsa* as a philosophical system. "... for it is in real truth not a system of philosophy, but rather of ritualism. It does not concern itself, like other systems, with investigation into the nature of soul, mind or matter, but with the solutions of doubts and discrepancies in regard to the *Vēdic* texts caused by the discordant explanation of opposite schools".[5]

This attitude certainly undermines the valuable contribution of *Pūrva Mīmāṃsa* to the Indian philosophy. Once we look into the significance of Mīmāṃsa doctrines and their place in the Indian thought, we will know why the remarks of William M.M. need not be over-emphasized. Given the peculiar position of Mīmāṃsakas, they cannot be denied to be philosophers. While it is possible to read non-secular motives underlying their doctrines, we should not overlook the fact that *Mīmāṃsakas* are no less interested in philosophical discussions than any other philosopher of any other system. Indeed, *Pūrva Mīmāṃsa* produced some of the greatest minds of high philosophical eminence in the history of Indian thought. Mīmāṃsa deserves the status of philosophy, which is rightly attributed to it in Indian tradition. Afterall. It is one of the most significant systems of traditional Indian philosophy and philosophy is not extraneous to the structure of Mīmāṃsa system.

Now, let us see what exactly makes Mīmāṃsa a respectable system of philosophy despite its non-philosophical objective of interpreting the *Vēdic* texts. Why does Mīmāṃsa undertake interpretation of *Vēdic* passages? The purpose behind the exegetical work is 'to know what is *Dharma*'. The very first *Sūtra* of *Jaimini Sūtras* explains that the object of Mīmāṃsa is 'enquiry into *Dharma*'.[6] This explicit object of Mīmāṃsa is the nucleus of all its philosophical endeavours. Jaimini defines *Dharma* as 'the object qualified by an injunction'.[7] *Dharma* or duty is what is expressed by an injunction. Further, Jaimini claims the *Vēda* to be the only source for knowing *Dharma*. The only authoritative injunctions are the *Vēdic* injunctions. This claim presupposes the absolute authority of the *Vēda*. Hence, rationalization of the *Vēdic* ritual injunctions invariably involves establishing the absolute authority of the *Vēda*. This is the position which *Mīmāṃsakas* vigorously attempt to defend philosophically. In the process of proving the validity of *Vēda* as absolute and self-sufficient, *Mīmāṃsakas* had to grapple with certain philosophical doctrines of other schools which question such validity.

Jaimini refuses all other modes of apprehension, except *Śabda* or Authority, as incapable of acquiring knowledge of *Dharma* or duty.[8] Sources of knowledge like perception and inference can give us the knowledge of sensuous things which come into contact with senses. So, they are capable of exposing only those things that can come into contact with senses. *Dharma* is, however, a supresensuous thing and as such cannot come into contact with senses. Here, Jaimini makes a difference between 'is' and 'ought'. 'Ought' is different in its nature from the external objects. It is an abstract notion which can be known only through the teaching of the *Vēda*. As Perception, Inference etc., can manifest only whatever exists in the sense of 'is', but *Dharma,* in the form of 'ought', cannot be known through these sources.

In connection with the above position of jaimini, Vrittikāra indulges in the investigation of sources of knowledge. He is followed by later commentators who take the epistemological discussion to further heights. Their interest in these discussions appears to be negative, in the sense that they are interested in showing how these *Pramāṇas* cannot be sources for knowing *Dharma.* However, we come across the positive epistemological polemics of Mīmāṃsa, when the validity of the *Vēda* is argued for. Kumārila and Prabhākara differ as to the number of *Pramāṇa.* According to Prabhākara, Perception, Inference, Verbal Testimony, Anology and Presumption are the five valid sources of knowledge. Kumārila accepts the five and adds non-cognition as a seperate *Pramāṇa* while Prabhākara includes it in Inference. Both of them reject Possibility and Rumour as *pramāṇas.*

Jaimini explains that *Śabda* is the exclusive source of knowing duty. Only *Śabda* can express an injunction. *'Śabda'* in its wider sense means 'sound' and in a narrower sense used to mean 'words'. The character of imposing duty belongs only to words. Only words are capable of compelling one to action. Other sources of knowledge are passive, in the senses that they are not capable of expressing norms of human conduct. On the other hand, words are endowed with the potency to drive one for action. *Śabda* as a *Pramāṇa* or a source of valid knowledge, refers to knowledge derived from words. Mīmāṃsa again distinguishes between humaṇ assertions and the assertions of the *Vēda* which are devoid of any author, human or devine. According to Jaimini, it is the assertions of the *Vēda* which are absolutely authoritative, eternal and self-sufficient. Hence, in order to establish the *Vēda* as the exclusive source of *Dharma,* the eternality, the self-sufficiency and the absolute authority of the *Vēda* should be first established.

Theory of Eternal Sound

The *Vēda* is an instance of *Śabda Pramāṇa* i.e., words as a source of valid knowledge. A word is nothing but a sound used to denote an object of apprehension. The eternality of the *Vēda* thus implies the eternality of words. Mīmāṃsa, as it claims the eternality of the *Vēda*, argues for the eternality of sound in general and of words in particular.

Mīmāṃsa holds that sound is a quality of *ākāśa* or there. Sound exists eternally though its apprehension stands in need of some manifesting agency. In the case of word sounds, the manifesting agency is the human utterance. Utterance manifests a word in the consciousness of the listeners. Words have no production or destruction but eternally existing and all pervading. Sound as a quality of *ākāśa,* subsists in it. As there is eternal and all-pervading, sound, as its quality, is also eternal and all-pervading. To understand the peculiarity of Mīmāṃsa theory of sound, we may refer to the theories of sound held by other schools, in this connection.

Indian thought offers distinct views on sound and its nature. For *Sāṃkhya*, sound is a quality of tangible substances and subsists in them like colour, smell etc. and liable to manifestation. Vaiśēṣika takes sound to be a quality of *ākāśa* and is liable to production and destruction. Thus it is a non-eternal quality of the ether. Buddhists argue that sound does not subsist in anything. It is rather a production of vibrations in the elements and thus subject to production and destruction. Nyāya, following Vaiśēṣika, treats sound to be a quality of the ether and thus subject to production and destruction. So, it is non-eternal as opposed to the Mīmāṃsa view that it is eternal. Though Nyāya-Vaiśēṣika and Mīmāṃsa share the view that sound is a quality of the ether, Nyāya-Vaiśēṣika differs from Mīmāṃsa regarding its eternal character.

The significant discussion on the nature of sound in Indian philosophy boils down to the debate between Mīmāṃsa and Nyāya. It is interesting to see that the Naiyāyikas, despite their overt veneration for the scriptures, are the ardent opponents of eternality of the *Vēda*. Though they explicitly argue for the authority of the *Vēda*, they do so on quite different grounds.[9] We will later see how the so called arguments in favour of the *Vēdic* authority are nothing but mere lip-service to please the orthodoxy.

Gotama, the founder of Nyāya, objects the eternality of sound on the following grounds: 1) because it has beginning in time, 2) because it is apprehended by sense organ and such apphension implies series of sounds, and 3) we use the verb 'make' with reference to sound and this implies that sound is a product.[10] The first of these grounds means that sound has a cause. When it is caused, it comes into existence and thus has a beginning in time. At a later moment it ceases to exist and thus has an end too. Whatever has a beginning in time cannot be called eternal. It may be argued that a jar after destroyed would not come into existence again and thus its non-existence after destruction *(vidhvamsābhāva)* is eternal though has a beginning. Uddhyōtkāra answers the above argument saying that the absence of jar has a cause i.e., destruction of the jar. It was not there before the jar existed or during its existence. Moreover, non-eternality, as an abstract noun, denotes something positive whereas non-existence prior to the jar and after its destruction is sheer absence.[11] So, when a thing is said to be non-eternal, it means that it does not have absolute existence.

Naiyāyikas explain the apprehension of sound through existence of series of sounds caused by the effort that produces sound. For example, when a piece of wood is being cut, the conjunction and disjunction of the axe with the piece of wood produces sound and this initial sound produces other sounds in all directions. The latter sounds produce further sounds. In this way, sound proceeds in series, each duller than the preceding one. Of those series, the one which reaches the *ākāśa* in the ear of the hearer alone is apprehended. This is the reason why we hear the sound much after the impact of the axe on the wood has ceased. The hypothesis of sound series impairs the eternalist notion of sound, by showing the limited temporal existence of each series. The fact that sound is heard at a distance after its cause has ceased establishes the view that the impact of the axe has not manifested but produced the sound.

Kumārila argues that utterance manifests a word but does not produce it as a lamp manifests a jar and does not produce it.[12] But Naiyāyikas make a point against this argument also, saying that there is a difference between the two instances. It is true that light of the lamp manifested the jar. The lamp is said to have manifested the jar because as soon as the light has ceased, there would be no apprehension of the jar. So, in the case of manifestation, the manifested object ceases to be apprehended as soon as the manifesting agency ceases. However, in the case of sound it is heard even after the effort, which is said to have manifested the sound, ceases. So, it is clear that the effort, be the ùtterance or impact of the axe, has rather produced the sound.

Moreover, the Naiyāyikas argue, sound is spoken of as a product. We say sound is loud or soft, as we say pain is acute or dull. Only a product can be spoken of in this fashion.[13] It is argued that the character of loudness or softness belongs the manifesting impact and not to the sound itself. This can be illustrated by the case of colour, which remains the same while its apprehension becomes brighter or duller by the light that manifest it. Vātsāyana says that this argument is untenable, for in the case of sound there is the phenomenon of suppression (abhibhāva).[14] The sound of a drum suppresses the sound of the lute only when it is loud, and not when it is deadened. If the loudness belongs to the drum and not to the sound of it, the sound of the drum must always suppress the sound of the lute. However, the sound of drum does not always suppress the sound of the lute but only when it is loud. This shows that loudness belongs to the sound itself and not to the drum. On the other hand, we do not find the colour of one object suppressing the colour of another object. If sound is manifested like the colour of an object, it cannot suppress the sound of another object. So, suppression can be explained only when loudness belongs to sound. When there are two different series of sounds, produced by the drum and the lute, a loud sound can suppress a soft sound if they reach the ear at the same time.

Mīmāṃsakas argue that in ordinary language, we also speak of eternal *ākāśa* as we speak of non-eternal objects. We speaks of 'part of *ākāśa (pradeśa)*. Similarly, we are prone to speak of eternal sound as we speak of a product. But mere speaking of eternal *ākāśa* and sound as we speak of products, does not make them non-eternal. Naiyāyikas argue that in the case of *ākāśa*, we figuratively impose the word 'part' to it though in reality, *ākāśa* is devoid of parts. The basis of this imposition is the similarity of *ākāśa* to things that have real parts, in the sense that its contact does not pervade over the whole of it. Even the *ākāśa* has no parts, the contact is not deprived of its substratum; it subsists in the *ākāśa* itself. Moreover, sound is a non-pervasive quality of *ākāśa*. Pervasion means subsistence all over the substratum. When a jar is seen, its colour is seen. So, colour is a pervasive quality. Whenever a few cows are perceived, the universal 'cowness' is perceived. So, the universal is pervasive. However, sound is not perceived whenever its substratum i.e., *ākāśa* is perceived. This proves that sound is a non-pervasive quality.[15]

In this connection, Gotama advances a positive argument in favour of non-eternality of sound:

"(Sound is non-eternal) because there is non-apprehension of it before it is uttered and also because there is non-apprehension of obstruction (that could explain the non-apprehension of the sound)[16].

The first part of above argument recognizes sound as an effect of utterance. Whatever is a product of an effort cannot be eternal. The second part argues that if sound is eternally existing in its substratum, it should be apprehended as there is no veil to cover it from senses. Kumārila objects to the first part of argument saying whatever is apphended after an effort need not be non-eternal. Even the eternal *ākāśa* is apprehended, in particular cases, after an effort:

The *ākāśa* too, being eternal, — when it happens to be covered up under the earth or water, — is rendered visible only by the removal of these (earth and water) by means of digging and pumping. And thus we see that here we have perception (of *ākāśa*) only after an effort. Consequently your reasoning — "since it (word) is perceived only after an effort" — becomes doubtful *(Slōkavārttika*, Eternality of words. 30-32, P. 414).

Against the argument of Kumārila, it may be pointed out that we do not perceive *ākāśa* everytime after an effort as in the case of a word. Even the above instance does not militate either eternality or pervasiveness of *ākāśa*. All the empirical objects subsist in the eternal and all pervading *ākāśa*. Even earth and water, like other objects, subsists in *ākāśa*. When an object, say a jar, is removed from a position, we apprehend *ākāśa* in its previous position as a result of our effort. It does not mean we produced or created space. It only proves its pervasive character. Similarly, when we apprehend *ākāśa* after digging or pumping, we do not produce *ākāśa*. We do not apprehend *ākāśa* due to out effort but due to the pervasive character of *ākāśa*. Whereas, sound is produced by our efforts for there is no other instance of its apprehension, except after on effort.

Regarding the argument of Gotama that if should is eternal, it must be apprehended persistently as there is no apprehension of any viel covering it, Mīmāṃsakas raise an objection. They claim that obstruction exists because there is non-apprehension of the non-apprehension of the obstruction. Vātsāyana says that this is no argument, because non-apprehension is of nature of the negation of apprehension. Non-apprehension is negation of a positive apprehension. So, there cannot be non-apprehension of non-apprehension. The non-apprehension of sound is thus to its sheer absence.

The important positive arguments of Mīmāṃsa are in connection with instruction and repetition. The sound must be eternal otherwise no instruction would be possible. In the case of instruction, teacher imparts words to his pupil. If a word ceases to exist as soon as it is uttered, how could it explain the fact of teaching? But, Naiyāyikas argue, sound is not persistent as it is not heard in the space between the teacher and the pupil. It is true that word-sounds are taught. The teaching is possible through the imitation by the pupil what he finds in the teacher. As in the case of teaching of dance, pupil just imitates what he finds in the teacher. Dancing as an act ceases but it will be imitated by the student who learns it while so imitating. So, the case of instruction does not prove eternality of sound.

The case of repetition, *Mīmāṃsakas* argue, certainly proves the eternality of sound. What one reads for several times must persist all the time. But, according to Naiyāyikas, the repetition involves different acts giving different and thus distinct sounds though they are figuratively said to be repetition of one and the same sound. We can take the example of dance enacted twice, though it may be called repetition of the same dance. But they are two different acts as such. We call it a repetition due to their similarity in form though they are distinct acts.

Similarly when the word 'cow' is ultered many times by a person or by many person at different times, what makes all those utterances of the word refer to the word 'cow' is the generic concept of the word 'cow'. It is due to the similarity of their form, all the utterances are said to be of the word 'cow'. But similar is the case of the universal notion of 'cow' which includes all the instance of individual cows.

Jaimini, in his *Sūtras*, observes that "... it (sound) is eternal by the reason of its manifestation being for the sake of others".[17] Here, Jaimini wants to explain that the purpose of words it to instruct someone (the hearer) about a particular thing. Words are used and also learned through injunctions. When a hearer acts upon a verbal injunction, it shows that he has comprehended its meaning. Such comprehension presupposes the eternality of the word. Unless the word already existed, it cannot be comprehended. However, Naiyāyikas argue that whatever is for the sake of others need not be eternal as is the case with lamp, cloth etc. Again, whatever eternal may not have any use as is the case with atoms which are devoid of any use. So, being for the sake of others does not prove the eternality of sound.[18] The comprehension of meaning, on the other hand, depends upon recognition of the word as used earlier. Such recognition is due to remembrance of the form of the word, as in the case of jar which is seen in a new light is remembered as the same old jar because of its form.

The eternalists also argue that sound is eternal because we perceive no cause for its destruction where as we see causes for the non-eternal objects like jar. To this Nyāya replies that cause for the destruction of sound is actually perceived. Each sound series is destroyed after giving raise to another sound series. The sound which reaches the ear perishes after producing impact on the sense. Again, we can stop the ringing bell with our hands. So, the obstruction by hand destroys sound.

To recapitulate the whole debate, we may look at the basic differences between the respective positions of Nyāya and Mīmāṃsa with reference to sound and its nature. Naiyāyikas, do not suppose seperate ontological non-sensuous existence of sound over and above its empirical existence as it is apprehended. For them sound is an empirical phenomenon produced by an effort and it ceases to exists when it is not apprehended. For anything to exist, it must be apprehended through some valid sources of knowledge. There is no sound apprehended before an effort so it does not exist before such effort and ceases to exist when it is ceased to be apprehended.

On the other hand, *Mīmāṃsakas* presuppose the existence of sound even when it not apprehended. Utterance or an effort only makes it manifest, while Naiyāyikas say that it is a product of an effort. Though Nyāya and Mīmāṃsa generally agree as to the process of utterance and its apprehension, they differ as to the mode of sound reaching the sense-organ. Mīmāṃsakas oppose the hypothesis of sound series, and hold that sound reaches the hearer though the force of the wind. However, the Mīmāṃsakas oppose Nyāya theory keeping in view its further implications on their fundamental doctrine of *Dharma*. Refutation of any cause for the existence of sound helps the Mīmāṃsakas in establishing its self-sufficiency, especially in showing that *Vēdas* as collection of sounds, are uncaused and eternal. This will be clearer when we proceed to understand and how Mīmāṃsa looks at *Śabda Pramāṇa* and its validity.

Verbal Authority

As the scriptures are a specific instance of *Śabda Pramāṇa*, the validity of the scriptures depends upon the validity of *Śabda Pramāṇa* in general i.e., words as source of knowledge.

In other words, recognition of the *Vēdas* as a *Pramāṇa* rests upon recognition of knowledge of words as a *Pramāṇa* in general. Kumārila mentions the Buddhists and the viśēṣikas as those who do not recognize words to be a seperate *Pramāṇa*.[19] The Buddhists and the viśēṣikas include words in Inference.

As they do not accept *Śabda* in general as an independent source of knowledge, they also refuse the *Vēdas* as a seperate *Pramāṇa*. Kumārila realizes the adverse effects of including the *Vēda* in Inference and thus insists that seperate validity of *Śabda Pramāṇa* in general has to be proved:

"...An further (if verbal authority be accepted to be a form of Inference) then there would be no end to the counter-arguments (proving the invalidity of the *Vēda)*...For these reasons it is only when verbal authority, in the *Vēda* as well as in human utterances, *has its validity apart from the character of Inference* (which is sought to be thrust upon it), that the validity of the *Vēda* can be established".[20]

The Buddhists as they are committed only to perception and Inference as valid sources of knowledge, they view all other *Pramāṇas*, including verbal authority, as either invalid or as included in the two *Pramāṇas* they accepted.[21] They identify verbal cognition with Inference on the grounds that both involve an identical process and are different from perception. They argue that we arrive at the cognition of the meaning of a word in the same way we arrive at existence of fire after perception of smoke. The apprehension of physical sound lead to the cognition of its meaning as apprehension of smoke leads to the knowledge of fire. This process of cognition is different from that of perception in as much as perception is direct apprehension. So they conclude, verbal cognition is yet another from of Inference and hence should be included in Inference as a source of knowledge.

Sāṃkhyas who also consider verbal authority as a distinct *Pramāṇa*, want to distinguish *Śabda pramāṇa* from inference by showing that in the case of the former we have verbal specification while in the case of Inference we do not have verbal specification. The cognition of smoke is different from cognition of sound (word) in the sense that smoke is devoid of utterance.

This argument of *Sāṃkhyas* inadequate and at best serves as a counter-argument. Kumārila observes that even among Inferences of such objects as "smoke", "non-eternality". "Horned-ness", etc., there is difference; but that does not make any difference in their common character of "Inference".[22]

Śabara advances more substantial and adequate grounds for non-identity of *Śabda Pramāṇa* with *Anumana*. Śabara defines verbal cognition to be "that knowledge of imperceptible things which is derived from words".[23] With this definition, Śabara distinguishes verbal authority from Inference which has three specific features. Verbal authority is not inference because it is devoid of three characteristic features of Inference. Kumārila, following Śabara shows that *Śabda* as a *Pramāṇa* is different from Inference fro the former does not share the tripartitie character of Inference.

The characteristic features of any Inference are its Major Term, Minor Term and the conclusion. For instance, in the case of inferring existence of fire from the cognition of smoke on the mountain, The Major, Minor and the conclusion are as follows: (1) Wherever there is smoke, there is fire (2) There is smoke on the mountain (3) Therefore, there is fire on the mountain.

The Major premise expresses the relation between probans and probandum. The relation is of invariable concomitance. Smoke invariably coexists with fire. This relation is the basis of the inference. The Minor premise expresses the cognition of probans as specified with mountain. The conclusion expresses the inference of probandum arrived at. The Major premise asserts a universal relation and when this is applied to a specific cognition of probans lead to the conclusion regarding the existence of probandum.

The Buddhists argue that the process of verbal cognition is similar to that of Inference, because even in the case of verbal cognition, the object of cognition proceeds from the precognition of its relation with the word. The word uttered leads to the cognition of its objects because the relation between the word and its object is already known. Here the word uttered is the probans and the cognition of its object is the probandum. The Major term is the invariable relation between the two.

Mīmāṃsakas argue that verbal cognition is devoid of the above three features of Inference. First of all, the relation between probans and probandum has to be definitely ascertained. However, in the case of the word and its object no such relation can be ascertained. The word and its object are not related in the same way as smoke and fire are related. There is no invariable concomitance between a word, say 'tree', and its object, an actual tree cognized. We do not find the existence of tree wherever the word 'tree' is uttered. The word is not a property of any such subject as the tree. Until the probans are definitely cognized to be possessed of the probandum, the inference of the probandum cannot proceed from it.

The subject of the inference is the object cognized. If the subject is yet to be cognized how it be said to have any character belonging to it? If the subject is already cognized, what is the ned for Inference as such? As the word and its object do not exist at the same place because the word is always found to be wherever the speaker is. Nor the object exists at the same time as in the case of the word 'Aśōka'. Even the eternal existence of words cannot prove their concomitance with their objects. Because if it were so, as all words are qually eternal and all pervading, any particular word should make all the objects present when ever it is uttered. In that case, there can be no negative concomitance i.e., the absence of the words whenever there is absence of the objects.[24]

With the above arguments, Śabara distinguishes verbal cognition from inference by showing that former does not share the tripartite character of the latter.

Kaṇāda, the founder of Vaiśēṣika, also considers verbal authority as a part of Inference.[25] He does this on the grounds that the validity of all personal utterances depend upon the trustworthy character of the speaker. So, verbal cognition is inferred from the trustworthy character of the speaker.

This criticism does not effect Mīmāṃsakas, as we would see later, but it is directed against the Nyāya which holds such relationship between the speaker's character and the word. The Buddhists also subscribe to this argument. Gotama answers the above objection by saying that the validity of verbal cognition depends upon the trustworthy person, but the cognition as such is derived from words whether uttered by a trustworthy person or a mischievous person. As far as cognition of words is concerned, the utterances are sufficient to bring about cognition irrespective of the speaker's character.[26] So, the above criticism is irrelevant.

Quite interestingly, *Prabhākara* use the above argument of *Kaṇāda* to show that the *Vēdas* are the exclusive instance of *Śabda- Pramāṇa*. As all human utterances are Inferential in character, the *Vēdas* alone constitute *Śabda Pramāṇa* as they are devoid of human authorship.[27]

However, Kumārila rejects the above view of Prabhākara and insists upon independent character of verbal cognition in general. In the both cases of human assertions and *Vēdic* assertions, the words are common. The *Vēdic* words, though do not have any personal author, are words in general. Hence, to prove the independence of the *Vēda* from Inference, the verbal cognition in general has to be accepted apart from Inference.

Even Naiyāyikas refute the Buddhist theory that verbal cognition is just an instance of Inference. Gotama argues that the invariable concomitance between a word and objects is absent, as er do not find words like food etc. accompanied by the action of filling etc.[28]

Though both Naiyāyikas and Mīmāṃsakas are equally interested in proving the status of words as a *Pramāṇa* apart from Inference, they differ as to the definition of *Śabda Pramāṇa* and its validity. They uphold two extremely opposite views, on the validity of *Śabda*, which focus on the validity of cognition in general. Let us first see the difference between their definition of *Śabda Pramāṇa*.

As we have already noted, Śabara defines verbal authority as that knowledge of imperceptible things which is derived from words. The words are of two types: human *(pauruṣ ēya)* and super-human *(apauruṣeya)*. He distinguishes between ordinary human utterances and the eternal super-human scriptures. The scriptures *(Vēdas)* are devoid of human agency.

On the other hand, Gotama defines *Śabda Pramāṇa* as "communication of *āpta*".[29] It is of two kinds: that which refers to perceptible objects and that which refers to objects not perceived.

Vātsāyana in his *Bhāṣya* explains the views Gotama on *Śabda Pramāṇa*. Word is that by which an object is spoken of or made known. *Śabda Pramāṇa* is the verbal communication of *āpta*. An *āpta* is one who has direct or intuitive knowledge of things, who wishes to make known, and who is capable of speaking about them. In otherwords, an *āpta* is a trustworthy person who wishes to communicate things as he has seen them. This definition is secular and includes all the person whether sages, āryas or Mlēcchas.[30]

The definition given by Gotama precludes the *Mīmāṃsaka* classification of words into human and super-human. According to Gotama, all words are human utterances and there are no super-human utterances. Further, the validity of words arises from the trustworthy character of the speaker. Even the *Vēdas* are the utterance of sages and thus depend on the trustworthy character of sages for their validity.

Gotama's definition proves dangerous for the self-sufficient character of the *Vēda*. On the one hand it does not distinguish the scriptures from ordinary human utterances. If the distinction is not there, the scriptures would be devoid of sanctity attached to them. On the other hand the validity of the *Vēdas* are made to be knows from the trustworthy character of their authors, while the major plank employed by Mīmāṃsakas to prove the self-sufficiency of the *Vēda* is the argument that the scriptures are devoid of authorship, human or devine. Hence the Nyāya definition of *Śabda Pramāṇa* goes against the validity of the scriptures in general and their self-sufficiency in particular. Mīmāṃsakas vehemently oppose Gotama's definition as far as it considers verbal cognition as communication of a trustworthy person. They want to ascertain verbal authority as a 'trustworthy assertion' rather than 'assertion of trustworthy person'. They argue that words owe their existence not to any individual. They are rather eternal and thus independent from human production. Human utterances only manifest eternal words and do not produce them. Words denote objects naturally due to their own nature and connection between them is eternal. So, the definition must be devoid of human interference.

On the otherhand, Naiyāyikas consider words as products of human efforts. Hence, they owe their existence to the human usage. Again, words denote their objects due to convention *(samaya)*. Knowing words is nothing but knowing the conventional usage of words. We come to know what a word means only when we know that a particular word is used to denote a particular object. If words and objects are naturally connected, we should know the corresponding object whenever we hear a word and the corresponding word whenever we see the object.

Mīmāṃsakas argue that the world of objects is eternal and the words also eternal. So, there is no beginning to their connection and it is also eternal. Mīmāṃsakas also see language being learnt by the young people by observing their elders and understanding the conversation. This process, Mīmāṃsakas argue, is not possible unless the words are eternal. Naiyāyikas, however, say that the process shows how children learn the conventions regarding usage of words. Again, if words are independent of human beings, what is the ground for knowing the validity and invalidity of the cognitions brought about by words?

Here they enter the important question — whether validity of cognitions depend on any extraneous factors or is it inherent to the cognition itself? The answer to this question has decisive bearing upon the self-sufficiency of the scriptures.

The Naiyāyikas and the Mīmāṃsakas arrive at two opposing views on this issue. The Naiyāyikas argue that the authoritativeness of cognitions depends on extraneous factors. A cognition gives merely the knowledge of things and by itself cannot express its validity. Validity of the cognition is in need of another cognition which can ascertain the excellences of previous cognition. This theory is known as parataḥ prāmaṇyavāda.

Mīmāṃsakas, on the other hand, view every cognition as self-evident and is prima facie valid. Only its invalidity can be shown by other factors. A cognition, by the virtue of its being a cognition, is valid in itself. This theory is known as svataḥ prāmaṇyavāda.

The debate between Mīmāṃsakas and Naiyāyikas concerning the validity of cognitions in general, including that of verbal cognitions, has acquired a lot of significance in Indian Epistemology. Keeping in view the influence of this debate on the divergent epistemological commitments of the rival schools, we try to understand it in detail in the following section.

Svataḥ Prāmaṇya Vāda

Nyāya and Mīmāṃsa accept the distinction between valid and invalid cognitions. But they differ as to the ground on which such distinction can be made. For the Naiyāyikas, the validity of cognitions depends on the excellences of the cause of the apprehension. So, the criteria for the validity of a cognition is external to the cognition. A cognition is, hence, unauthoritative in itself unless it is supplemented with validity by another cognition of excellences of the cause of previous cognition.

Kumārila opposes the Nyāya view in detail.[31] A cognition cannot be validated by factors extraneous to it, because those that are by themselves false cannot be proved to be true by any means. Again, validity and invalidity cannot be both inherent to the cognition itself, because they are contradictory in character. Nor can both of them be extraneous to cognition, because in that case there would be no definiteness in the cognition.

The Naiyāyikas argue that invalidity, being a negative factor, cannot be due to extraneous causes i.e., discrepancies in the origin. On the other hand, validity, being a positive entity, is always based upon the excellences of the cause. So, cognition by nature are invalid and their validity is inferred from cognition of the excellence of the cause of its apprehension. This theory explains how dream cognitions are inherently invalid and they cannot be validated by further cognitions because the dream cognitions are devoid of perfection in their cause.

However, Kumārila argues, a cognition in itself cannot be invalid because if it were so, it can never proved to be valid.

Though every cognition has some originating cause, it does not depend on such cause for its efficacy to illumine the object. Again, if the validity of a cognition is ascertained by another cognition, we need another cognition to validate the cognition which is supposed to validate the first cognition. This way we will end up in infinite regression to know the validity of a single cognition. So, a cognition can never be valid.

On the other hand, cognition is valid in itself, by the virtue of its being a cognition. Its invalidity is due to extraneous causes such as discrepencies or lack of excellences in the originating cause. The invalidity of a cognition does not need infinite regression of cognition. Whenever the validity of a cognition is doubted for any reason, we can seek other cognitions. Whenever the validity of cognition is doubted for any reason, we can seek other cognition. If there is any cognition which sublates the former cognition, then the former cogniton stands unauthoritative. The later cognition is valid in itself and, for that reason, can vouch for the invalidity of the former cognition. If there appears another cognition which invalidates the later cognition, then the first cogniton would be valid. Hence, with a few cognitons we can ascertain the validity of a cogniton, unlike the Naiyāyikas.

With *Svataḥ Prāmāṇya Vāda*, the invalidity of dream cognitions can also be explained. Dream cognitions as cognitions are valid. But their invalidity is shown by the later waking cognitions which sublate the dream cogniton. However, there are no further cognitions to invalidate the waking cognitions. So, the invalidity of dream cognitons is ascertained by the unsublated waking cognitions. Prabhākara explains the erroneous nature of dreams that the objects present in the dreams, though they seem to be directly apprehended, are objects remembered. Memory as such is not valid. So, dreams are invalid.[32]

The theory of *Svataḥ Prāmāṇya Vāda* proves the self-sufficiency of the *Vēda*, so far as it takes all cognitons as intrinsically valid. Kumārila, however, makes the difference between human assertions and the *Vēdic* assertions. Both are valid prima facie according to svataḥ prāmaṇya vāda. However, in the case human utterances, there is a possibility of invalidity due to the character of the speaker. In the case of the *Vēda*, there is no possibility of doubt because there is no author for the *Vēdas*. So, their self-sufficient authority is proved by their intrinsic validity and further impossibility of sublating cognitions.

While the theory of eternality of sound and independent nature of words to denote objects help to establish the eternality of the *Vēda*, the theory of self-evident character of cognitions and freedom from human authorship help to prove the self-sufficient character of the *Vēda*. These two theories i.e., of eternal sound and *Svataḥ Prāmāṇya Vāda,* are cardinal doctrines of Mīmāṃsa as far as absolute authority of the *Vēda* is concerned.

The rejection of conventional theory of meaning estranges language of its human origin. This view of Mīmāṃsa, as Keith rightly observes, "... can hardly be regarded as anything else than an attempt to bring the doctrine of verbal testimony into harmony with their traditional beliefs in the nature in the *Vēda*, which doubtless long preceded their speculations on the nature of the relation of word and meaning".[33] This further leads to a peculiar position that only sanskrit words are naturally capable of denoting objects. All other languages are degenerated forms of sanskrit. They signify objects due to their origin from sanskrit.[34]

The *Svataḥ Prāmāṇya Vāda*, recognizes truth as simple and natural to cognitions. But *Parataḥ Prāmaṇya Vāda* understands Truth belonging to a system in which each element depends on other. These two theories of Truth are extremely

desirable thing or avoid an undesirable thing, they are found to be valid. The validity of the spells and medical scriptures is guaranteed by the reliable character of their authors and their capacity to yield the desired results. Similarly in the case of the *Vēdic* injunctions, their authority is derived from the reliable character of the seers who composed them and by actual observation of their yielding results.

In connection with sacrifices yielding the attached results, the *Vēda* is charged of untruth. The sacrifice is not always followed by the intended conseques proves that the *Vēdic* injunctions are false. Gotama meets this objection by saying that the result not falling in order could be due to the deficiencies in the act, the agent and the means.[37]

Vātsāyana further explains that when *Putrakāmēṣṭi* sacrifice is performed by a couple, they should give to a son. Here, the couple being the agents, the sacrifice being the means, their connection with the sacrifice is the act. The results may not accrue due to the deficiency in any of the factors. The agent might be immoral or the materials offered might not be properly consecrated or the *mantra* might not be properly recited or any other deficiency might be pertaining to the whole sacrificial act. *The results would not come along even if the act of procreation itself is defective. In the case of defective method of sexual intercourse or defective semen or uterine decease the child may not be conceived.* If everything is allright, the result is accomplished. If the result does not appear, it is due to various defects.[38]

The above defence of sacrifices is spurious. What is Vātsāyana's point in telling that if all the physical conditions for procreation i.e., male sterility, lack of uterine diseases and proper method of intercourse are there, there would be the birth of child? It is nothing but conceding indirectly that the performance of sacrifice has got nothing to do with bearing a child.

In fact, Vacaspati, in his *Nyāya Vārttika Tātparya Tīka,* makes the point clearer:[39] "When the sacrifice is said to bring about the son's birth, it does not mean that there is any such positive and negative concomitance between the son's birth and the sacrifice as 'whenever the sacrifice is performed the son is born' or 'whenever the sacrifice is not performed the son is not born'. What is meant is that the scripture lays down that the sacrifice only assists in the son's birth. If the son is born without performing sacrifice, it can be assumed that the son is born as a result of sacrifice performed in the previous birth. If the son is not born even after the performance of the sacrifice, it must be assumed that the potency raised by the sacrifice is neutralized by some unseen obstruction."

Now it is cleat that Nyāya's attitude towards the *Vēda* and the sacrifices is only superficial veneration. Despite their desperate attempts to please the *Vēdic* orthodoxy, Naiyāyikas take up serious fight against the Mīmāṃsa theory of eternal *Vēda*. Vātsāyana concludes that the eternality of the *Vēda* means nothing more than the continuity of tradition, practice and use; these are though all ages past and future. So, Mīmāṃsakas use the word 'eternality', in a figurative sense to mean 'continuity of tradition'.

Coming back to the main discussion, we may proceed to see how Mīmāsakas analyse *Dharma* or Duty, with their epistemological commitments on hand.

Vidhivākya and *Arthavāda*

Given the absolute of the *Vēda* as the exclusive source of Duty, Mīmāṃsa takes to the investigation into *Dharma*. Jaimini defines *Dharma* as 'an object sanctioned by the *Vēdic* injunction'. It is known through the scriptural imperatives which inculcate certain acts as Duty. By the whole *Vēda* is not a collection of mere injunctions. There are several kinds of passages in the *Vēda* which are not imperative. Hence the *Vēda* has to be classified into systematic heads so as to decipher which part of the extensive literature directly deals with *Dharma*.

The *Vēdic* passages are devided into two broad heads: Mantra and *Brāhmaṇa*. *Mantras* are the hymns which have to be recited in the sacrifice. *Brāhmaṇas* are the injunctive passage or *Vidhivākya* which enjoin the sacrificial acts and rules thereof. They include both prescriptive and prohibitive injunctions. Besides, *Arthavāda* and *Nāmadhēya* passages are also part of *Brāhmaṇas*. *Arthavāda* passages are those which do not contain injunctions but describe the merits of undertaking a sacrifice or avoiding prohibitions. They are descriptive and directly or indirectly influence one to undertake the sacrificial acts. So, they have the function of instigating one for action and for that reason, are closely connected with vidhi or injunctions. *Nāmadhēya* are the names in a *Brāhmaṇa* passage which neither serves as an injunction nor can be taken as *Arthavāda*.

While the whole *Vēda* is described as the source of *Dharma*, it is the *Vidhivākya* and the *Arthavāda* passages which are of paramount importance, because they directly deal with the Duty. *Mantras* are, though not formally defined, rather considered as instruments of offering. They too are important due to their connection with the sacrifice.

Mantras are devided into three parts *Ṛk, Yajus* and *Sāman*. *Ṛks* are the hymns which have specific metre and devided into well defined parts *(pāda)*. *Ṛks* contain definite number of syllables in each *pāda*. *Sāman* are nothing but *Ṛks* set to music. When *Ṛks* are sung, they are supposed to be more efficient in bringing about the results. *Yajus* are the hymns which are neither *Ṛks* nor *Sāman*. Yajus are devoid of material feet and are nor set to music.

The *Mantras* being marginally important as instruments of the sacrifice, the essence of the *Vēda* lies in the injunctive passages, for the Mīmāṃsakas. Prabhākara emphasizes the

Vidhivākya as the nucleus of the scriptures. Not only in the case of the *Vēda,* but even in the case of ordinary speech, it is the injunctive sentences that play a vital role. Prabhākara advances the theory that meaning of words are learnt only through injunctions. He says, we come to know the denotation of words only as and when they occur in imperative sentences. Words by themselves are not expressive unless they are connected with a verb which incites for an action. In the sentences *Gamānaya* i.e., 'bring the cow', the word *'gam'* can be understood only through its connection with *ānaya* i.e., 'bring'. This theory of Prabhākara is known as *Anvitābhidhānavāda*, according to which words express meaning only as parts of sentence, to be specific, an injunctive sentence.

Kumārila differs from Prabhākara in this connection. For Kumārila, on the other hand, words denote their object individually and when these individual words are combined into a sentence, it expresses a unitary idea. So, words do not owe their meaning to a sentence in which they are parts. This theory of Kumārila is called *Abhihitānvayavāda.* Nevertheless, both Prabhākara and Kumārila agree upon the view that the primary teaching of the *Vēda* lies in its *Vidhivākya* par excellence. All other passages are subsidiary to the *Vidhivākya.* This position of Mīmāṃsakas is controverted by the Vēdāntins. For them, the more direct teaching of the *Vēda* does not lie in enjoining something to be done i.e., *Vidhivākya* but in pointing out to the established fact i.e., existence of *Brahman.* This divergence between Mīmāṃsakas and the Vēdāntins can be understood when we see that the passages on which they lay emphasis are different. For the former it is the *Brāhmaṇas* which constitute the most important passages of the *Vēda*, while for the latter, it is the *Upaniṣads*. From the above observation, it follows that both of them do not mean the same texts by the word *'Vēda'*.

The divergence also effects their views as to what texts constitute *Arthavāda*. For Mīmāṃsakas, all descriptive passages are subsidiary to the injunctive passages and thus constitute *Arthavāda*. The descriptive passages of *Upaniṣads*, for them, are *Arthavāda* and thus directly or indirectly connected with sacrifices. On the contrary, for the Vēdāntins, while the descriptive passages of *Upaniṣads* directly deal with the reality as Brahman, the injunctive passages are supposed to be *Arthavāda* which indirectly purport the existence of supreme spirit.

This divergence culminates in an unbridgable gulf between them, in connection with the reality of the material world. They come out with mutually untenable metaphysical views concerning the ontological status of the physical world. We will realize the importance of this issue when we actually analyse the materialistic outlook of Mīmāṃsakas in the forthcoming section.

Coming to the present discussion, the Mīmāṃsakas consider the *Vidhivākya* to be the direct preaching of the *Vēda*. The *Vidhivākya* are divided into five classes with reference to the aspects of the sacrifice: (1) The *Karmōtpattivākya* is one which enjoins a specific act — e.g. 'one should perform the *Agnihōtra*'; (2) The *Guṇavākya* enjoins certain necessary details in connection with the prescribed act — e.g. 'one should perform the *hōma* with curds'; (3) The *Phalavākya* refers to the results which follows from the performance of an enjoined act — e.g. 'one desirous of attaining heaven should perform the *Agnihōtra*'; (4) The *Phalayaguṇavākya* mentions both the result and necessary details — e.g. 'one desirous of having efficient sense-organs should perform the *hōma* with curds'. This injunction is a combination of *Phala* and *Guṇa Vākyas*; (5) the *Saguṇakarmōtpattivākya* enjoins an act with an accessory detail — e.g. 'one should perform the sacrifice with enjoins an act with an accessory detail — e.g. 'one should perform the sacrifice with *Sōma*'. This kind of injunction is a combination of *Karmōtpatti* and *Guṇa Vākyas*.

While the first three kinds of injunctions enjoin an act, its accessory and its result respectively, the other two kinds of injunctions are mere combinations of the second and the three, again the second and the first respectively. There is another classification of *Vidhivākya* pertaining to the nature of activity they enjoin i.e., positive or negative or preclusive character of the injunction.

According to this classification, injunctions are divided into (1) the *Apūrvavidhi* or original injunctions known — e.g. 'the grains should be washed'; (2) the *Niyamavidhi* or Restrictive Injunction enjoins one method of doing something among various possible modes of doing the same thing — e.g. 'the corn should be thumped' while it is also possible to remove the chaff pealing off with hand; (3) the *Parisānkhyavidhi* precludes some among other possible alternatives — e.g. precluding the use of a particular *mantra* in a particular act. While both *Niyamavidhi* and *Parisānkhyavidhi* are restrictive in a sense, the former enjoins a positive restriction i.e., prescribes a particular method, the latter enjoins a negative restriction in the sense that it prescribes a method which should not be adopted.

Arthavāda passages gain importance only through their reference to *Vidhivākyas*, as we have already noted. They can be divided into two broad heads: Eulogistic and Deprecatory. The Eulogistic passages praise the enjoined act or the result or the agent who performs the act. The Deprecatory passages condemn some act as undesirable or the adverse effects which follow the act or the agent who does the act. As a matter of fact the *Arthavāda* passages freely use quite fanciful hyperbolae. What is surprising about Mīmāṃsa view of the *Arthavāda* is that there is not hesitation to consider even those passages which are totally irrelevant to the performance of sacrifices as

Arthavāda. For example, the descriptive *Upaniṣadic* passages are generally the speculative assertions about the ultimate reality. Mīmāṃsa, as a rule, assumes some connection between those passages and *Vidhivākya*, not always successfully. The important negative function of this view is to explain away the irrelevant and sometimes contrary passages as *Arthavāda*. Kumārila adopts the same technique in explaining away the theistic references and the theory of creation, which are found in the *Vēda*. The passages, though go against the philosophical spirit of Mīmāṃsa, are supposed to be supporting *Vidhivākya* in a disguised form.

Given the importance of *Vidhivākys* and *Arthavāda* as the sources of knowing what to be done, *Dharma* has to be understood as what is enjoined by them. Now, there arises a doubt as to what exactly corresponds to *Dharma*. Is it the action enjoined or the result thereof? Again, if the action i.e., sacrifice is supposed to bring about the corresponding results, how does it do so? How are the action and its results are connected? What way is the agent related to the act? Once, Mīmāṃsakas establish the acts enjoined by the *Vēda* as *Dharma*, they have to advance a comprehensive theory of action to clear off all the doubts pertaining to it. In the following section we shall deal with the Mīmāṃsa theory of action and its relation with *Dharma*.

Dharma and *Apūrva*

In order to substantiate their theory of *Dharma* in connection with the *Vēdic* sacrifices, the Mīmāṃsakas have to explain how the agent, the act and the result are connected and how do the *Vēdic* mandates have a bearing upon the three factors. In otherwords, they have to advance a systematic theory of action in the light of their theory of *Dharma*. For this purpose, the Mīmāṃsakas deal with the process in which the *Vēdic* injunction is carried out into a *vēdic* sacrifice and how the enjoined act bring about the desired consequences. The

Mīmāṃsaka's explanation of action is relevant not only to the *Vēdic* sacrifices but also to the moral actions as such.

Actions in general are classified into worldly *(laukika)* and the *Vēdic (uaidika)*. The *Vēdic* actions are distict from the ordinary worldly actions in as much as they are not unnecessarily this worldly. They are mostly devoid of worldly purport. The *Vēdic* actions have their source in the *Vēda* whereas worldly actions are devoid of this feature and, for this reason, worldly actions do not accrue spiritual merit. As far as spiritual merit is concerned, the worldly activities, if not irrelevant, are of not much important.

The *Vēdic* actions are again devided into *Nitya* (unconditional duties), *Naimittika* (occasional duties) and *Kāmya karmas* (desired actions for a particular result). Performance of everyday *sandhya* is an unditional *Nitya karma;* sacrifice on lunar or solar eclipse is an instance of occasional *Naimittika karma*; sacrifice for attaining son or village or cattle is an instance of *Kāmya karma*. In the case of the former two, there is no specific desire as a motive. They are rather part of one's adherence to one's Duty. There is no option regarding these actions. There is an option in the case of *Kāmya karmas* as they are binding only when the agent has a desire to be accomplished.

However, the three kinds of actions are supposed to be virtuous because they are equally prescribed by the *Vēda*. The *Vēdic* injunctions give rise to an impulse in the mind of the agent to perform the enjoined act. The impulse or impact is known as *'Bhāvana'*. The *Bhāvana* prompts one to action. *Bhāvana* stands for the psychological process intervening the cognition of duty and actually discharging it. It is two kinds — *Ārthi* and *Śabdi*. *Ārthi Bhāvana* is referred by the injunctive affix of the word *'yajēta'* which urges the agent to put forth his efforts towards a definite act. *Śabdi Bhāvana* is what accompanies i.e., the verbal propting from the injunction.

Prabhākara explains that the *Vēdic* injunctions leave the impression of what to be done *(Kartavyatājñāna)*. Such impression leads to mental determination *(cikīrṣa)*. The determination proceeds to know the possibility of action *(Kritisādhya)*. Then volition *(pravṛtti)* arises. *Pravṛtti* leads to overt action *(chēṣta)*. Overt action finally accomplishes the performance of enjoined act.

However, what is important in explaining the *Vēdic* sacrifices is to explain the process in which the action accrues the result. The act itself being transitory, how can it lead to the results which are supposed to come at a later time?. When a sacrifice is performed to attain heaven, the agent is not led to heaven as soon as he completes the sacrifice. So, the sacrifice and its result are temporally separated. Now, the question is — how does the ephemeral action, which perished as soon as accomplished, gives rise to a result at a later time? The action which does not exist in the intervening period between the sacrifice and its result cannot, for that reason, immediately precede the result. If it does not do so, it cannot be called the cause of the result.

The Mīmāṃsakas resolve the problem by postulating an unseen energy brought out by the sacrificial act. The unseen potency is called *'Apūrva'*. Though the act perishes, it gives rise to a new potency which endures the time intervening the act and its result. *Apūrva* culminates in the result of the act. This energy called *Apūrva* is presumed not only to explain the temporal separation between the act and its result, but also to avoid other incogruous explanations of the same. Prabhākara, by postulating *Apūrva*, avoids the explanations that (1) the action is everlasting (2) the action incites certain faculty in the agent (3) the results are accomplished by the favoures of the deities. Prabhākara summarily rejects these assumptions. It is against all evidence to consider the action as everlasting. The self, itself being inactive, cannot be supposed to bring the result through any facility. Nor can the deities or their favours do it. The sacrifices are not to appease the deities. Even the offerings cannot reach them because the deities are neither eternal nor omnipresent. There is no possibility of their receiving the offerings and showering favours. Hence, results are not due to the favours of the deities. This issue, thus, can be sufficiently explained by postulating *Apūrva.*[40]

It is interesting to note the observation made by Prabhākara regarding the *Vēdic* deities. It gives us an important clue as to the anti-theistic commitment of Pūrva Mīmāṃsa. The early *Vēdic* hymns, where the deities are eulogised, give us the impression that the whole sacrificial practice is directed to propitiate the *Vēdic* deities. But in the *Brāhmaṇas* the place of the deities is occupied by the sacrifice itself, where they are treated as mere datives in the injunction and as subsidiary to be the sacrifice. This development leads to the Mīmāṃsa view which reduces the stature of *Vēdic* gods to mere manes which form accessories for the sacrifice. Prabhākara thus conceives the sacrificial results as independent of the favours of the deities. It is only peculiar force or potency of the act itself that can accomplish its results.

Kumārila understands *Apūrva* to be a new force or faculty arising out of the performed action which brings along the result attached to it. But it is not identical with the sacrifice or its results.[41] It is rather a latent potency pertaining to these. It resides as a faculty in the agent till it realizes itself as the result. Prabhākara opposes this view and claims that it cannot be a faculty in the agent because if the results are accomplished by the faculty of the agent, then they are not produced by the action. If action is said to be the cause of the results, the potency must belong to the action, not to the agent.[42]

However, there is an objection to the view held by Prabhākara. *Apūrva* being a product of the action, is transient. If it is transient, it cannot continue till the appearance of the result. The transient potency cannot be treated as causing the results, unless it subsides in the agent who continues to exist from the time of sacrifice till the appearance of the result.

Apūrva is employed not only in the case of Kāmya karma which are connected with certain results, but also in the case of unconditional duties where no specific results are attached. Even those unditional duties accrue spiritual merit through *Apūrva*. *Apūrva*, in general, connects the results and the agent by the virtue of his connection with the act.

Apūrva also accounts for discrimination among various actions enjoined by the *Vēda*. There are primary and subsidiary acts enjoined by the *Vēda*. The primary action is one which directly results in an independent *Apūrva*. The subsidiary acts are those which are undertaken to complete the primary act. They do not produce independent *Apūrva* but only as part of the primary act of which they are subsidiary acts. *Apūrva* is thus corresponds to the injunctive verb in the *Vidhivākya* which prescribes a primary act.

Now, what exactly corresponds to *Dharma*? Is it the act, the result or the unseen potency that corresponds to Duty? Prabhākara considering *Apūrva* to be what is mentioned by the injunctive verb, *Dharma* must be corresponding to the *Apūrva*. Kumārila, however, takes *Dharma* as belonging to the sacrificial act itself. Performance of Duty brings śreyas or bliss. It is achieved through the act, the materials and the auxiliaries. So, 'Duty' must correspond to these only. *Dharma* as an object cannot be identified with a faculty. *Apūrva* being a faculty cannot be signified by the word *Dharma*.[43]

Kumārila, while asserting that the prescribed acts themselves constitute *Dharma*, rejects other theories of *Dharma*. He rejects the *Sāṃkhya* doctrine according to which *Dharma* is a particular function of mind. Buddhists construe *Dharma* as a peculiar mental impression left by good and bad actions. The Jaina doctrine of *Dharma* relates it to the 'Body of virtue' *(Puñya pudgala)*. Vaiśēṣikas understand *Dharma* as a specific property of a person. Kumārila rejects all these theories categorically and along with them he also rejects the Prabhākara's theory of equating *Dharma* with *Apūrva*.[44]

Sāmkhya definition of *Dharma* is untenable for Kumārila because if *Dharma* were a function of the mind, it cannot be known through the *Vēda*. The Buddhist doctrine is also erroneous because if Duty is a mere mental impression it is devoid of the character of an action. Duty as an object of the scriptural injunction does not refer to a subjective impression but to an objective action. Further, the Buddhists do not accept an enduring self to which actions and their results can be attributed. The *Vijñanavādins* uphold the existence of a mental continuum which is nothing but a series of cognitions. The rejection of a substantial self leads them to define *Dharma* as a mere transient mental impression. Mīmāṃsa does not accept the view that a cognition is capable of having another cognition as its object. What is cognized is an object and not another cognition. Hence, they reject the theory that a series of cognitions constitute the mental continuum without a substantial self as their substratum. For *Mīmāṃsakas*, mind cannot operate without a self. *Mīmāṃsakas*, mind cannot operate without a self. *Mīmāṃsakas* establish a permanent self which performs actions as an agent and enjoys its result.

While *Sāṃkhyas* and Buddhists attribute *Dharma* to the mind, Vaiśēṣikas and Jainas attribute it to the individual. What is Duty cannot be property of an individual. Whatever is construed as individual cannot belong to others. Hence *Dharma* as Duty refers to an objective action which does not reside in any particular individual. Though Kumārila and Prabhākara differ as to what corresponds to *Dharma*, they agree upon non-individualistic objective character of it.

Given the objectivity of Duty, now a doubt arises as to its nature. Is it merely scriptural Duty or does it have any moral dimension? In other words, how is the ritualistic duty relevant to morality as a social practice? The answer is not as complicated as the question. In India, scriptuality is never seen as disconnected with morality. Spiritual discussions rather presuppose the moral problems of life. Mīmāṃsa, especially, does not undermine the ethical aspect of human activity. It is unfortunate the some of the modern scholars view Mīmāṃsa as a bundle of formal ritualism, seeking sanction from the scriptures. This view fails to understand the real implications of Mīmāṃsa world-view.

Mīmāṃsa definition of Duty is comprehensive and includes social conduct. For the Mīmāṃsakas, all that is prescribed by the *Vēda* is *Dharma*. The *Vēdic* prescription is not limited to ritual injunctions but includes certain norms of social conduct which are later codified in the law-books. Mīmāṃsa seeks to establish the authority of the *Vēda* for both ritual practices and other social, legal and political maxims supported by the scriptures. Hence, as far as social organization is concerned, Mīmāṃsa presupposes the *Varnāśrama Dharma* as laid down by the law-givers. The social codes derive their authority from the *Vēda* and Mīmāṃsa, by theoretically establishing the *Vēda*, endorses the codes as authoritative.

Mīmāṃsa, as part of its exegetical word, also interprets the *Vēdic* maxims in connection with legal concepts like — property Rights, Inheritance, Adoption etc. The influence of Mīmāṃsa on Indian legal literature will be discussed in a forthcoming section devoted for the purpose.

Meanwhile, it is important to see that the Mīmāṃsa view of *Dharma* is comprehensive. *'Dharma'* does not stand only for the rituals but all those actions, both spiritual and moral, prescribed by the *Vēda*.

Mīmāṃsa World-view

The Mīmāṃsa concept of *Dharma* will remain vague unless we elucidate it in the light of its world-view. Mīmāṃsa advances a thoroughly rationalistic view of the world which is quiet unexpected from such an ancient orthodox system. The misapprehensions caused by the orthodox character of Mīmāṃsa will be dispelled at once when we look at its Realistic world-view.

The nucleus of the world-view is its conception of the world as real, eternal and dynamic. This is further strengthened by rejecting the pessimistic view of life as a bondage from which some systems seek an ideal escape. Mīmāṃsa emphasizes the reality of the world and the place of human action in it. What is more surprising is its denial of theism in all its forms. Mīmāṃsa truly reflects and overwhelming positive spirit of life evident in the *Samhitas* and the *Brāhmaṇas*. It also attempts to bring the *Upaniṣadic* rendering of soul in line with the ritualistic understanding of the *Brāhmaṇas*, ofcourse not with much success.

Reality of the External world is a prerequisite for the practive of morality. All the axiological efforts would be fruitless if there are no real objects which correspond to our ideas. No relation between actions and their consequences can be established if the world is devoid of objective reality. The teaching of the *Vēda* would be groundless.[45] The concrete existence of the physical world is, thus, emphasized by the Mīmāṃsakas. Here, they had to grapple with the Idealists who go to the extreme of denying the reality of physical objects. While the Vijñānavādins conclude that there are no objects corresponding to our ideas and that ideas alone are real, the Vēdāntins describe the world as an indefinable superimposition which is ultimately unreal. The Sūnyavādins preach that both physical and mental worlds are void *(sūnya)* in the final analysis.

Despite of their minor differences, the above three schools equally demolish the reality of the physical world.

The vital argument of the Idealists is the anology of dream cognitions which are devoid of corresponding real objects. Similarly, they argue, the waking cognitions are also devoid of real objective because both dream experience and waking experience share the common character of 'cognition'. So, all the cognitions do not have objective basis. The above position makes the performance of duty meaningless. Kumārila says "It cannot be for the mere pleasures of a dream that people engage in the performance of Duty. Dream coming to man spontaneously, during sleep, the learned would only lie down quietly, instead of performing sacrifices etc., when desirous of obtaining real results. For these reasons, we must try our best, by arguments, to establish (the truth of) the conception of external objects (as realitiies)".[46]

Śabara argues that the falsity of dream cognitions does not arise from their being cognitions, bit from the fact that they are sublated by the waking cognitions.[47] As we do not find cognitions which sublate the waking cognitions, they are valid. This is true of not only dream cognitions, but also of all the doubtful and invalid cognitions.

Kumārila further shows that the Idealist anology of dream cognition goes against their own position:

"If a cognition be false, would it not be liable to rejection? If it were to be false even without being rejected, then there would be nor restriction as to the reality and unreality of a cognition. For us, dream cognition would certainly be falsified by the perception of a waking cognition contradicting it; while for you, what would constitute the difference between the reality of waking — cognition and that of dream consciousness, both of which are held by you to be equally false? Of waking cognition as such, there is no proper correct contradictory cognition, — the perception of which would establish the falsity of such waking cognitions as those of the post and the like. The fact of waking cognitions being the contradictory of dream-cognition is known to all persons and as such they differ from dream cognition (known only to particular individuals) just like the cognition, which serves to reject a particular dream-cognition".[48]

If it is objected that even waking cognition are sublated by some yogic-cognitions which serve as evidence for the falsity of waking cognitions, then we have our own *yōgins* who vouch for the contrary to your position.[49]

Prabhākara goes further and ascertains that even dream cognitions are not devoid of objective basis. The dream-cognitions are not altogether false, because they illuminate objects as external and these dream objects have their basis in the external objects. The dream objects are nevertheless objects, which are devoid of proper determination of time and space. In the case of waking cognitions, the objects are well-determined in terms of space and time.

Kumārila argues that it is the well-determined character of waking-cognitions on the strength of which they sublate the dream cognitions. The concrete existence of the objects is proved by the objective coercion they exercise on our cognitions. Even in the case of illusory cognitions, this coercion is evident. We can see an illusory snake only in a rope. The unreal objects can be seen as real only in those things which share some characteristic feature with the former. The snake has its substratum only in a real rope which shares the common character of length and shape with the snake.

Again, form belongs to objects alone and cognition has no form. Neither a cognition can be an object of another cognition. Hence the Buddhist argument that form belongs to cognition and the form of cognition is known through another cognition is untenable. The basis of all cognitions is the world of objects having form and other qualities. The objects are not creation of our ideas. They exist independently of ideas. They exist whether cognized or not. Hence the world is real, objective and independent of cognitions.

Kumārila thus explicitly attacks the Buddhistic schools. However, he also criticizes the *Vēdānta* view of the world implicitly. The *Vēdāntins* consider the world as an indescribable superimposition of ignorance. The physical world is a combination of the real and unreal. It is not real nor is it totally unreal. Viewed from the practical point of view it is real but from the transcendental point of view it is unreal. The self alone is real and all the worldly objects are conjured up by beginning — less ignorance or avidya. Kumārila does not accept the theory of two truths — i.e., practical and transcendental. Nor does he accept any third category of truth than real and unreal: "there can be no reality in *'samvṛti'* (Falsity); and as such how can it be a form of reality, how can it be *'samvṛti'*? If it is false, how can it be real? Nor can 'reality' belong, in common, to objects, false as well as real; because the two are contradictory; for certainly the character of the "tree" cannot belong in common to a *tree* as well as to a *lion*".[50] The words like *'samvṛti'* or *'mithya'* are used only to deceive people.

Kumārila's rejection of idealism establishes the positive reality of the world on which all the differences between virtue and vice, *Dharma* and *ADharma*, teacher and pupil etc., depend. Though Mīmāṃsa accepts the reality of soul and ideas, it does not ascribe them exclusive reality. The world cannot be said to have assumed or conditional reality but it is positively real.

The world is not only real but also eternal and dynamic. Though the particular objects of the world undergo change and destruction, the world as a whole is uncaused and eternal. It consists of objects which come into existence and pass away and thus dynamic in nature. The eternality of words will be groundless if the world is not eternal. Hence, according to the Mīmāṃsakas, there was not time when the world was not there nor does it pass away as a whole.

This view of the world faces a challenges from the theists. Theism in India is invariably connected with theories of creation. The god is viewed as material or efficient cause or both of the world. The Mīmāṃsakas refute all the theories of creation along with their theistic presuppositions. Acceptance of any theory of creation leads to the position that the world has a beginning. Hence, Mīmāṃsa vehemently opposes such theories.

Manu advances a theory of creation, as we noticed in the last chapter, in which the *Prajāpati* is the both material and efficient cause of the world. Vaiśēṣikas and the later Naiyāyikas also assume God to be the efficient cause of the world, the material cause being the atoms. The Vaiśēsikas are in a peculiar fix, The world is made up of atomic conjunctions. All the gross objects are nothing but atoms conjoined together. They face a question as to how the atoms first come together. The motion is viewed as external to the atoms. Then they themselves cannot come together. In search of an answer to this question, they end in assuming a theological entity which makes such conjunction possible. They further assume periodic creation and dessolution at which world comes to a state of suspended animation. The theological beings serves another purpose for them. The God is hell responsible for fixing names and their meanings. This position effects the eternality of the *Vēdas*.

Ḳumārila undertakes a detailed refutation of the theistic and creation theories. He argues as follows:

"At a time when all this earth, water etc. did not exist, what could have been the condition of the universe? As for *Prajāpati* himself, what could be his position? And what his form? If it be held that the world is by desire on the part of *Prajāpati*, then since *Prajāpati* is held to be without a material body, etc., how could he have any desire towards creation? And if he has a body, this body could not have been created by himself; thus then we would have to postulate another for his body, and soon, *adinfinitum*. If *Prajāpati's* body be held to be eternal, of what material would that body be composed? Then again, in the first place, how it that he should have a desire to create a world which is fraught with all sorts of troubles to living beings? For at the time of the beginning of creation he has not got any guiding agencies, in the shape of the virtue or sin etc., of the living beings themselves. Nor can creator create any thing, in the absence of means and instruments.... And if he were to depend upon Laws and Agencies, then this fact would deprive him of his boasted independence... what is that end which he desires, and which could not be gained without creating the world?...If the activity of the creator were due to a desire for mere amusement, then that would go against his ever-contendedness... And above all such a creator could never be known by anybody".[51]

Prabhākara equally objects to the theory of creation and the concept of an omniscient God. He argues that we actually observe the bodies of men and animals are produced by the functioning of parents. This fact will enable us to infer that the bodies of men and animals were so produced even in the past and this process will be there in the future also. There is no need to assume a supervening agency. Even *Dharma* and A*Dharma* do not need any supra-mundane supervisor. God cannot supervise individual merit and demerit for he cannot come into contact with them as they belong to individual souls. The contact can possibly be in two ways only — either conjunction or inherence. The individual *Dharma* or A*Dharma* cannot have conjunction with God because they are qualities. They can neither inhere in God because they can inhere only in individual souls, So, god can have no knowledge of individual merit or demerit.[52] The only instance of supervision is that of an individual soul on its body.

Mīmāṃsa does not accept any theistic assumptions in its world-view. However, Mīmāṃsa has to explain the theistic trends which are found in the *Vēda.* Manu rests his theory of creation on such theistic evidences found in the *Vēda.* The celebrated purusa sukta explicitly refers to a creator. Though it is a real difficulty to explain away those passages, Mīmāṃsakas do it easily. They ignore those passages as simply *Arthavāda.*

Kumārila observes that if the eternal *Vēda* existed before the objects created, then there can be no connection between the *Vēda* and the created objects. Therefore the passages occuring in the *Vēda* which appear to describe the process of creation must be interpreted as praising up some injunctions of sacrifices etc.[53] Neither the deities connected with sacrifices are considered to be substantial theological entities. The deities are neither eternal nor omnipresent. They are mere names having a subsidiary dative functioning in the sacrifice.

With these anti-theistic arguments, Mīmāṃsa establishes the eternal and uncaused character of the world. As to the nature of constituents of world, Prabhākara and Kumārila differ widely. Prabhākara admits eight categories of the constituents of the word i.e., substance, quality, Action, generality, Inheritance, Potency or Force, similarity and number. Prabhākara thus admits the first five categories from the list of Vaiśēṣikas but rejects the sixth Vaiśēsika category of particularity[54]. Kumārila, on the other hand, rejects the addition of three categories made by Prabhākara i.e., potency *(śakti)*, similarity and number. He also rejects Inheritance as a seperate category. Thus he admits the four categories admitted by Śabara i.e., Substance, Quality, Action and Generality and adds Negation *(Abhāva)* as a distinct category.

While enumerating substance, Prabhākara admits nine substances — Earth, Water, Air, Fire, Ether, the Self or Soul, Mind, Time and Space. Kumārila accepts the nine substances of prabhākara and adds Darkness and Sound among substances.

Prabhākara enumerates the following qualities which inhere in the substances — colour, taste, smell, touch, dimension, individuality, conjunction, disjunction, priority, posteriority, pleasure, pain, desire, aversion and effort.[55]. Kumārila following Praśastapāda admits twenty four qualities — colour, smell, taste, touch, number, individuality, dimension, conjunction, disjunction, priority, posteriority, gravity, fluidity, viscidity, cognition, pleasure, pain, desire, aversion, effort, impression, tone, manifestation and potency.

Though the Mīmāṃsakas agree that the tangible objects are made up of atoms, they do not think this position as binding on them. It is enough for them to prove the world as real, irrespective of proof for the existence of Atoms. Prabhākara and Kumārila offer interesting arguments in support of their enumeration of their substances and qualities. They owe much to the Nyāya-Vaiśēṣika in this connection.

However, what interests us is their rational materialistic explanation of the world. They entertain no theistic explanation of creation. Their rejection of Idealism is impeccable. Their world-view cannot be viewed as Mechanistic Materialism for they also render a moral-world in which Man has an important function.

Man is viewed as a part of the world and his essence consists in actions and reaping the fruits thereof. Prabhākara defines self as the doer and enjoyer. Though their view of physical world is thoroughly rational, they do not accept reason in the moral world. The morality has its source not in the internal source of reason but in the external source of the scriptures.[56]

The object of all actions is considered to be heaven. It is interesting to note that Heaven is not necessarily other worldly. "The word *'Svarga'* or 'Heaven' is applied to that happiness which is totally free from all touch of pain, and which, as such, is desired by all men".[57] Pleasure is not just negation of pain but a positive quality which is sought after.

Though Mīmāṃsa originally admits 'Heaven' as the highest ideal, the later it Mīmāṃsakas certain feel pressure to explain the *Vēdānta* ideal of *Mōkṣa* or deliverance. *Mōkṣa* as an ideal demands cessation of worldly activities and exhibits a negative interest in the ritual actions. The Mīmāṃsakas, though accept the reality of the soul, they do not afford to entertain the ideal of *Mōkṣa* at the cost of absolute reality of the world. If world is real, then the bondage of soul in the world is real. If the bondage is real, it can never be removed. Removal of the bondage eternally can be attained only if the bondage is illusory as Advaitins hold. Once, the reality of the world and thus reality of the bondage is established, there cannot be any deliverence due to knowledge. Kumārila makes this point very clear: "Barring its negative character, there is no other ground for the eternality of Deliverence. And no negation can ever be the effect of any action, therefore Deliverence cannot be held to be the effect of knowledge".[58] However, Kumārila attempts to brings the concept of deliverance in line with his theory of action. What Kumārila understands by *Mōkṣa* is that it is negation of future births. It is not a state of bliss as Heaven. Heaven again, unlike *Mōkṣa*, is perishable. Hence, he contends that *Mōkṣa* can be attained by fruction of actions, by not undertaking *Kāmya Karmas*, by discharging *Nitya* and *Naimittika* duties and by avoiding sin through prohibited actions.[59]

Now, it is clear that Mīmāṃsa world-view is no less rational than any other philosophical system. It is important to see that Mīmāṃsa does not appeal to the scriptures to defend its rational world. It takes the challenge on the level of profound logical argumentation. Except in as much as Mīmāṃsa looks at the scriptures for explaining *Dharma*, Mīmāṃsa in no other aspect can be discredited as a philosophical system. Neither its veneration for the scriptures can be made a reason to include it in theology *(Trayi)*, as did Kautilya, because no other so called rational systems denied the scriptures (save Carvaka), whatever the reasons may be. Mīmāṃsa is not a mere system of exposition but a systematic rational philosophy, discussion of which is relevant even today.

Reference

1. Keith A.B., *The Karma Mīmāṃsa*, p.6.
2. Śabara is supposed to have lived in the first century B.C. Cf. Jha, ganganath, *Prabhākara school of Pūrva Mīmāṃsa*, P.7.
3. Mandana Miśra, in the later literature, is identified with Surēswara who was a desciple of Samkarācharya. He is also known as a pupil of Kūmarila though not for certain.
4. *Arthaśāstra* II. i. 1-7. the term 'Yōga' applies to Nyāya-Vaiśēsika as they believe in connunction *(yōga)* of atoms which makes the world. Cf. D. P. Chattopadhyaya, *What is Living and What is Dead in Indian Philosophy*, P.240 ff.
5. Indian wisdom, P.98. Vol. I.
6. *Mīmāṃsa Sūtra* I. i. 1.
7. *Ibid* I. i. 1.
8. *Ibid* I. i. 4.
9. Gotama, *Nyāya Sūtra* II. 1.69.
10. *Ibid*, 2. 14 ff.
11. Uddhyōtakāra, *Nyāya Vārttika*, II. 2. 14.
12. *Slōkavārttika*, eternality of words - 42., P. 416.
13. Vātsāyana, *Nyāya Sūtra Bhāṣya*, II. 2. 14.
14. *Ibid*.

15. Uddhyōtakāra, *Nyāya Vārttika*, II. 2. 18.
16. *Nyāya Sūtra* II. 2. 19.
17. *Mīmāṃsa Sūtra*, I. i. 18.
18. Cf. *Slōkavārttika*, on Eternality of words, 231-236, P. 449.
19. Cf. *Slōkavārttika*, V. 6. 15, P. 209.
20. *Slōkavārttika*, V. 6. 50-51, P. 214.
21. Cf. *Tattvasangraha* of Santa Raksita, XIX. 1488, P.741. Vol.II
22. *Slōkavārttika*, V. 6. 16. P. 209.
23. *Mīmāṃsa-Bhāṣya* on I. i. 5.
24. Sāntarakṣita, *Tattvasamgraha*, XIX. 1496-97, P. 745.
25. *Vaiśēsika Sūtra*, I. 1.3; II. 2.32; VI - i. 1., etc.
26. Cf. *Nyāya-Vārttika*, II. 1. 49.
27. Cf. *Gangānāth Jha, The Prabhākara* School of *Pūrva-Mīmāṃsa*. P. 65.
28. *Nyāya Sūtra* Cf. II. 1, 49-54.
29. Ibid. I. 1.7.
30. *Nyāya Bhāṣya*, I. 1.7.
31. *Slōkavārttika* I. 2.34 ff.
32. for the detailed explanation of doubtful and wrong cognitions by Prabhākara, Cf. *The Prabhākara School of Pūrva Mīmāṃsa* P. 28 ff.
33. Keith, A.B., *The Karma Mīmāṃsa*, P. 36.
34. *Mīmāṃsa Sūtra*, I.3. 24-29.
35. *Slōkavārttika* I. 1. 127-28; 49-50. P. 20; 7.
36. *Nyāya Sūtra* II. 1, 68.
37. Cf. Nyāya Sūtra II. 1. 59.
38. Cf. *Nyāya Bhāṣya*, II. 1. 58-59.
39. *Nyāya Vārttika Tātparya Tīka*, II 1. 59.
40. Cf. *Gangānāth Jha, The Prabhākara* School of *Pūrva Mīmāṃsa* P. 160.

41. Cf. *Slōkavārttika* I. 2. 197-98. P. 51.
42. Cf. *The Prabhākara school of Pūrva Mīmāṃsa*. P. 165.
43. *Slōkavārttika*, I. 2. 200. P. 51.
44. Ibid I. 2. 195-6. P. 50.
45. *Slōkavārttika*, Nirālambanavāda, 1-3, P. 119.
46. *Slōkavārttika*, Nirālambanavāda, 12-13, P. 120.
47. *Śabara Bhāṣya*, on I. 1.5. P. 12.
48. *Slōkavārttika*, Nirālambanavāda, 87-91, P. 133.
49. Ibid., 94-95.
50. *Slōkavārttika*, Nirālambanavāda, 6-7, P. 119-120.
51. *Slōkavārttika*, Sambandhākṣēpa-parihāravāda, P. 356-7.
52. Cf. Prakarans Panchika, P. 137 ff.
53. *Slōkavārttika*, Samandhākṣēpa-parihāravāda, 62, P. 358.
54. *Prakaraṇapañchika*, p. 110-111.
55. *Prakaraṇa Pañchika*, p. 151.
56. Cf. *Slōkavārttika*. I. 2. 243-249.
57. *Prakaraṇa Pañchika*, P. 102-3.
58. *Slōkavārttika*, Sambandhākṣēpa-pariha l ravāda, 107, P. 367.
59. Cf. Ibid. 110. P. 367.

6

Ethics of the *Bhagavad-Gīta*

Introduction

The *Bhagavad-Gīta* is one of the celebrated sacred works of Hindus. It consists of the spiritual teaching of Lord *Kṛṣṇa* to Arjuna and thus acquires the name *'Bhagavad-Gīta'* which means 'the songs of the Lord'. The *Gīta* comes to us as a part of Bhīṣma Parva of the *Mahābhārata*, one of the grand Indian epics. The *Gīta* is narrated by Samjaya to the blind king Dhṛtaraṣtra and it contains seven hundred verses spread over eighteen chapters or discourses. Not only by virtue of being a part of the *Mahābhārata,* but also by its independent character, the *Gīta* is considered as an important peace of *Smṛti* literature. Keeping in view the significance of spiritual and moral teaching in it, the *Gīta* can be described as the heart of the epic. As a *Smṛti*, the *Gīta* is supposed to contain the essence of *Vēdic* wisdom. The *Gīta* is often considered as an *Upaniṣad* by itself.

The pronounced theism in the *Gīta* makes it a foundational text for Hindu religion in general and Vaiṣṇava sect in particular. However, it enjoys popular esteem not only for its theistic inclinations but also for its practical ethical purport. The ethical teaching of the *Gīta* decisively moulded the moral consciousness of Hindus over the ages. Even today, the *Gīta* is recited with utmost reverence in religious gatherings and one auspicious occasions.

The striking feature of the *Gīta* is the way it unified different methods of spiritual development in to a profound ethical vision. This ethical vision is backed up by a host of philosophical ideas borrowed from the speculations of Self, current in the *Upaniṣadic* period, and the theory of *guṇas* which later came down to us as the classical Sāmkhya system. These philosophical ideas are integrated with the theistic doctrines of Bhāgavata tradition which treats *Vāsudēva* or *Kṛṣṇa* as the Lord. The synthesis of philosophical and theistic doctrines makes one hesitant to call the *Gīta* a philosophical treatise. In fact, the *Gīta* is more a treatise on ethics than a serious philosophical text. As is the case with classical Indian *Smṛtis*, the religion is inseparable from the ethical thought in the *Gīta*. It lays more emphasis on moral teaching than on philosophical debates. One may find the philosophical ideas in the *Gīta* loosely connected but the moral teaching of it is nevertheless simple, direct and practical.

The inadequate theoretical rigour in the text can easily be understood in the light of the fact that it belongs to pre-*sūtra* period when the classical systems of philosophy were yet to be crystallized. The absence of systematic arrangement of topics, definition, classification, division and sub-division in the *Gīta* amply speaks of its antiquity to the *Sūtra* literature of various philosophical schools. In this regard the *Gīta*, like the *Upaniṣads,* lacks systematic exposition of ideas. It also lacks precision in the use of words. Many of the words are used in more than one sense and these words have not acquired the strict technical sense as in the *Sūtra* literature. The *Gīta* also comes out with incommensurable statements as they are made in different contexts. All these points make it evident that the *Gīta* dates far prior to the *Sūtra* period.

Though it is very difficult to be precise about its date, we have enough grounds to believe that the *Gīta* belongs to later *Upaniṣadic* or early post-*Upaniṣadic* period. This view is supported by some of the internal and external evidences.

The language of the *Gīta* is very lucid and simple. Frequent use of compounds and complex expression, which characterize the later classical Sānskrit literature, are absent in it. The similes used in the *Gīta* are also found in some of the early *Upaniṣads*. For example, the simile of ***lotus leaf untainted by water***[1] and the description of ***corporeal body as nine-gated city***[2] also occur in *Chāndōgya, Praśna* and *Śvētasvatara Upaniṣads*.

Further the *Gīta* always refers to the *Vēda* as threefold. It distinctly names *Ṛk, Yajus* and *Sāman* but does not mention *Atharva Vēda.*[3] The passage which refers to the three *Vēdas* could not possibly avoid *Atharva Vēda* if it existed because the passage in question is part of the description of the Lord's divine manifestations. Hence, in all probability, by the time the *Gīta* was composed, *Atharva* was yet to be recognised as a *Vēda*. What is more interesting is that from the *Gīta's* references to the *Vēda*, we get an impression that the *Gīta* does not recognize even the *Upaniṣads* as a part of the *Vēda*. The *Gīta*, whenever it concerns the teaching of the *Vēdas*, says that the *Vēdas* deal only with sacrifices and pleasures thereof.[4] The *Vēdas* are treated only as repositories of sacrificial injunctions.

This does not mean that the *Gīta* is not aware of *Upaniṣadic* thought. In fact, the *Gīta* does not know the *Upaniṣ ads* as a part of the *Vēda*. The *Gīta* recognizes the *Upaniṣadic* theory of soul as 'Science of the Self' *(Ādhyātma Vidya)* is mentioned as the Chief of the Sciences. The Lord identifies himself with the threefold *Vēda* and 'the science of the soul' separately.[5] This shows that the two i.e., the triple *Vēda* and science of the soul are conceived as distinct.

In the *Upaniṣads*, we find a declining interest towards ritualistic practices. Knowledge of the soul is deemed to be superior to the practice of rituals. While the *Brāhmaṇas* conceived Heaven *(svarga)* as the highest goal, the *Upaniṣadic* thought aims at self-realization and internal peace. The change in the conception of *summum bonum* resulted in looking down upon material sacrifices. The domination of theoretical philosophical speculations over the ritualistic practice is evident in *Chāndōgya* and *Mundaka Upaniṣads*.[6]

The *Gīta* shares the same attitude towards the ritualistic practice and conceives knowledge of the soul as superior to ritualism. The *Vēda* which prescribes specific acts for specific purposes is said to be of no use for an enlightened brāhmaṇa.[7] Here, the *Vēda* is compared to a small reservoir of water whereas the knowledge of the soul is described as all flooding water. The *Gīta* also suggests indifference to the *Vēda*.[8] Here, the point to be noted is that by the word 'the *Vēda*', both the *Gīta* and *Upaniṣads* mean 'repository of sacrificial commands'.

However, the claim that the *Gīta* belongs to a period close to the *Upaniṣads* might be objected on the ground that it alludes to 'Vēdānta' and *'Brahma Sūtra'*.[9] But on a closer examination, the objection does not make much impact. It is true, for us 'Vēdānta' means *the Upaniṣads* but it need not be so for the *Gīta*. In fact, as Telang suggests, "...in the passage referred to in Chapter XV, the word Vēdānta probably signifies the *Araṇyakas*, which may be regarded as marking the beginning of the epoch, which the composition of *Upaniṣads* brought to its close".[10] It might be the *Araṇyakas* rather than the *Upaniṣads* which are mentioned as 'Vēdānta'.

Even the reference to *'Brahma Sūtras'* cannot be taken as referring to the *Vēdānta Sūtras* which are also known as

Brahma *Sūtras*. As Prof. S.N. Dasgupta rightly observes, "Since there is no other consideration which might lead us to think that the *Gīta* was written after the *Brahma Sūtras*, the verse *'Brahma Sūtra padaischaiva hetamadbhir vinischitah'* (XIII 4) has to be either treated as an interpolation or interpreted differently".[11] Samkarāchārya, commenting on the passage, takes the phrase *'brahma sūtra padaischaiva'* to mean suggestive words about *Brahman*.[12] Hence the *Gīta*'s use of the words 'Vēdānta' and *Brahma Sūtra* need not be overemphasized. On the other hand, *Vēdānta Sūtras* mention the *Gīta* as an older *Smṛti* and refers to some of the ideas of the *Gīta*.[13]

The *Gīta* must be much earlier to *Āpastamba Dharma Sūtras*, which clearly indicate their post-*Upaniṣadic* origin. Though Manu is referred to in the *Gīta,* he is not identified as the law-giver.[14] The description of caste duties in the *Gīta* are different from that in *Manu Smṛti* and *Āpastamba Dharma Sūtras,* in as much as the *Gīta* enumerates the virtues of serenity, self-restraint, austeriy, purity, forgiveness, uprightness, knowledge, wisdom and faith as the duties of *Brāhmaṇas*.[15] In Āpastamba and Manu we find, on the other hand, the duties of study, instruction, sacrificing, officiating sacrifices, making gifts and accepting gifts. The *Gīta* enumerates the specific qualities to be adhered by a *Brāhmaṇa* while the law-books give the social privileges as the duties. Hence, the legal codes exhibit an advanced stage of social administration. Again, *Sama Vēda* occupies the place of honour in the *Gīta* whereas the legal codes ill treat and prohibit the recitation of the hymns of *Sama Vēda* where other hymns are recited.[16] This development shows that the *Gīta* is much earlier to the legal codes.

We find a number of parallel verses to those of the *Gīta* in the *Upaniṣads*. *Upaniṣads* like *Īśa, Mundaka* and *Kathaka* contain some of the *Gīta* passages. It is more likely that both *Gīta* and the *Upaniṣads* borrowed those passages from a common tradition. The *Vēdic* literature also refers to Lord *Kṛṣṇa*, son of *Dēvaki* who taught the *Gīta* to Arjuna. *Ṛg Vēda* refers to *Kṛṣṇa* as a sage, descendent of *Angīras.*[17] The *Chāndōgya Upaniṣad* identifies *Kṛṣṇa*, son of *Dēvaki*, as a pupil of *Ghōra Angīras.*[18] The *Ghata jātaka* also speaks of *Kṛṣṇa* or *Vāsudēva* as son of *Dēvaki*. The *Mahābhārata* describes *Kṛṣṇa* as *Vāsudēva*, *Sātvata* and as the chief of *Vṛṣṇa*. *Vṛṣṇa* is the race of Yādavas of which *Sātvata* is a tribe.[19] The *Gīta* also mentions *Kṛṣṇa* as *Vārṣnēya*. In the *Gīta* Lord *Kṛṣṇa* identifies himself as *Vāsudēva* of *Vṛṣnis.*[20]

As far as the religious aspect of the *Gīta* is concerned, it is closely connected with the *Sātvata* faith of the Yādavas, who worshipped Lord *Vāsudēva* with their ritual practices. This *Sātvata* faith has its source in the *Bhāgavata* tradition of Pañcha-rātra. The Chief doctrine of the religious sect is adoration of Lord *Hari* or *Vāsudēva* according to some specific rites of worship without any desire for gains. This is also called *ekāntin* faith. The Pañcha-rātra tradition is known for its image worship and the *Gīta* clearly refers to the image worship with flowers, leaves, water etc.[21] Hence, the *Gīta* is probably one of the earliest works of *Bhāgavata* tradition which is founded on the worship of *Vāsudēva* as the Supreme Lord.

As to the question whether the *Gīta* is a part of the *Mahābhārata*, there appears to be some ambiguity among scholars. Such a long ethical discussion in the midst of a battle field appears to be an arbitrary inclusion and gives rise to a doubt concerning its genuinity. In the *Gīta*, though Kapila is mentioned, the theory of *Prakṛti* and *guṇas* is not attributed to him. Though the words 'Sāmkhya and Yōga' are used, they do not denote the classical systems which came down to us with these names. However, in the *Mahābhārata*, Sāmkhya often means Kapila's system. Again, nowhere in the *Gīta* do we find Vaiṣṇavism, whereas the *Mahābhārata* makes a definite reference to it as a religious sect. The *Mahābhārata* is quite aware of Manu as a law-giver, while the *Gīta* hardly acknowledges it.

Given the advanced social and ethical views expressed in the *Mahābhārata,* we are forced to presume that the *Gīta* was composed earlier than the epic. According to Prof. S.N. Dasgupta, "the *Gīta* may have been a work of the *Bhāgavata* School written long before the composition of the *Mahābhārata,* and may have been written on the basis of the Bhārata legend, on which the *Mahābhārata* was based. It is not improbable that the *Gīta* which summarised the older teaching of the *Bhāgavata* School, was incorporated into the *Mahābhārata*, during one of its revisions, by reason of the sacredness that it had acquired at that time".[22] Though *Mahābhārata* has certainly undergone revisions, the *Gīta* appears to have been hardly tampered with. We do not find any alternative readings of the *Gīta* and the *Gīta* is preserved as a holy religious piece.

The authorship of the *Gīta* is traditionally attributed to Vyāsa, the author of the epic. However, as we have seen, the *Gīta* which existed as a *Smṛti* might have been incorporated into the epic at a later date. So, the *Gīta* may have been composed by the Scholars of *Bhāgavata* School and was handed down as a *Smṛti* in Hindu tradition. The date of the *Gīta*, though it leads to unending chronological disputes, could be fairly ascertained as 7th century B.C. which roughly corresponds to the later *Upaniṣadic* period.

A Brief Note on the *Gīta* Literature

There are numerous commentaries on the *Gīta* by various distinguished scholars with different philosophical and religious affiliations. The lack of philosophical rigour in the text gave room for these commentators either to interpret its doctrines as supporting their own systems or to graft their own doctrines on the *Gīta*. This resulted in a variety of interpretations, sometimes amazingly incommensurable, each claiming fidelity to the original teaching of the *Gīta*. However, the *Gīta* still stands as an independent text, inspiring even modern thinkers, as a source of valuable ethical and spiritual precepts.

The foremost among the commentators is Śamkarāchārya of Advaita School, whose commentary is called *Bhagavad-Gīta Bhāṣya*. Among the other commentators Rāmānujachārya, Sridhara, Mādhavācharya, Nīlakanta are the most prominent, while among the modern scholars Tilak and Aurobindo are considered to be the most prolific. Śamkara's commentary was not the first but the earliest commentary available. Śamkara himself refers to the existence of earlier commentaries in his *Bhāṣya*.[23] Ānandagiri, one of the commentators on Śamkara's *Bhāṣya*, suggests that Śamkara refers to Bōdhayana, the *Vṛttikāra* of *Brahma Sūtras* who also might have written a *Vṛtti* on the *Gīta*. However, while we are not certain about the predecessors of Śamkara, we are nevertheless certain that Śamkara was not the first to comment on the *Gīta*. There are two commentators on Śamkara's *Bhāṣya* - Rāmānanda and Ānandagiri. Ānandagiri's work is called *Bhagavad-Gīta Bhāṣya Vivaraṇa* and Rāmānanda's work is known as *Bhagavad-Gīta Bhāṣya Vyākhya*.

Śamkara's *Bhāṣya* ascribes a thorough going Vēdantic view to the *Gīta* and attempts to explain its doctrines in the light of *Vēdantic* doctrines. The main thesis of Śamkara's commentary is that works and knowledge cannot be combined for they are mutually incompatible as the works presuppose 'agency and multiplicity' while knowledge denies agency and teaches unity'.[24] Knowledge of ultimate reality leads to natural cessation of all activity. The works have only marginal significance as they lead to purification of mind *(sattvaśuddhi)* and the final liberation necessarily involves renunciation. According to Śamkara, "the aim of this famous *Gīta Śastra* is, briefly, the supreme Bliss, a complete cessation of *Samsāra* or transmigratory life and its cause. This accrues from that Religion (Dharma) which consists in steady devotion to the knowledge of the Self, preceded by renunciation of all works..."[25]

Śamkara understands that injunctions of the *Vēdas* and *Smṛtis* are only meant for the ignorant but not for the wise.[26] The wise who realize the ultimate redity need not obey those injunctions. The non-performance of obligatory duties, by a samnyāsin does not accrue sin, for nothing positive results from a mere negation. The non-performance of scriptural duties, thus, cannot result in a positive sin. On this point, Rāmānuja holds a diametrically opposite view to that of Śamkara.

Rāmānuja interprets the *Gīta* on Viśiṣṭādvaita lines and follows the view of his preceptor Yāmunāchārya whose brief work on the *Gīta* is known as *Gītārtha Samgraha*. Yāmuna and Rāmānuja conceive devotion *(bhakti)* as the highest ideal preached by the *Gīta*. Rāmānuja asserts that the path of action *(Karma Yōga)* is superior to the path of knowledge *(Jñāna Yōga)* for, he thinks, the former naturally leads to and includes the latter. No one can transgress the allotted duties, even one who pursues the path of knowledge.

So, Rāmānuja, contrary to Śamkara, makes the scriptural duties imperative even to a man of wisdom. According to Rāmānuja, the path of knowledge cannot itself lead to liberation and it can be attained only through observing obligatory and occassional duties *(nitya-naimittika)* with sincere devotion to God. Hence, he subordinates both knowledge and action to devotion and highlights the theistic aspect of the *Gīta*.

Madhvāchārya in his *Gīta-Bhāṣya* explains the ontological superiority and excellence of God over everything. Everything follows the will of God and hence, there is no wisdom in our attachment to the external objects. Mādhva's theory sounds like a kind of fatalism with God as the source. Madhva also differs from Śamkara with reference to ontological Monism. Madhva holds that God is ontologically and substantially different from his creation.

The later commentators follow either Śamkara or Rāmānuja in their exposition of the *Gīta's* ideas, and occassionally differ as to the minor details. Tilak, the modern commentator, emphasizes that the *Gīta* essentially preaches action rather than renunciation. Aurobindo conceives the divine action, preached by the *Gīta*, as the central teaching of the text. Irrespective of their theoretical differences, all the commentators unanimously accept that the *Gīta*, aims at spiritually elevated moral conduct of men and that its teaching is essentially ethical.

Philosophy of War

The holy dialogue of the *Gīta* itself is peculiar when viewed from the ethical point of view, It is immensely interesting. The *Gīta* takes place on the battle field, amidst the two great armies of Kauravas and Pāndavas. The war is remembered as the greatest legend in India. The best of warriors of the time participated in the war. The whole *Kṣatriya* class itself appears to have got ready for the doom. The beginning of such a grand war gave rise to the holy dialogue recorded in the *Gīta*.

Arjuna, the chief warrior among the Pāndavas asked his Charioteer Lord *Kṛṣṇa* to place the chariot in the midst of the two warring armies. Then he was depressed by the sight of the warriors who are all his friends, teachers and relatives whom he had to fight. Arjuna was overcome by grief thinking that he had to kill them all and therefore refuses to fight. What is highly significant is that the reasons for which Arjuna wants to withdraw from war are ethical rather than physical or psychological. It is very important to note the reasons given by Arjuna for his grief and reluctance to fight.

Arjuna supposes that the wealth, dominion and pleasures are sought for the sake of friends, relatives and Kinsmen. It being the case, he does not see any point in killing them for the sake of dominion or wealth. He questions *Kṛṣṇa*: 'how can we be happy, O Mādhava, after slaying our own people?'[27] This reminds us of the spirit of *Ṛg Vēdic* people who sought all the dominion, wealth, progeny and welfare for the sake of the community as a whole comprising of their kinsmen, relatives and friends. The *Ṛg Vēdic* hymns exhibit a similar spirit of attachment for the collective communal life which is expressed by Arjuna. Śamkara rightly explains that the cause of Arjunas despondency is his feeling that 'I am theirs and they are mine.'[28] It has to be noted here that it is an intra-tribal war in which both the warring factions belong to the tribe. This war is against the fundamental principle of tribal unity.

Further, Arjuna supplements the cause of his despondency saying that extinction of families in the war results in disappearance of the immemorial family rites, impiety among women and intermingling of castes.[29] Hence, Arjuna opposes war on the grounds of community spirit on the one hand and its social consequences on the other.

Here, we find the seeds of reflective morality which advances a critique of existing system based on the grounds of earlier *Ṛg-Vēdic* spirit of life and war. This critical reflection of Arjuna naturally makes him think that the war is unwarranted and evil producing. What is remarkable about the reflection is that it is truly ethical in nature.

Lord *Kṛṣṇa* explains Arjuna that his grief is baseless and unbecoming of warrior. He begins with a statement that the wise grieve neither for the living nor for the dead.[30] He justifies the war and killing people by referring to the wisdom which He names 'Sāmkhya' and the art of discharging duties which He calls *'Yōga'*.

The Wisdom of Sāmkhya is the realization that soul is different from body, and is eternal and imperishable and passes through different perishable bodies; that all experience is transitory and does not affect the soul; and that soul is neither the agent nor the object of action.[31] From this doctrine, the Lord deduces the justification for war, explaining that the indestructible soul neither slays nor is slain and that the bodies which are slain anyway have an end.[32] Hence, one need not grieve either for the soul, because it is indestructable, or for the body, because it is anyway destructable. The Lord also suggests that if one thinks the soul to be impermanent and perishable with the body, even then there is no reason for grief, because whatever born is certain to perish.[33] In both the cases i.e., whether the soul is taken to be eternal or otherwise, there is no point in grieving. With this the Lord shows Arjuna's despondency as baseless. He justifies killing in the war with reference to the permanence of the soul in everyone's body which can never be killed. Therefore Arjuna should not grieve for any creature.[34]

The Sāmkhya wisdom enlightens one to discharge one's bounden duty without any regard for pain or pleasure which arises from it. Hence, the Lord preaches Arjuna to discharge his lawful duty, as a warrior, and to take part in the war. The Lord also shows the consequences, if Arjuna refuses to perform his own duty. If Arjuna fails at discharging his bounden duty as a *Kṣatriya*, he not only incurs sin but also contempt of other warriors and shame.[35] The Lord finally makes the point that there is no loss in the war: 'if you win you will enjoy the earth (dominion) and if you lose your life in the battle, you will enjoy the heaven'.

After teaching the wisdom of Sāmkhya, the Lord teachers Arjuna what *Yōga* is. *Yōga* is defined as the equanimity of mind.[36] *Yōga* is the only way to peace and is described as the *Brahmic* state.[37] The precondition for *Yōga* is subjugation of passions and discharging duties without an eye for their fruits. *Yōga* is attained through withdrawing senses from the attachment of their objects, casting off desires, and transcending the pairs of extremes. *Yōga* thus consists in the discharge of one's duty with control over senses, passions and desires. *Yōga*, in brief, is the art of performing actions.[38]

Though Sāmkhya and *Yōga* appear to be two different paths, on a closer look they both culminate in passion-free moral attitude towards the world. Hence, Sāmkhya and *Yōga* form the theoretical and practical aspects of the same teaching. They both aim at internal peace through equanimity of mind. The *Gīta* suggests, through Sāmkhya and *Yōga*, internal peace as the remedy for external turbulences.

The gist of the whole discussion is that the *Gīta* addresses itself to an ethical problem and thus it is more an ethical treatise than anything else. Arjuna's problem and the Lord's solution to it pertain to the ethical conduct of man in general and moral dilemma concerning war in particular. The ethical solution given by the Lord chiefly consists in rising above the pretty material interests and acting with an unprejudiced mind devoid of all attachments.

Here, we see the germs of reflective morality taking the place of objective ritualism. The *Gīta* exhibits a new spirit of looking at problems of life, both social and individual. The Society, witnessing frequent wars and unreflective ritualism, was in search of ideals of peace and meaningful moral life. The *Gīta*, as an attempt towards these ideals, advances a world-view which seeks to give rise to a better ethical understanding of man and his conduct.

The World-View

The *Gīta*'s world-view is predominantly Sāmkhyan. It incorporates the doctrines of *Puruṣa, Prakṛti* and its evolutes as its cardinal points. The *Gīta* explicitly commits itself to

Satkāryavāda by saying that what exists cannot perish and what does not exist cannot come into being.[39] The *Gīta* accepts *Prakṛti* and *Puruṣa* i.e., matter and spirit as the two ontological categories which cause the world. However, the *Gīta* conceives a supernatural divine entity called God who is above the matter and spirit. He is called *Puruṣōttama* or the Supreme Self who possesses matter and spirit as His two-fold nature. The two ontological categories are viewed as integral to the super natural personality of God. God, through His two-fold nature *prakṛti* i.e., Matter and Spirit, produces the world.

God places His germ in *Prakṛti*, which is described as His womb, and this fertilization by God results in the origin of living beings.[40] *Prakṛti*, thus fertilized, gives rise to the three characteristic qualities or dynamic tendencies called — Sattva, Rajas and Tamas. These *guṇas* produce all other forms. They pervade all material manifestations of *Prakṛti* and all existences including the gods in the heaven.[41] *Prakṛti,* thus under the supervision of God, produces all moving and unmoving world.[42]

This divine fertilization is nothing but figurative description of the process in which matter and spirit come together. God is held responsible for the contact between spirit and matter, which are treated as His twofold nature. Through the introduction of God, the *Gīta* overcomes the difficulty of explaining how spirit and matter come together to form an individual entity. The two-fold nature of God i.e., *Puruṣa* and *Prakṛti* are held to be eternal and beginningless entities which together produce the world.[43] *Prakṛti* is the cause of all effects, instruments and agency while *Puruṣa* is the cause which holds together all experience of pleasure and pain.[44] *Puruṣa* when seated in *Prakṛti* i.e., as an individual soul in a corporeal body, experiences the qualities of *Prakṛti* and through his attachment to those qualities undergoes transmigration and rebirth.[45]

Puruṣa, which is called the higher nature of God, is the life principle *(Jīvabhūta)* of the universe. *Prakṛti*, the lower nature of God, constitutes the eight-fold categories of Earth, Water, Fire, Air, Ether, Thought *(manas)*, Intellect *(budhi)* and Egoism.[46] Among these categories, mind *(manas)* is higher to senses. Intellect *(buddhi)* is higher to *manas*, and Ego is higher to intellect.

The most important feature of this doctrine is that it makes the Sāmkhya concepts of *Prakṛti* and *Puruṣa* as integrally belonging to the nature of God. Though a distinction is maintained between matter and spirit, the world is said to have a unitary source in God, because matter and spirit form the super natural personality of God.[47] The reality of matter is unambiguously or clearly accepted, though as God's nature. *Prakṛti* is said to be the female element and God is viewed as the father with reference to the world.[48]

Commenting on this, Śamkara brings in the concept of *Māya* in between God and *Prakṛti*. In order to bring the metaphysics of the *Gīta* in line with that of Vēdānta, Śamkara introduces *Māya* as the illusion which creates the world. According to Śamkara the supreme Self, which is referred to as God in the *Gīta,* alone is real as the cause of the world and the world as an effect is unreal or illusory. The Self is the only reality without a second. The *guṇas* are only forms of avidya or nescience.[49] *Prakṛti* is the *Māya* made up of three *guṇas*. Śamkara thus reduces *Prakṛti* to illusory creation or *Māya*.

However, the *Gīta* does not view the world as an illusion and nowhere does it appear to think on those lines. For the *Gīta*, people live in a real world and perform real actions. The multiplicity of objects is not an appearance though it has its source in the Supreme spirit. The world is not an illusion but an emanation from the Supreme Self. Though the word *'Māya'* occurs in the *Gīta,*[50] it does not correspond to the illusory appearance of the world, as in Vēdānta, but means the unpentratable power of the God. This diffusive power consists of *guṇas* because, due to the operation of *guṇas* on mind, man cannot know God.[51] *Prakṛti* being part of God's nature, the diffusive power of *guṇas* also belong to God. But this does not mean *Prakṛti* and *guṇas* are not real. The only delude a person by covering his wisdom.

Now, coming to the *Gīta*'s conception of an individual, it treats an individual as the combination of the mind-body complex is called *Kṣētra* and the individual Self is called *Kṣētrajña*, or the knower of *Kṣētra*. *Kṣētra* consists of the five great elements (Earth, Water etc.,) Egoism, Intellect, the Unmanifest, Mind, Senses (cognitive and conative), five objects of senses (like sound, smell etc.). The modifications of *Kṣētra* are desire, aversion, pleasure, pain, body, consciousness *(cētana)* and courage.[52] *Kṣētra* thus corresponds to the constituent categories of mind-body complex as well as all their modifications as forms of experience. What is remarkable about this description of *Kṣētra* is that even consciousness, which is generally attributed to the Self, is also part of the *Kṣētra*.

Kṣētrajña is the individual Self which illumines the body as the sun illumines the world.[53] He is the enjoyer of *guṇas* and experiences all forms of *guṇas* through the body and senses. He is a passive on-looker and all activity belongs to *guṇas*. *Kṣētrajña* is said to be a ray of the Supreme Self or God. God is the *Kṣētrajña* in all bodies.[54] Hence, God is the higher *Puruṣ a* or *Paramātman* and the individual Self is nothing but a ray or reflection of the Supreme Self. God, as the higher *Puruṣa*, is present in the heart of everyone.[55]

Hence, the presence of *Kṣētrajña* implies the presence of God as the higher Self in the body. However, the higher *Puruṣa* is unattached to the *guṇas* and their forms while the lower *Puruṣa* or the individual Self is affected by them. It is this divine presence or the presence of higher *Puruṣa* in the individual accounts for moral elevation and spiritual development. While the union with this Patamatan stands as the positive moral ideal for the individual Self, detachment from the influence of *guṇas* forms the negative aspect of the moral ideal. The moral progress of an individual consists in elevation of the Self by the Self.[56] The *Gīta* prescribes various methods for self-elevation i.e., wisdom, medition, performing works, worship etc., These methods of union with the higher Self are dealt with by different discourses in the *Gīta*. The *Gīta* calls for raising above the *guṇas* through sense-control and seeking the higher Self which is the ultimate goal of morally commendable life.

The *Gīta* also speaks of *Brahman* as the essence of God. *Brahman* is the undivided and unmanifest essence of God. God is the abode of the undifferentiated ultimate which is described as the immortal, the immutable, the eternal *dharma* and the unfailing bliss.[57] Unlike Vēdānta, the *Gīta* does not describe *Brahman* as pure consciousness. *Brahman* is primarily seen as the differenceless unmanifest essence of God. The word '*Brahman*' is also used sometimes synonymous to God and at places, it is used to denote the *Vēdas*.[58]

The *guṇas* are the dynamic tendencies which act as a downward pull and make the Self indulge in sense-objects. They inevitably lead to action and make an individual helpless in this regard. However, the scope for human exertion lies in man's capacity to be unattached to the fruits of action and desire thereof. Man can participate in the world of affairs with an equanimous mind. He can see things right even while being engaged in them. In fact, the central teaching of the *Gīta* consists in this. We will discuss in a later section various ways prescribed by the *Gīta* to attain the state of perfect moral vision.

The *Gīta*'s world-view, in many respects, resembles that of Kapila's Sāmkhya. However, it differs from the latter on certain important points. Though *Gīta* accepts *Satkāryavāda*, it differs from Sāmkhya proper with regard to the doctrine of creation. While Sāmkhya conceives the world as a product of self-transforming evolution of *Prakṛti*, the *Gīta* regards it as a creation. This creation has its source in the ultimate principle called God. Again, while in Sāmkhya *Prakṛti* is conceived as an independent ontological principle, the *Gīta* treats *Prakṛti* primarily as a part of God's nature. Even though *Prakṛti* is referred to as a beginningless entity, it is made subservient to God and functionally dependent on him. The *guṇas* are said to be produced from *Prakṛti* as a result of God's fertilization or impregnation while in Sāmkhya the *guṇas* verily constitute *Prakṛti*. The *Gīta* does not talk about the state of existence of *Prakṛti*, before such impregnation. *'Avyakta'* is used to mean 'unknowable' and 'unmanifest' and God is said to be *Avyaktam. Avyakta* is also spoken of as different from God from whom all manifest world comes.[59] Hence, two *Avyaktas* are referred to, the other being imperishable *Avyakta.*[60] However, it is not clear whether the inferior *Avyakta* corresponds to the pre-evolutionary state of *Prakṛti*, because nowhere it is mentioned as pertaining to *Prakṛti*. The *Gīta* lacks precision in relating various aspects of God i.e., *Brahman, Prakṛti, Avyakta*, categories, and *Puruṣa*. However, we find an attempt in the *Gīta* to present a world-view in terms of Sāmkhya principles however loosely connected. As Prof. S.N. Dasgupta rightly comments, "it is easy to notice here the beginnings of a system of thought which in the hands of other thinkers might well be developed into the traditional Sāmkhya philosophy".[61]

The *Gīta* also records some of the traditional views concerning the world. The worldly life is figuratively described as the indestructable Banyan *(Asvattha)* tree having its roots above and branches below.[62] The *guṇas* are described as its branches, sense objects as its buds, *Vēdic* hymns as its leaves and actions as its roots. This figurative tree can be cut at its root by dispassion. The idea of *Asvattha* tree also appears in *Katha Upaniṣad*[63] and in some of the *Purāṇas*.

Theory of Action

Given the *Satkāryavāda* and the conception of the material world as a modification of *Prakṛti* and *guṇas*, the *Gīta* pays special attention to the analysis of human action in view of centrality of this to its ethical vision. Probably, the *Gīta* is the first text which endeavours a systematic exposition of human action. It presents a strictly materialistic analysis of action and explains it in terms of materialistic *guṇas*. Action is primarily viewed as a function of *guṇas* acting upon *guṇas*.[64] The objects of senses, the senses, the impulse for action and the body, which stands as locus for action, are all conditioned by *guṇas*, and the action is nothing but a product of *guṇas* and is characterized by them.

The mechanism of action consists in the function of five elements or factors. They are the substratum *(adhiṣṭānam)*, the agent *(karta)*, the instruments *(karaṇam)*, the movement *(chēṣta)* and unseen forces *(daivam)*.[65] All actions have these five constituent elements.

Kṣētra is the substratum of action. The body which is the abode of senses, mind and intellect acts as the locus of action. The second factor i.e., the agent needs a brief discussion. What constitutes the agent has to be carefully analysed. The *Gīta* time and again mentions that Self is not the agent. This is a queer observation because the agency, in all most all the systems of philosophy, is generally attributed to the Self. But the *Gīta* attributes agency to *Prakṛti* than to Self. It clearly states that the right understanding of action lies in the realization that it is *Prakṛti* alone that acts and not the Self.[66] Having no beginning and no qualities, the supreme Self, though dwelling in the body neither acts nor is tainted.[67] As the all-pervading *akasa* is, from its subtlety, never soiled, so the Self seated in the body is not soiled.[68]

Those who think 'I am doing', I am acting are supposed to be deluded. They are attributing the agency to Self while

Prakṛti alone is acting. A wise man rightly sees that all actions are done by *guṇas* and realizes the Self to be above these *guṇas*,[69] while the deluded suppose the Self to be the agent. Now arises the question — if *guṇas* are the real agent in action, what is the role of the Self in action? The answer is clear — the Self is just an on-looker. The Self sustains and illumines the senses and other categories of *Kṣētra* indifferently. The Self on its own does not lead to action. The impulse for action, volition and deliberation are subscribed by *guṇas*. As we have already noted, even consciousness is attributed to *Kṣētra* and thus volition also belongs to *Kṣētra* and not to the Self. *Guṇas* make the passive Self to take up action and experience the fruits thereof. It is *svabhāva* or disposition, which is determined by *guṇas* that leads to action. While the Self is unconcerned with action, *guṇas* make the Self bound to action. The Self, being devoid of qualities, cannot act on its own except making the senses and other categories function. The Self is described as the spectator, permitter, supporter and enjoyer of the action but not as the agent of action.[70] The Self does not instigate actions nor does it tend towards fruits of those actions. The Self stands as the enjoyer or experiences only in relation to the body. Though it experiences the outcome of actions, it does not stand in need of them. It only makes pain and pleasure possible and holds together all experience. It is explicitly said that *Prakṛti* is the cause of effects, instruments and agency *(Kārya kāraṇa karthṛtva hētu)*, while the soul is the cause of experiencing pleasure and pain which accrue from an action.[71] Hence, the place of Self in the texture of action is that of a passive enjoyer, rather than an active agent.

Among the *guṇas*, which are together held to be the agent, it is *Rajas* which is mainly responsible for action and attachment. *Rajas* is the source of thirst, passion, attachment.[72] However, the existence of *guṇas*, on the whole, makes action indispensable. The *guṇas* characterize the individual's subjective disposition which is called *svabhāva*. Action follows the *svabhāva*, or naturally flows from *svabhāva*. In this way, *guṇas* manifest through *svabhāva*. In terms of the *guṇas* that predominate an individuals *svabhāva*, agents are divided into three types — *Sāttvic, Rājasic* and *Tāmasic*. When an individual's *svabhāva* is characterized by non-attachment, non-egoism, firmness, vigour, and indifference to success and failure, the agent is *Sāttvic*. *Rajasic* agent is passionate, aspirant for fruits of action, greedy, cruel, impure and subject to joy and sorrow. *Tāmasic* agent is one who is unsteady, vulgar, unbending, deceptive, indolent, desponding and procrastinating.[73] Hence, the agent is primarity determined and characterized by *guṇas*.

'Karaṇa' corresponds to various instruments and implements which are used to carry on the intended action. Śamkara takes it to mean various sense-organs. Sense-organs by perceiving their respective sense-objects, discharge the function of instruments. *'Cēṣṭa'* corresponds to overt movement on the part of the agent and includes the life functions and biomotor activities of the body which make the movement possible.

Coming to the last factor i.e., *daiva*, there appears some ambiguity among commentators and scholars. Śamkara suggests that this factor corresponds to the gods like *Āditya* who aid the eye and other organs discharge their functions.[74] Following Śamkara, Mr. Telang translates *'daiva'* as deities.[75] Allusion to the deities presiding over sense-organs is found in *Aitarēya, Praśna* and *Mundaka Upaniṣads*. However, this notion of deities forming a factor in human action appears to be unacceptable, because, nowhere else in the *Gīta* do we find such idea. Nowhere deities are said to have any control over human action in any manner. Moreover, in such case, deities should be included in the instrumental cause along with the senses but need not be mentioned as a separate factor. Prof. S.N. Dasgupta understands *'daiva'* to mean 'unknown objective causal elements' or 'all-controlling power of God'.[76] The first suggestion is more probable than the alternative. The *Gīta* explicitly states that God does not create agency or objects for the world. Nor does He unite fruits with action.[77] Hence, *'daivam'* might mean uncontrollable external contingencies than the power of God.

'Daiva' in the sense of destiny or uncontrollable external force operating on the action is found in *Yōgavāśiṣṭa*. The destiny of action is determined by external forces on which man does not have any control. This might be due to counteracting efforts of other or due to one's own past actions.[78] Tilak also takes *'daiva'* in somewhat similar sense: "...there are also several other activities in the world, of which men are not aware, and which are either favourable or unfavourable to the efforts he makes; and these are known as DESTINY; and this is said to be the fifth reason for any particular result coming about".[79] Tilak's understanding of the fifth factor is more appropriate and convincing.

All actions by mind, speech or body have these five factors. The *Gīta* mentions this theory as a Sāmkhya doctrine.[80] Śamkara interprets 'Sāmkhya' in the passage as Vēdānta and takes it as a Vēdānta doctrine. However, this doctrine of five factors is described in *Caraka Samhita* as a Sāmkhya doctrine.[81] Hence, it is a distinctly Sāmkhya doctrine and cannot be a Vēdānta theory as Śamkara views.

The *Gītā*'s conception of *Vēdic* sacrifices as an instance of human action deserves special attention. The origin of sacrifices is attributed to *Prajāpati* who created mankind together with sacrifices. *Prajāpati* prescribed sacrifices to human beings in order to nourish the gods. Gods, nourished by the sacrifices, in turn bestow all kinds of enjoyments on human beings whoever enjoys food without offering to gods is a thief. From food creatures come forth, food comes from rain; rain comes forth from sacrifice; sacrifice is born of action;

action comes from the *Vēda (Brahman)* and the *Vēda* comes from the eternal imperishable being. This is the wheel set in motion and whoever does not follow this wheel is sinful.[82]

The above theory of sacrifice is very archaic. Here, the sacrifice is seen as the cause of living beings through bringing forth rain and food. This idea of living beings supported by the sacrifices is an ancient belief, which is also acknowledge by *Manu Smṛti*.[83] At another place, the *Gīta* defines action in this sense, "the offering which causes the origin of physical beings is called action".[84] Here, the important point to be noted is that the purpose of a sacrifice is to support the living beings and sustain them. The *Gīta* supports performance of sacrifices for the welfare of living beings. Sacrifices undertaken with a view to upholding the cosmic order or the great wheel of the universe are devoid of bondage brought forth by actions because the motive of sacrifice here is not selfish but altruistic. That is what the *Gīta* means when it says that except in the case of action done for sacrifice's sake, this world is action bound.[85] Hence, sacrifice, in the true sense, is an action without attachment and selfish gains.

The *Vēda* prescribes certain sacrifices for personal gains such as obtaining a son, heaven, a village, fame, wealth etc.. The *Gīta* explicitly criticizes performance of sacrifices for selfish gains and individual pleasures. The aim of sacrifices is not heaven but to continue the cosmic order. The original sacrifices which once formed the collective activity of Aryan community were at a later period became pursuits for individual gains. The purpose of collective welfare was substituted by personal desires to obtain specific purpose. The *Gīta* seriously opposes the contemporary practice of performing sacrifices with individual motives and supports the older ideal of sacrifices for collective well-being and upholding the cosmic order.

As the Lord says, "no conviction of resolute nature is formed in the minds of those who are attached to pleasures and power, and whose minds are drawn away by that flowery speech which the unwise — enamoured of *Vēdic* utterances, declaring there is nothing else, full of desire, having *Svarga* as their goal — utter, a speech which promises birth as the reward of actions and which abounds in specific acts for the attainment of pleasure and power.[86] Actions with specific motives and purposes involve *guṇas* while the performance of sacrifices as a duty and for the welfare of the world is devoid of *guṇas* and attachment. Hence, Lord *Kṛṣṇa* advises Arjuna to rise above the three *guṇas*, pairs of opposites, and to be free from the sense of acquisition and preservation.[87]

A sacrifice which is performed with devotion and without desire yields no bondage to *guṇas*. In the case of such sacrifices, *Brahman* is the offering, *Brahman* the oblation, by *Brahman* is the oblation poured into the fire of *Brahman*. *Brahman* verily shall be reached by him who always sees *Brahman* in action.[88] Here the point is that when an action is discharged either as a duty or for the welfare of the world or with an intention to please the Lord, such action, being devoid of materialistic individual gains, does not involve *guṇas* and their products as a result. In such an action, the only point of reference and purpose being the Lord or *Brahman*, it is not said to be an action involving *guṇas* but an action which transcended them. Having transcended the mire of *guṇas*, it does not result in bondage thereof. Here we have a clue as to the notion of freedom in the *Gīta*. The point to be gleaned here is that the *Gīta* supports performing only those sacrifices which are devoid of materialistic individual objective and despises all the *Kāmya Karma* prescribed by the *Vēda*. The *Gīta* criticizes those who undertake *Kāmya Karmas* by saying - "Self - honoured, stubborn, filled with pride and intoxication of wealth, they perform sacrifices in name with hypocrisy and without regard to ordinance".[89]

Further, we find a wide application of the word '*Yajña*' in the *Gīta*. It describes various spiritual efforts as *Yajña*. The

Gīta refers to wisdom sacrifice, which consists in knowledge of the Self as everything, sacrifices to gods, sacrifice of Self by the Self i.e., subduing lower Self to the higher Self,[90] Sacrifice of wealth, sacrifice of senses in the fire of self-restraint, sacrifice by austerity, sacrifice by *Yōga*, sacrifice by reading and reciting, sacrifice by ascetic vows.[91]

The *Gīta*'s description of self-control, *prāṇāyāma* and other yogic practices, dispassion towards objects, restraint of senses etc., as different types of *Yajña* is noteworthy. It reflects the growing enthusiasm for symbolic spiritual sacrifices which were taking the place of ritualistic material sacrifices prescribed by the *Vēda*. Meditation and psycho-physical discipline were given more significance than the strictly ritualistic practices. Here we find the shift of interest, in the *Upaniṣadic* period, from heaven to freedom. While the *Vēdic* rituals aim at heaven, these spiritual practices help towards the goal of internal freedom. This freedom and internal peace find immense importance in the *Gīta* and it conceives freedom in a unique way.

Determinism and Freedom

Action is indispensable for all living beings. The *guṇas* born of *Prakṛti* would not allow one to remain inactive even for a moment.[92] The body which is conditioned by *guṇas* necessarily leads to some action or other. One is bound to act even for the maintenance of one's body.[93] While the *guṇas* make one helpless to do action, one's *svabhāva* or natural subjective disposition determines the way one acts. One's *svabhāva* determines one's conduct even against one's will.[94] Even a man of knowledge acts in conformity with his own nature.[95]

So far, the *Gīta* advocates strict determinism of action by holding *guṇas* as inevitable force and *svabhāva* as the unopposed determinant. Now, the question is how can a man attain freedom from *guṇas* and their attachment? Where is the scope for human exertions and teaching of śāstra? The scope lies in the fact that though man is inevitably lead to some action or other, he can nevertheless mould his attitude towards the action with constant practice and knowledge. Though one cannot physically cease to do actions, he can give up the attachment for fruits and thus avoid the bondage of *guṇas*. Man can transcend attachment to sense-objects in the form of love or hatred toward those objects by wilfull exertion, and by avoiding love and hatred one can be detached to action.[96]

Though physical abandonment of action is not possible, actions can be abandoned in thought and mind, and this is the only way to abandon actions. The Mind can exercise control over the senses and the intellect can influence the mind. Hence, Arjuna is advised to take shelter in Buddhi which can control the mind.[97] Before we further discuss freedom, let us first see how bondage arises and operates.

When a man thinks of objects, attachment for them arises. By constant brooding over objects, man develops love or hatred towards those objects. This attachment gives rise to desire for either to obtain or to avoid the object. From desire arises wrath; from wrath delusion; failure of memory from delusion; from this loss of conscience and once intelligence or conscience is lost, man loses everything.[98] In this way senses disturb the mind through desire and all the evils follow due to that. Desire which is born out of Rajas is the chief enemy. Rajas urges man to action through desire and attachment. Desire covers wisdom as smoke covers fire.[99] Senses, mind and intellect are the seat of desire. Wisdom covered by desire does not see things right and leads to bondage of the soul.

However, there is a way out. As the first step towards liberation or freedom, man, should first control his senses. Keeping senses in control, one should avoid love and hatred towards objects. When the dangerous senses, which carry away the mind of man, are kept under control, his mind would be steadfast and his wisdom would be clear of all delusion. The mind, which is restless, turbulent, strong and obstinate, is as difficult as wind to be controlled. However, by practice and by indifference or dispassion *(abhyāsa* and *vairāgya)* it can be controlled.[100] Unless mind is restrained, there is no point in restraining organs of action. He who, restraining organs of action, sits thinking in his mind of the sense-objects, self-deluded, he is said to be one of false conduct. On the other hand, one who restraining the senses by mind, even if engages in action, he is not bound by organs of action and is esteemed.[101]

The mind which is controlled leads to steadiness of wisdom *(prajña)*. Then wisdom, free from delusion, looks at things in the right way in equanimity. The man whose wisdom is steady neither loves nor hates objects, neither depressed not exhaulted in failure and success. He is called *sthita prajña* or a wise man.[102] This equanimity of mind is called *Yōga*. Only steady minded can acquire wisdom and only a wise man can meditate and only a meditating man can attain peace and happiness can be there only to one who is peaceful.[103] Only in peace there is an end of all miseries.

A wise man clearly sees that all actions are function of energies of *Prakṛti* and upholds Self by Self. He kills desire by subjugating his lower Self to the higher Self.[104] He is free from egoism. Free from desire, with the mind and Self controlled, having relinquished all possessions, doing merely bodily action, he incurs no sin. When an action is done without desire and attachment it is equal to inaction. He is liberated from action. Such a liberated man, even if kills all the people, kills not and is not fettered.[105] The man attains peace, who abandoning all desires, moves about without attachment, without selfishness and without vanity. This is the *Brahmic* state in which none is deluded.[106]

The clue to freedom from *guṇas* consists in the possibility of controlling senses through practice and dispassion. The *Gīta* prescribes various methods of self-discipline to animate this process. The higher Self stands as the goal to be attained and by recognizing the unattached divinity in the body one successfully kills desire. While the binding nature of *Prakṛti* suggests determinism, the unbinding nature of the higher Self suggests freedom. When the individual Self raises above the *guṇas* and seeks union with the higher Self, it is liberated.

Though *guṇas* lead to action, *Sattva* is the quality which helps the process of liberation. When *Sattva* predominates there arises knowledge and wisdom. Hence, though *guṇas* are the source of bondage and they also help in liberation. *Rajas* when dominated by *Sattva*, yields to the process of freedom. One has to develop a *Sāttvic svabhāva* or temperament in order to attain liberation. One has to make one's mind steady by developing *Sattva* which helps liberation from action while acting.

The concept of liberation according to the *Gīta* is not the same as that of Vēdānta. Unlike the *Gīta*, Vēdānta aims at total freedom from worldly affairs. However, according to the *Gīta* freedom from worldly affairs does not mean giving up active life in the world. Freedom only means giving up attachment but not rejecting the reality of the external world. It suggests detached participation in the world rather than non-participation in the world. Here, Vēdānta and the *Gīta* differ as to the significance of action and renunciation.

Action and Renunciation

As mentioned earlier, the words 'Sāmkhya' and '*Yōga*' do not refer to the systems of Kapila and Patanjali, in the *Gīta*. Though it incorporates the theory of *Prakṛti* and its evolutes, *Gīta* does not subscribe it to the Sāmkhya of Kapila. By 'Sāmkhya', the *Gīta* means philosophical and discriminated wisdom in general.

Similarly, though the *Gīta* is aware of certain *Yōgic* practices like *prāṇāyāma* or breathe control and *Dhyāna* (meditation), it does not use the word *'Yōga'* to denote those practices, which are later systematized by Patanjali. It uses the word in a broad sense of association, union, or devotion. There are two aspects of this *Yōga*. *Yōga*, in its positive aspect refers to the achievement of equanimity of mind and union with the divine higher Self while in its negative aspect refers to disassociation with lower passions, mundane objects of desire and bonds of action. With these two aspects, we can understand *Yōga* in relation to moral action.

Śamkara, in his commentary, takes renunciation of all actions as a necessary corollary to philosophical knowledge of soul i.e., Sāmkhya. Hence, he understands Sāmkhya as leading to or as synonymous to renunciation. On the other hand, he takes *Yōga* to mean devotion towards actions and thus incommensurable with philosophical wisdom. Hence, Śamkara views Sāmkhya and *Yōga* as two distinct insulated paths. However, for Śamkara, it is only Sāmkhya that leads to final liberation and *Yōga* is subordinate or instrumental to the former.

Though Sāmkhya and *Yōga* are mentioned as separate paths, the *Gīta* does not view them as incommensurable or opposed to each other. In fact, the *Gīta* unmistakably shows the unity of Sāmkhya and *Yōga*. Lord *Kṛṣṇa* says that it is children, not wise, speak of Sāmkhya and *Yōga* as distinct. He who is rightly devoted to even one obtains the fruits of both. That state which is reached by Sāmkhyas is reached by Yōgins also. He sees, who sees Sāmkhya and *Yōga* as one.[107]

So, Śamkara's analysis of Sāmkhya and *Yōga* as opposite to each other is not in the right spirit of the *Gīta*, though it might be on line with the Vēdāntic philosophy. The *Gīta* differs from Vēdānta not only in as much as it treats philosophical wisdom as not opposed to works, but also as to the notion of *Samnyasa* or renunciation of works.

Śamkara repeatedly argues that knowledge and works cannot be combined as they presuppose opposing notions of unity and multiplicity respectively. He also conceives renunciation as a natural consequence of philosophical wisdom of the soul. He relentlessly argues in favour of the view that renunciation means abandoning all works, even the obligatory and occasional duties *(nitya and naimittika karma)* prescribed by the scriptures.

The *Gīta's* view is quite different from that of Śamkara in this regard. The *Gīta* without ambiguity states that *Samnyāsa* is not abandoning action as such but performing duties without depending on or hoping for the gains. A *samnyāsin* is one who acts without attachment to fruits but not one who is without fire (obligatory duty) and without action.[108] Such a man is a *samnyāsin* and *yōgin*, who performs bounden duty being inadvertent about the gains in discharging them. Here, *samnyāsin* and *yōgin* are identified. *Samnyāsa* consists in renouncing love and hatred for action but not action itself. A perpetual renouncer neither hates nor desires and is free from the pairs of opposites and bondage.[109] *Samnyāsa* is abandoning interested works *(Kāmya karma)* but not work as such. Obligatory duties have to be performed without fail.

The *Gīta* itself an address to the dilemma concerning renunciation. Some learned men declare that action should be abandoned as an evil. Some others declare that acts of sacrifice, gift and austerity should not be given up. In this regard, the *Gīta* supports the view that practice of sacrifice, gift and austerity should not be given up. They are purifiers of men. However, they should be performed without attachment and being indifferent to the fruits.[110]

Abandonment of action is said to be of three kinds. When obligatory duties are abandoned out of ignorance, it is *Tāmasic* abandonment. If they are avoided because it is painful to observe them, it is *Rajasic* abandonment. *Sāttvic* abandonment consist in due performance of duties and giving up the thought of their fruits. This is the real spirit of renunciation.[111] As action cannot be physically avoided, it has to be renounced in thought by being indifferent to the fruits thereof.

Now, the question arises as to why at all the Lord distinguishes Sāmkhya and *Yōga* if they result in identical goal. The answer is clear — Sāmkhya and *Yōga* are distinguished only in as much as the former consists in theoretical understanding of the nature of the soul while the latter consists in practical attitude towards the world of action. They together make one system of ethical vision. Knowledge and practice are not incommensurable. Unlike Śamkara, the *Gīta* views theory and praxis as inseparable and necessarily unified. It does not sacrifice active life of man for the sake of philosophical wisdom but shows how the philosophical wisdom should guide the active life.

Central Teaching

The central teaching of the *Gīta* consists in its viewing ethical self-elevation as possible and its prescription of different methods or paths to achieve that ideal. The aim of such self-elevation is the attainment of steadfastness in wisdom and internal peace or the state of being *Brahman* or Brahmic state, the union with the higher Self. The Self is said to be both a friend and foe for a man, depending upon its role in this ethical process. If the individual Self seeks union with the higher Self, it is deemed as a friend, an if it seeks the bondage of *guṇas*, it is said to be a foe.[112]

The *Gīta* does not stop there but also prescribes various methods of attaining this ethical ideal. It speaks of philosophical wisdom (Sāmkhya), devoted actions (Karma *Yōga)*, mediation on the supreme Self *(Dhyāna Yōga)*, and worship of God *(Bhakti Yōga)* as the four methods to attain union with the higher Self.[113] Through any of these modes of *Yōga*, man can attain absolute tranquility of mind and soul.

As we have already discussed, the wisdom of Sāmkhya consists in realization of eternal and unattached nature of the soul. The wisdom leads a man to see all the affairs of the world as a play of *guṇas* and therefore to realize the soul in its transcendental aloofness. Such wisdom is said to be peerless purifier which reduces all actions of a man to ashes and liberates him.[114]

The *Gīta* classifies wisdom into — *Sāttvic, Rajasic* and *Tāmasic. Sāttvic* wisdom consists in seeing the one indestructable Reality in all beings i.e., unity in diversity. *Rajasic* wisdom differentiates and distinguishes various kinds of entities in all creatures and sees only diversity and multiplicity. *Tāmasic* wisdom clings to one aspect of Reality as if it were the whole, without reason and corresponds to a narrow conception of Reality. Among these, it is the *Sāttvic* wisdom which leads to the highest goal. It leads to equanimity and freedom. This *Sāttvic* wisdom comes through faithful commitment *(śradha)* to the pursuit of knowledge.

Such a wise man sees action in inaction and inaction in action.[115] He sees inaction where the unwise see action and vice-versa. He can be active in inaction and can be inactive while acting. He takes off notion of personal agency from the mechanism of action and is therefore not bound by it. A wise man is of the conviction that 'I do nothing at all'.[116] In whatever he does, he does not claim agency. He casts off both good and bad deeds, in the sense that he transcends good and bad.[117] He is self-content and is satisfied with whatever comes to him by chance.[118] He does not crave for anything. His engagements involve no desire nor purpose. He attains supreme peace.[119] He is called a sage.

Here arises an important question. As the *Gīta* suggests inevitability of action even for a sage, how can there be an action without a purpose or motive? Naiyāyikas, especially, cannot conceive an action without a purpose. Even the involuntary bio-motor activity serves the purpose of bodily functions. A voluntary action presupposes a specific purpose or motive for which it is undertaken, no matter whether such purpose is really served or not. However, when the *Gīta* says that a sage's action is devoid of motive, it only means that the action does not involve personal gain or purpose as the sage is free from the sense of agency. The action is not undertaken to satiate one's personal ego. The *Gīta* does not take love or aversion towards objects as a necessary condition for action. The *Gīta* teaches to substitute desire with devotion in the texture of action.

Further, Lord *Kṛṣṇa* states in clear terms that a sage should undertake actions with a view to set example to others. He sets himself as an example and says that though he does not have anything to achieve or attain in this world, he is still engaged in actions for the purpose of guiding the masses.[120] He also refers to Janaka, the kingly sage, who attained perfection through action. A wise man's actions set a standard for others to follow. Sages undertake actions being intent on the welfare of all beings.[121] Hence, sage's actions transcend the realm of personal gain.

Karma Yōga pertains to performing bounden duty and, in fact, all actions without craving for their fruits. Abandoning fruits *(phalatyāga)* is the key concept in *Karma Yōga*. All actions have to be performed, not for personal gains but with a sense of duty. When actions are thus performed with a sense of duty, they lead to the achievement of unperturbed mind and through it to the ultimate goal of ethical perfection. *Karma Yōga* is the art of performing action without being affected by them. It is achieving non-action through action. Here, both

Sāmkhya and *Yōga* culminate in the same attitude towards the object of action. While in Sāmkhya *Yōga*, the dispassionate attitude towards the world is attained through philosophical wisdom in *Karma Yōga* it is attained through devotion to the idea of duty. Action when done with a strict sense of duty, does not bind the Self. Except this difference in origin, Sāmkhya and *Yōga* are the same as far as the effect is concerned.

The path of meditation *(Dhyāna Yōga)* is another important method of self-elevation. The *Gīta* considers *Dhyāna Yōga* as a superior way, and, at the same time, a tough way to attain perfection. The aim of meditation is to gain control over the mind and to attain quiescence thereof. A yōgin's thoughts would be steady like a lamp in a sheltered spot which does not flicker.[122] Through the tranquility of mind, yōgin attains peace.[123] The balance of mind involves control over passions and external influences. The yōgin, gaining control over mind, avoids longing for the objects of desire. Without abandoning thought of objects, one cannot be a yōgin.[124] The mind, as a result of severe practice of meditation becomes single-pointed and becomes free from passions and desires.

Such a yōgin is unperturbed even in great distress or in pain. *Dhyāna Yōga* in its negative aspect causes severance with pain[125] and in its positive aspect leads to peace.[126] A yōgin attains equanimity when he sees Self everywhere and everything in the Self. He realizes ultimate truth through meditative intuition. He is called *Yōgaruda* then. This is the highest stage in meditation, in which the yōgin spontaneously relinquishes all objects of desire and desists passions and attachments. He enjoys meditative union with his higher Self in a Godly existence.

The *Gīta* is also aware of breathe-control of inhalation and exhalation *(prāṇa* and *āpana).*[127] It also speaks of offering *prāna* and *āpana* in the fire of restraint. Severe physical austerities are also referred to. However, these are not mentioned in the chapter on *Dhyāna Yōga*. They exhibit a rudimentary form of psycho-physical discipline which is elaborated and systematized later by Pantanjali. The *Gīta* holds control of thought through moderate discipline as the aim of *Yōga* while Patanjali holds absolute extinction of ideas and mind as the supreme goal of *yōgic* practice. The *Gīta* aims at controlled and balanced mental inclination towards the world through *Yōga* and not total cessation of the worldly thought.

Answering one of the questions of Arjuna, Lord *Kṛṣṇa* says that those who fail in this *Yōga* need not be disappointed. They will take birth in a wealthy family or in a family of yōgins. They will retain the memory of past life and will continue their efforts in *Yōga*. Meditation is praised as superior to knowledge and devotion to works. Mere knowledge of this *Yōga* is supposed to raise one superior to the followers of the *Vēda*.

Bhakti *Yōga*, the last and most important path enunciated by the *Gīta*, lays foundation for Hindu religion with its profound theistic inclinations. Though we find the germs of theism in *Puruṣa Sūkta* of *Ṛg Vēda* and later elaboration of it in *Śvētasvatara Upaniṣad*, it is the *Gīta* which advances a comprehensive theistic theory, incorporating the ethical conduct of man as its nucleus.

As the discussion on *Bhakti* necessarily involves clear conception of God and His existence, a brief description of the *Gītā's* idea of God or the Supreme Self is in order. The *Gīta* combines different aspects of theism in its conception of God as the source of the world, the creator, the upholder, the sustainer, the all-pervading, the transcendental substratum and as the liberator.

God is the ultimate source of all existence. He is viewed as both material and efficient cause of the world. *Prakṛti, Brahman*, individual souls, moving and unmoving world are the manifestations of His devine nature and parts of His super natural personality. He pervades the whole world and is still above it. He is both immanent and transcendent to the world. He is the father of the world, the mother, the dispenser and grandsire; He is the knowable, knower and the knowledge; He is the goal, the purifier, the sustainer, the Lord, the witness, the abode, the shelter, the friend, the origin, dissolution and stay, the treasure house and the seed imperishable.[128] He pervades the world but not exhausted in it. The world is only a part of His being.[129] He is the essence of all existence good or bad. All qualities and substances are eminations from His being. The whole world comes from and goes back to His nature at the time of creation and dissolution. God sends forth the multitude of beings again and again but He is not bound by the acts of creation and dissolution.[130] All beings rest in Him as wind rests in the *ākāśa*.[131] But He transcends all the worldly existence as the substratum of it.[132] He is the rapidity of water, heat in the fire and essence of all qualities and substances.

The above description of God in the *Gīta* unifies pantheism, transcendental theism and deism. A more peculiar feature of the *Gīta* is that it not only views God as the ultimate reality, but it also sees Him as a participant in the world of affairs as persion. Lord *Kṛṣṇa* is an incarnation of the supreme God and claims Lordship over the whole creation. He declares all the best things of a class as His own manifestation. He states that the unmanifest, unborn and eternal God incarnates Himself in human form through His divine illusive power. He also promises to do so whenever there is spread of irreligion and whenever the *Vēdic* religion is affected.[133] The idea of incarnation of God in human form is peculiar to the *Gīta*, which is shared by later literature of *Bhāgavata* school, and distinguishes the *Gīta* from *Vēdic* theism. God, in addition to being the transcendental source and immanent essence of the world, is also established as a personal being in human form capable of interfering the world of affairs. God is seen in intimate relationship with man as a friend, relative and preceptor. This possible intimate relationship between man and God is the central feature in the path of Bhakti.

The idea of personal God is the contribution of *Bhāgavata* tradition to Hindu religion. God in human form, though is somewhat inconsistent with transcendentalism, serves an important purpose. It is the ethical purpose of establishing personal relationship between man and God as possible, and making it the goal of ethical progress. *Bhakti* presupposes union with God not only as possible but also as desirable. It is the ultimate goal to be achieved.

Bhakti *Yōga* consists in viewing God as the ultimate principle of all existence and seeking union with Him by surrendering oneself to Him. When whatever one does, whatever one eats, whatever one sacrifices, whatever one gives and whatever austerity one undertakes are all done as an offering to God, God delivers one from bondage.[134] By realizing God as the goal of all activity, one transcends the realm of egoistic exertion and by overcoming the idea of personal agency in action and through surrendering oneself to God, man attains freedom from action and its bondage.

Bhakti also presupposes some personal qualities of God such as grace, compassion and love. God secures gain and safety to those who worship Him, meditate on Him as the ultimate.[135] God delivers even the evil minded if they surrender themselves to God. They should be treated as righteous for they are resolved rightly.[136] Even people of sinful birth — women, *Vaisya* and *Sūdras* as well can attain the ultimate goal through *Bhakti Yōga.*[137] In this sense, *Bhakti* is more universal and an easily accessable path to self-elevation. Due to this possibility, *Bhakti* has preferability over other paths of perfection. While meditation on the unmanifest is hard to achieve, it is relatively easy to surrender oneself to personal God through devotion. Even those who think of God on death bed are said to be liberated through God's grace.[138]

The *Gīta* mentions four kinds of worshippers — the distressed, the seeker of knowledge, the seeker of material gains and the wise man.[139] Among these worshippers, the wise man is more dear to God for he lives in constant union with God without a desire to obtain anything. Here, the wise man is one who seeks union with God through any of the prescribed paths.

The *Gīta* also refers to the worship of other gods and non-*Vēdic* forms of worship. Men of desires engage in worship of petty gods under the influence of their own nature. However, the supreme God is said to ordain their objects of desire, irrespective of the form they are devoted to.[140] Those worshippers are said to be the worshippers of the supreme God Himself though under ignorance.[141] Elsewhere, worship of *Yakṣas, Rākṣasas, Prētas and Bhūtas* is also mentioned. *Sāttvic* worshippers profitiate gods, *Rājasic* men worship *Yakṣ as* and *Rākṣasas* whereas *Tāmasic* people worship *Prētas* and hosts of manes.[142] Worship is also distinguished in terms of *guṇas*. *Sāttvic* worship is offering made by men desiring no fruit, in accordance with scriptures, with a fixed resolve in the mind that they should merely worship. *Rājasic* worship is undertaken with a view to rewards and for ostentation. *Tāmasic* worship is one which is contrary to the ordinances, in which no food is distributed, which is devoid of *mantras* and gifts, and is devoid of faith.[143] It is only *Sāttvic* faith which liberates the devotee from bondage.

The most important aspect of *Bhakti* is offering all actions to God and being unattached to both actions and their fruits. Those who worship God, renouncing all actions in God as the supreme and meditating on Him with exclusive devotion, are said to be delivered by God out of mortal *samsāra*.[144]

Any of the four paths mentioned would liberate man. Thus Lord *Kṛṣṇa* advises Arjuna as follows: "Fix your mind exclusively in Me, apply your intellect to Me. You will no doubt live in Me alone hereafter. If you could not fix your mind, then by *Yōga* of constant practice seek Me. If you could not practice that either, then you be intent on doing actions for My sake. Even by doing actions for My sake, you will attain perfection. If you are unable to do even this, then taking refuse in Me, you abandon fruits of all actions, self-controlled".[145] Here, knowledge, meditation, devotion and abandonment of fruits are shown as alternatives to attain the perfection. In this connection, knowledge is said to be superior to practice *(abhyāsa)*; meditation better than knowledge; abandonment of fruits is better than meditation. On abandonment, peace follows immediately.

Hence, the central teaching of the *Gīta* consists in its prescription of the above mentioned methods of perfection towards the ultimate goal of spiritual purity and absolute peace. What is remarkable about it is the way the *Gīta* weaves all these methods into a unitary ethical vision, conceived in terms of man's capacity to regulate his conduct for a better ethical world devoid of selfish gains and petty egoism.

Morality in the *Gīta*

According to the *Gīta,* a morally commendable life consists in discharging the normal duties of life without regard to the consequences and attaining tranquility of mind and internal peace thereby. In this regard, self-control forms the negative moral ideal while equanimity of mind and peace form the positive moral ideals. Further, moral value of an action is determined not by external consequences but by the subjective attitude of the agent towards the object of action. In brief, these are the foundational principles of the whole moral discussion in the *Gīta.*

Though self-control as the precondition for knowledge and liberation occurs in the *Upaniṣads* and other philosophical systems, it finds an important place in the *Gīta* and its moral teaching mainly insists on self-control. Many of the virtues enumerated by the *Gīta* pertain to self-control and thus are negative in character. Fearlessness, harmlessness, being free from anger, egoism, desire, hatred, pride, ostentation, arrogance, insolence, self-conceit, ignorance, sensesual enjoyment are some of such negative virtues which are conducive to self-control. Self-control is the first step in all the paths of perfection. Suppression of sensual carvings and control of mind have to be achieved necessarily for the attainment of *Yōga*.

The *Gīta* also mentions some positive moral virtues such as purity of heart, steadfastness in wisdom and *Yōga,* alms-giving, worship, austerity, uprightness, study, truthfulness, compassion towards creatures, gentleness, and modesty which are called divine lot for they help the process of perfection. Among these various positive virtues, equanimity of mind needs special mention. The *Gīta* gives a place of honour for equanimity, both internal and external.

Passions, desires and attachment are said to be mystifying or obscuring the faculty of judgement, *prajña. Prajña* is the mental inclination with which man attends the worldly functions. When a man is self-content and casts off all the desires in the mind, his *Prajña* will be steady and unperturbed. He is called a *Sthitaprajña* or a man of steady wisdom.[146] He neither exaults not hates. For him, all experience is ineffective transitory phenomenon. He is the same in cold and heat, pleasure and pain, and in honour and disgrace. He transcends all pairs of opposites and endures everything silently. This state of equanimity is called *Yōga*.[147] He is the wise man. He sees the same in a learned *Brāhmaṇa*, in a cow, an elephant, a dog and in a outcaste.[148] For him a lump of earth, stone and gold are equal. He is of the same mind to good hearted, friends, foes, the indifferent, the neutral, the hateful, relatives, the righteous and unrighteous.[149] The Man, who is subjectively equanimous in all subjective experiences and objectively equanimous to all the objects of the world, is said to have crossed beyond *guṇas* and is thus called *'guṇātīta'*.[150]

This equanimity should not be confused as indifference. Indifference is a negative attitude towards objects while equanimity is a positive attitude towards action. Indifference leads to inaction while equanimity, as a positive attitude, leads to well balanced moral exertion. In fact, an action can be judged properly only by a mind which is devoid of prejudices, preferences and selfishness. All moral contradictions primarily arise from these. Here, the *Gīta* exhibits a great insight into the nature of moral judgment. The *'Prajña'* which corresponds to the faculty of intellectual comprehension is rightly said to be covered by desire, preferences and others passionate attachments. When these elements are cleared off, the *'Prajña'* will be transparent and such transparent *Prajña* helps man to look at the world clearly as one can see the objects clearly after removing dust on spectacles. Hence, equanimity is the perfect moral character of the faculty of judgement which leads to right comprehension and right exertion. The *Gīta* recognizes equanimity of mind as the only way to peace.[151]

Peace is the ultimate goal of all ethical and spiritual endeavours. Peace is what aimed at by all knowledge, actions, meditation and devotion. The *Gīta* looks at it as the highest virtue and perfect goal to be achieved. In peace, there is end of all miseries. Only a steady minded *(Sthitaptajña)* can attain peace and to the peaceless person, there is no happiness.[152]

He attains peace, into whom all desires enter as waters enter the ocean, which, though filled from all sides, remains undisturbed.[153] Peace is the characteristic of Godly existence and divine life. Peace is the positive mark of liberation. Peace is thus called *Brahmic* state which is beyond delusion.[154] Peace is said to be the immediate result of successful practice of *Yōga*. The man who clings to any one of the four paths of perfection attains peace spontaneously. Knowledge, devoted action, meditation and worship are said to be leading to peace immediately.[155] Peace follows subjugation of senses and mind through any of the prescribed paths. Only a peaceful man can realize the ultimate reality but not a disturbed man.

The *summum bonum* of the *Gīta*'s ethics is union with the supreme Self or God. This is called liberation or ultimate freedom. The liberated Self is in constant communion with God and stays in the God's essence. Śamkara attempts to graft the Vēdāntic conception of liberation on the *Gīta*. According to him, liberation is necessarily the result of philosophical knowledge of the Self and there is no other means to it. All other means are only instrumental in gaining the philosophical wisdom. However, the *Gīta* widely differs from the Vēdānta in this respect as far as it understands liberation as possible through alternative means. Even on the nature of liberation the *Gīta* differs from the Vēdānta philosophy. Liberation in the *Gīta* does not means absolute cessation of body, mind and all physical phenomenon. It is not necessarily an after death achievement. It can be attained in the earthly life itself.[156]

The *Gīta* conceives liberation as union with God and cessation of rebirth and all that follows. The idea of cessation of transmigratory life needs a bit of discussion. Lord *Kṛṣṇa* time and again states that those who reach Him will never return, while even the heaven is subject to return. Those who follow the *Vēdic* prescription of sacrifices attain the heaven as a result but will be back to mortal world after experiencing the fruits of those sacrifices. Even the heaven is said to be pervaded by *guṇas* and thus does not mark cessation of rebirth. But the union with God, which transcends *guṇas* and their afflictions, leads to the cessation of transmigratory life. Liberation from *guṇas* and rebirth is possible through any of the paths mentioned earlier.

The question now is, how can philosophical wisdom, devotion to actions, meditation or worship explain the absolute freedom from rebirth? The clue lies in the *Gīta*'s conception of action and rebirth. According to the *Gīta*, just as in this body the Self passes from childhood to youth and to old age, so also the Self passes from one body to another.[157] This transmigration of the Self is due to the attachment it acquires through various actions and objects. As attachment leads to rebirth, non-attachment leads to cessation of rebirth. As we have already seen, an action without attachment is ehtically equal to non-action. In *Yōga*, the attachment is relinquished and thus action is also relinquished. When there is no action and no attachment, there should naturally be no rebirth. All the paths of self-elevation stop rebirth by stopping acquisition of attachments. This is what corresponds to liberation in its negative aspect. It is freedom 'from' rebirth and *samsāra* or transmigratory life. This is the negative side of freedom i.e., freedom 'from'. The positive side of liberation consists in the permanent peaceful existence in God or the higher Self. This is what corresponds to freedom 'for'. Lord *Kṛṣṇa* unambiguiously states as follows: "Having attained to Me, they do not attain birth again, which is the seat of pain and is not eternal, they having reached highest perfection.[158]

The Vēdānta, however, explains cessation of transmigratory life in terms of the illusory character of *samsāra* and rebirth. According to the Vēdānta, the world, birth and death are illusory phenomena caused by *avidya* or nescience. *Avidya* is the principle in which the phenomenal world has its roots. Even birth and death are nothing but illusions conjured up by this indefinable principle of avidya which is beginningless but not without an end. The beginningless indefinable *avidya* comes to an end on the dawn of right knowledge concerning *Brahman*. As a result, along with avidya, the illusory world of birth and death also ceases to exist. The *Gīta*, however, does not view birth, death and the world as illusory. It does not trace their origin to the indefinable metaphysical principle of *avidya*. The world and all physical phenomena are rather emanations from God. Hence, they are as real as God Himself. The attachment of sense object is caused by the conjunction of the Self with the corporeal body which is a product of *Prakṛti*. This *Prakṛti*, though said to be capable of detluding, is never viewed as illusory. The *Gīta*, thus, takes desires and attachments as given and prescribes definite methods of uprooting them.

Hence, the *Gīta*'s views on liberation are not an outcome of strict metaphysical deliberation but a product of moral reflection dressed in a religious garb. It is more ethical than mystical. The *Gīta* always talks about control over mind and never suggests, even remotely, extinction of mental phenomenon.

As far as moral action is concerned, the *Gīta* advances a subjectivist theory of morality. The moral value of an action is determined by the motive of the action. If the action is motivated by selfishness, lust or greed, then the action is viewed as evil producing. An ethically commendable action is one which is performed out of a sense of duty and without attachment to consequences or results. The consequences or fruits of an action have no bearing on the moral value of an action. The objective consequences of action are irrelevant as long as the action is done with the sense of duty or welfare of the living beings as its motive. The consequences affect the agent only when he is attached to the results of action. Hence, morality as a value is more a subjective truth than an objective quality. The sense of duty does not correspond to confirmation to external law but is a subjective attitude which is reflected in the performance of all actions.

The *Gīta* goes to the extent of saying that one who is without egoism and whose mind is not tainted, even though he kills all the people, and he is not fettered by the deed.[159] On the face of it, the statement appears to be bewilderingly a moralistic as far as it is extremely inadvertent to the consequences.

However, the *Gīta* means only that when an action is done as a duty and attended with mere sense of duty, without a selfish motive, such action is absolutely moral, irrespective of its consequences. If man's duty, without a taint of selfish purpose, demands killing of people, it has to be accepted as moral action. Precisely in this spirit, Lord *Kṛṣṇa* advises Arjuna to fight, without regard for external considerations but as a duty of *Kṣatriya*. This advise of the Lord is not only justified in terms of the ethical discussion in the *Gīta*, but is also based on the social duty of Arjuna as a warrior. Here comes the question of social conduct of men.

The *Gīta*, as far as social conduct of men is concerned, accepts scriptures and customary moral precepts. It explicitly supports the social and political system which have their source in the tradition. So far, the *Gīta* is orthodox in its attitude towards the order in the society. The *Gīta* does not suggest any disturbance in the existing social order. However, it prescribes a definite subjective attitude or inclination with which the social order should be adhered to. The duties demanded by one's caste and particular station in life have to be discharged with utmost sincerety and without a selfish motive. The adherence to one's duties should not involve any personal interest or purpose.

The *Gīta* ascribes origin of the four castes, which together constitute the traditional form of Hindu social organisation, to God Himself. Lord *Kṛṣṇa* states that He only created the four castes according to the division of nature and actions.[160] Though God is the source of the four castes, He should not be treated as the author of them. God is said to be the Creator only in as much as everything has its source in Him. It is the *guṇas* and actions which determine the division of castes. Duties of the four castes are divided according to the *svabhāva* or individual nature.[161] This *svabhāva* is a product of one's own previous actions. Hence, it is the law of Karma which operates in determination of one's caste and God is only the transcendental source of existence of the beings of all the castes. In this sense, man is the author of his own destiny.

The *Gīta*'s enumeration of caste duties is also interesting. Serenity, self-restraint, austerity, purity, forgiveness, uprightness, knowledge, wisdom and faith are the duties of a *Brāhmaṇa.*[162] On the other hand, Manu enumerates study of the *Vēda*, teaching of the *Vēda*, sacrificing, officiating other's sacrifices, giving alms and taking gifts as the six duties of *Brāhmaṇa*. These are rather social privileges in the guise of duties, through which a *Brāhmaṇa* makes a living. However, the *Gīta* declares the virtues to be held by a *Brahman* as his duties. They are more responsibilities than privileges. Hence, it is clear, Manu *Smṛti* and other law-books, being later works, show an advanced level of political consciousness, highly stratified social functioning, and strict heirarchy of the castes.

Bravery, boldness, fortitude, promptness, not flying from battle, generosity and lorliness are the duties of *Kṣatriyas*. Ploughing, cattle rearing and trade are the duties of Vaiśyas. It is remarkable that *Vaiśyas* are referred to as of sinful birth *(papa yōnija)* along with women and *Sūdras*. But by the time of Manu, Vaiśyas gained social ascendency and respect. Service is the only duty of *Sūdras*. These duties follow from the nature of an individual, in the *Gīta*. Manu, however, derives the social functions, privileges and duties of the four castes from the infallible sanction of the scriptures. The *Gīta* emphasizes more on the subjective qualities than on the objective scriptural sanctions.

By being devoted to his own caste duty, man attains perfection. Proper discharge of caste duties, in the spirit of worshipping the supreme lord, leads to perfection. One should stick to one's duty and perform actions demanded by it, in a dispassionate mode. The *Gīta* emphasizes the idea of *Svadharma* or one's bounden duty and any transgression is viewed as bad.

Better one's own duty than the duty of another well discharged. Better is death in one's own duty. The duty of another is productive of danger.[163] One has to stick to one's duty even if it is faulty, because all endeavours are surrounded with some evil or other as fire with smoke. No duty is absolutely faultless.[164]

Though the *Gīta* accepts customary moral law as far as the social conduct of men is concerned, it insists that these caste duties and other social functions have to be done with a pure mind devoid of attachment. The so called duty, if it is performed out of selfish motive, is as bad as any other evil action. Hence, duty is more an internal attitude than just a mechanical observation of ordained action. Though the *Gīta* refers to scriptures as the source of knowledge of what is to be done and what is to be avoided.[165] It prescribes, the specific attitude with which all actions, including caste duties, have to be discharged.

Any action which is characterized by lust, wrath and geed is held to be evil-producing, even if it is an ordained action. Lust, wrath and greed are described as the triple gate to hell.[166] Even sacrifices have to be performed as a duty, with the motive of welfare of the world and for the purpose of upholding the cosmic order but not for selfish gains. The *Gīta* explicitly despises *Kāmya karma*, even though they are ordained by the *Vēda*. Hence, the *Gīta* does not accept the *Vēda* as immutable in all respects. However, it does not revolt against the established social order nor does it suggest any objective change in the existing system. It only attempts to show how human actions, including ordained duties, can be carried out with a balanced mind in an unattached manner.

The *Gīta* does not advocate a strict code of moral discipline like the law-books but encourages a definite mental inclination in all actions. Though it does not give a rigorous scheme of individual and social behaviour, it distinguishes three kind of worship, austerities, food, worshippers, gifts, abandonment, knowledge, action, agents, intellect, firmness, pleasures etc., in accordance with *Sattva, Rajas* and *Tamas.*[167] Here, everything *Sāttvic* is acclaimed as desirable, everything *Rajasic* as marginally acceptable and everything *Tāmasic* is to be rejected as despicable. All actions and phenomena which are characterized or predominated by *Sattva* are helpful in the process of ethical perfection. Man has to consciously chose *Sāttvic* things in order to be morally perfect. Hence, man is volitionally free to opt for anything even though he is conditioned by his *svabhāva* to an extent. He has to deliberately attempt to demystify his faculty of judgement, *Prajña* through self-control and employ his moral freedom in the right path.

References

1. The *Gīta* V. 10.
2. The *Gīta* V. 13.
3. The *Gīta* IX. 17.
4. e.g. *The Gīta* II. 42-45.
5. The *Gīta* X. 32.
6. Cf. *Chāndōgya* IV. 1-4 and *Mundaka*.
7. The *Gīta* II. 46.
8. The *Gīta* II. 52.
9. The *Gīta* XV. 15 and XIII. 4.
10. Introduction to the *Bhagavad-Gīta*, p. 18. *Sacred Books of the East*, Vol. 8.
11. *A History of Indian Philosophy*, Vol. II, p. 549.
12. Śamkara's *Bhagavad-Gīta Bhāṣya* on XIII-4.
13. *Vēdānta Sūtra* II.3-45.
14. The *Gīta* IV.1.
15. The *Gīta* XVIII.42.
16. *Āpastamba Sūtras* I. 13.17.18: *Manu* IV. 123. 124.

17. *Ṛg-Vēda* VIII. 74.
18. *Chāndōgya* III. 17.6.
19. Cf. *The Mahābhārata* VII. 7662.
20. *The Gīta* X-37.
21. *The Gīta* IX-26.
22. *A History of Indian Philosophy,* Vol. II, p. 552.
23. *Bhagavad-Gīta Bhāṣya* on II.10. Translation by A. Madādēva Śāstri, p. 23.
24. *Bhagavad-Gīta Bhāṣya* , p. 25.
25. *Bhagavad-Gīta Bhāṣya,* Introduction, p. 4.
26. *Bhagavad-Gīta Bhāṣya* on II. 21, p. 44.
27. The *Gīta* I. 37.
28. *Bhagavad-Gīta Bhāṣya* on II. 10, p. 22.
29. The *Gīta* I. 39-44.
30. The *Gīta* II. 11.
31. The *Gīta* 13-19.
32. The *Gīta* II. 20, 21.
33. The *Gīta* II. 26-28.
34. The *Gīta* II. 30.
35. The *Gīta* II. 31-35.
36. The *Gīta* II. 48.
37. The *Gīta* II. 70, 71.
38. The *Gīta* II. 50.
39. The *Gīta* II. 16.
40. The *Gīta* XIV. 3.
41. The *Gīta* XVIII. 40.
42. The *Gīta* IX. 10.
43. The *Gīta* XIII. 19.
44. The *Gīta* XIII. 20.

45. The *Gīta* XIII.
46. The *Gīta* VII. 4-6.
47. The *Gīta* XIII. 30.
48. The *Gīta* XIV. 4.
49. Śaṃkara on the *Gīta* XIV. 5.
50. cf. The *Gīta* IV. 7.
51. The *Gīta* VII. 13,14.
52. The *Gīta* XII. 5,6.
53. The *Gīta* XIII. 33.
54. The *Gīta* XIII. 2.
55. The *Gīta* XIII. 17.
56. cf. The *Gīta* XIII. 24.
57. The *Gīta* VIII. 3.
58. The *Gīta* III. 15; IV. 32.
59. The *Gīta* VIII. 18.
60. The *Gīta* VIII. 20.
61. A *History of Indian Philosophy*, Vol. II, p. 467.
62. The *Gīta* XV, 1.
63. Katha *Upaniṣad* III. 2.1.
64. The *Gīta* III. 27,28.
65. The *Gīta* XVIII. 14.
66. The *Gīta* XIII. 29.
67. The *Gīta* XIII. 31.
68. The *Gīta* XIII. 32.
69. The *Gīta* XIV. 19.
70. The *Gīta* XIII. 22.
71. The *Gīta* XIII. 20.
72. The *Gīta* XIV. 7.

73. The *Gīta* XVIII. 26-28.
74. Śamkara on The *Gīta* XVIII. 14.
75. The *Bhagavad-Gīta*, Sacred Books of East Series, Vol.8, p. 123.
76. Cf. *A History of Indian Philosophy*, Vol. II, p. 515.
77. The *Gīta* V.14.
78. *Yōgavāśiṣṭam* II. 25 ff.
79. *Gīta Rahasya*, Vol. II, p. 1182.
80. The *Gīta* XVIII. 13.
81. *Caraka Samhita*, IV. I. 54.
82. The *Gīta* III. 10-16.
83. *Manu Smṛti* III. 76.
84. The *Gīta* VIII. 3.
85. The *Gīta* III. 9.
86. The *Gīta* II. 42-44.
87. The *Gīta* II. 45.
88. The *Gīta* IV. 24.
89. The *Gīta* XVI. 17.
90. It is interesting to note that here Self is referred to as '*Yajña*'. Cf. Śamkara on IV. 25.
91. The *Gīta* IV. 25-28.
92. The *Gīta* III. 5.
93. The *Gīta* III. 8.
94. The *Gīta* XVIII. 60.
95. The *Gīta* III. 33.
96. Cf. The *Gīta* III. 34.
97. The *Gīta* II. 49.
98. Cf. The *Gīta* II. 62-63.
99. The *Gīta* III. 38.

100. The *Gīta* VI. 35.
101. The *Gīta* III. 6,7.
102. The *Gīta* II. 57.
103. Cf. The *Gīta* II. 67.
104. Cf. The *Gīta* III. 43.
105. The *Gīta* XVIII. 16.
106. The *Gīta* II. 71, 72.
107. The *Gīta*, V. 4,5.
108. The *Gīta*, VI. 1.
109. The *Gīta*, V. 3.
110. The *Gīta* XVIII, 3, 5 and 6.
111. The *Gīta* XVIII, 7-9.
112. The *Gīta*, VI. 5,6.
113. The *Gīta* XIII, 24,25.
114. The *Gīta* IV. 37-39.
115. The *Gīta* IV. 18.
116. The *Gīta* V. 8-9.
117. The *Gīta* II. 51.
118. The *Gīta* IV. 22.
119. The *Gīta* IV. 39.
120. The *Gīta* IV. 22,23.
121. The *Gīta* V. 25.
122. The *Gīta* VI. 19.
123. The *Gīta* VI. 15.
124. The *Gīta* VI. 2.
125. The *Gīta* VI. 23.
126. The *Gīta* VI. 15.
127. The *Gīta* V. 28.

128. The *Gīta* IX. 17,18.
129. The *Gīta* IX. 4,5.
130. The *Gīta* IV. 14, IX. 9.
131. The *Gīta* IX. 6.
132. The *Gīta* VII. 30.
133. The *Gīta* IV. 7.
134. Cf. The *Gīta* IX. 26.
135. The *Gīta* IX. 22.
136. The *Gīta* IX. 30,31.
137. The *Gīta* IX. 32.
138. The *Gīta* VIII.5.
139. The *Gīta* VII. 16.
140. The *Gīta* IX. 20-22.
141. The *Gīta* IX. 23.
142. The *Gīta* XVII. 4.
143. The *Gīta* CVII. 11-13.
144. The *Gīta* XII. 6-7.
145. The *Gīta* XII. 8-11.
146. The *Gīta* II. 55-56.
147. The *Gīta* II. 48.
148. The *Gīta* V. 18.
149. The *Gīta* VI. 8,9.
150. The *Gīta* XIV. 25.
151. The *Gīta* V. 12.
152. The *Gīta* II. 67.
153. The *Gīta*, II. 70.
154. The *Gīta*, II. 72.
155. The *Gīta* XII. 12.

156. The *Gīta*, V. 19.
157. The *Gīta*, II. 13.
158. The *Gīta* VIII. 15.
159. The *Gīta* XVIII. 16.
160. The *Gīta* IV. 13.
161. The *Gīta* XVIII. 41.
162. The *Gīta* XVIII. 42.
163. The *Gīta* III-35.
164. The *Gīta* XVIII. 48.
165. The *Gīta* XVI. 24.
166. The *Gīta* XVI. 21.
167. The *Gīta* XVII and XVIII Chapters.

7

Conclusion

Foundations of Indin Ethics

Right from the *Ṛg-vēdic* times to the present times, the evolution of Indian ethical values is a continuous process which forms a grand uniform tradition, despite local variations in customs.

Ṛg-vēda is the fountain head of many of the fundamental moral ideas which took theoretical form in the later literature. *Ṛta* is one of such foundational concept. It denotes a universal order, both cosmic and moral. *Varuṇa* is the chief diety who guards *Ṛta* and punishes the transgressors.

Ṛta and *Varuṇa* are the most prominent in the earlier portions of the Ṛg-vēda which depict harmonious communal living of Āryans. The sacrificial rituals, which were primarily aimed at fostering *Ṛta* came to be identified with *Ṛta*. As the cosmic and moral order, *Ṛta* is identified with Truth. Thus whatever is false is called anrta. *Ṛta* is ensured by certain communal values like harmony, comradeship, equality, brotherhood, cooperation and collective living.

With the increasing warfare with aboriginal *Dāsyus*, *Indra* the war-god comes into limelight. *Indra* supersedes

Varuṇa and, along with *Varuṇa*, *Ṛta* goes into oblivion. Inclusion of *Dāsyus* as the fourth *Varṇa* into the *Āryan* society witnessed a radical shift in the *Āryan* religion, economy and world-view. End of warfare and rise of new social order brought creator gods and sustainer gods into prominence. *Puruṣa, Prajāpathi, Brahman* etc. were projected as creators and sustainers.

In the *Brāhmaṇa* period, priestly class engaged in fabricating detailed and complex rituals. Along with rituals certain moral precepts, principles of social organization, and theosophical speculations were developed. The notion of three debts, the concept of *Dharma* as religious duty, *Brahman* as the origin of all that is, castes and caste duties were all developed in this period. The *Brāhmaṇa* period marks a vital transition from naturalistic religion to theosophical speculation. This intermediary stage witnessed rampant ritualism.

In the *Araṇyakas* we find the beginning of theosophical speculations along with some genuinely philosophical questions. These rudimentary speculations find their culmination in the *Upaniṣads*. Theories of *Ātman, Brahman,* their identity, *Karma*, transmigration and liberation are some of the most important theories of *Upaniṣads*.

The *Upaniṣadic* theories of *Karma*, transmigration, *Ātman* and liberation are the foundational theories which occur in different ways in the Indian schools of thought. These are central to the whole spectrum of Indian ethical thought with varied treatment by the philosophical schools. Thus a proper articulation and development of ethical thought in India owes much to the *Upaniṣads*. Apart from the intellectual exercises, the *Upaniṣads* developed a moral perspective on life. They condemn formal ritualism and insist on knowledge. The *Upaniṣads* crystalized the moral concepts by making them part of their idealist world-view.

The *Sūtra*-period, which can be considered as the most productive period in the history of Indian philosophical literature, made creative use of the fundamental ethical concepts available in the vedic texts. This is the time various philosophical systems arose independent of the vedic influence. Heterodox religions such as Jainism and Buddhism too arose in this period. This period thus witnessed prolific flow of contending theories and views.

The philosophical systems borrowed certain foundational theories like *Karman, Ātman,* transmigration etc. and used them in their own ways to suit their metaphysical and epistemological purposes. However, the original meaning and significance of these ethical concepts is not lost but enriched. This is called *Darṣana* period in which the original *Sūtra* literature is expanded and commented upon by eminent exponents of each system.

The most important contribution is made by *Smṛtis* and Itihasas in making the original vedic morality and customs popular among Indian masses. They moulded the moral conscience of Indian people by controlling their social and political conduct, and by imbibing the traditional moral ideals deep into their minds.

The *Dharma* śastras were comprehensive in their character in touching the Indian ṣocial, legal, political, economic and spiritual life of the people. They claimed their authority in all matters. They derived this authority from that of the vēdas.

The social codes gave room for change and variation according to the times. They also accommodated local customs and other traditional variations. However, they are mainly responsible for some of the institutions which had adverse impact on Hindu society throughout the ages. They, however, helped in bringing stability and peaceful order to the society. They played an important role in establishing and administrating great empires.

The medical, astronomical, metallurgical and other scientific treatises, which were developed in the Gupta period, through enhanced scientific temperament, could not sustain it for various reasons. The Hindu society fell a victim to formalism again.

The Muslim invasions on India and establishment of Mughal empire created new history in development of arts, architecture and influenced Hindu ethos too. Both Islam and Hinduism were influenced and benefited by each other. Religious toleration and co-existence became superior values. But the cloud of ritualism and superstitions was growing big. The earlier humanistic values were slowly occupied by excessive formalism.

This was the time when Sūfīs and Hindu poet seers tried to inject human values into the Indian social life. In the place of ritualism and pomp, devotion and simplicity were preached. The fellow men are considered as representatives or manifestations of god. Love and devotion are eulogized. Brotherhood of men and the mercy of god are sought after.

The humanistic values and ethos are revived in the nineteenth century when India was again caught in ritualistic excesses. This marks the Indian Renaissance, father of which is Rājā Rām Mōhan Rōy.

The eighteenth and early nineteenth centuries witnessed traditional degeneration. Formalism, superstitions and cruel practices were having their sway. Social evils like *Sati*, child marriage, neglect of women were awefully frequent. The general degeneration in the Indian morale due to British rule and loss of identity were reflected in social life.

Though British rule had adverse influence on India in all the spheres, it also had certain accidental benefits. Through British education many of the Indian youth came into contact with the west and the modern western thought. Liberalism, fraternity, equality and freedom were the new ideals which gave a fresh breath to the educated youth of India.

Rājā Rām Mōhan Rōy was one of those who had advantage of English education and also had strong traditional roots. He reinterpreted the Hindu scriptures and showed that the real spirit of these scriptures does not entail brutal superstitious practices. By this time even British government was also taking interest in Indian social practices and made appropriate laws to curb inhuman practices.

Rājā Rām Mōhan Rōy established *Brahmō Samāj* which preached "brotherhood of men and fatherhood of god". His theological monism made him a religious cosmopolitan and resurrected the religious toleration. He fought against idolatry and abandoned all pompous rituals and festivals.

Many of the youth were attracted by Roy and joined *Brahm Samāj*. He also influenced two of great personalities in modern Indian history — Vivēkānanda and Gandhi.

Rationalising Hindu culture and reading sense into ancient scriptures began with Roy and was continued. Swāmi Vivēkānanda, disciple of Rāma Kṛṣṇa Paramahamsa, made Vēdānta a source of universal religion, equality, and national rejuvenation. He awakened the youth and the nation in general, with his influencing and thought provoking messages.

Tilak carried the torch of nationalism by revoking the grand Indian traditional ethos. Gandhi later took up the mission and brought India freedom. He made "Truth and Non-violence", the age old Hindu virtues, two powerful weapons in acquiring independence from the British. For the first time in the history of mankind was there a peaceful national revolt of grandscale on the lines of non-violent moral indignation and suffering.

Kālidās Bhattachārya preached *'Swarāj'* in ideas. Aurobindo, who is exposed to both western and Indian thought, revitalised Indian spiritual tradition on rational grounds.

The contemporary Indian life, though influenced by the west, still has not lost its identity. The ancient texts are still viewed with reverence and ancient moral virtues are still having their influence on moral life of the people. Religious tolerance and liberal ideas of freedom, equality and fraternity are finding stronger roots.

As the largest democracy of the world, India has its cultural and ethical roots so strong that Indian moral life has peculiar characteristics of its own. The popular morality and ethical beliefs have their sources in ancient humanistic ethos.

Today, the ancient virtues are still cherished as a part of cultural heritage. Throughout the long history, India sustained its ethical and traditional identity despite occasional relapses.

There are certain fundamental notions which run throughout the history as 'the foundations of Indian ethics'. These foundations give Indian ethics an identity of its own. They are common to all the systems of Indian thought and serve as the launching pads for further creative development of theories in the field of ethics.

These foundations are not merely part of intellectual or ethical speculations but form the nucleus of a living tradition. Despite variations in geographical and climatic settings, despite differences in local customs and forms of life, despite changes in material ways of living, the foundational ethical concepts are still meaningful in the lives of Indian people.

The following can be identified, in the light of analysis undertaken in the thesis, as the foundations of Indian Ethics:

Ordered moral universe
Retributive moral action
Eternal moral agent
Transmigratory moral career

Possibility of Emancipation
Authority of the Vēda
Immutable moral virtues
Fusion of Ethics and Metaphysics
Religion as a vehicle of change
Secular life.

Indian mind conceived an ordered moral universe in which everything material and non-material has its place. *Ṛta* as cosmic and moral order expresses itself through the workings of natural phenomena and the conduct of men. What is really noteworthy here is that there is no dichotomy between 'fact and value' or 'is and ought'. There is only one order which sustains, 'is' and promulgates 'ought'.

The western paradigm of 'fact-value' dichotomy not only deprives all values of their cognitive content but also deprives facts of their inherent value. This is a double tragedy.

The logical positivist, taking 'is-ought' distinction to its heights, stripped the world of all values and made all values mere matters of taste or arbitrary choice. Values are thus made non-cognitive and of no justification. Hence the ethical world is rendered impossible. Emotivism conceives no ethical world but offers a mere possibility of choice of taste. This impossibility of an ordered ethical universe is due to its estrangement from cognitive world. Thus, the fact-value dichotomy deprives us of an order moral world.

On the other hand, this dichotomy deprives us of even the physical world. The theory of value-neutral world made up of atomic facts denies Nature any regard for it. Nature is a mere mechanistic soul-less automation. According to the new creed of scientism, human and social development depends on how effectively we can manipulate the natural laws and exploit it. We achieved tremendous industrial development but at the cost of environmental and ecological balance. The scientistic inductionist world-view which puts man outside Nature as its master, considers Nature as devoid of reason and intelligence. The culmination of this world-view can be seen in the environmental crisis the world is facing today.

Any world-view which undermines the organic relationship between Man and Nature and fails to see the meaningful order in Nature is bound to miss the essential ethical significance of the nature. Our relation to the nature is not mechanical nor one of master and slave, but an ethically organic one.

In this context of loss of both moral and physical worlds, *Ṛta* is still relevant as an alternative model of man-nature relationship. Man and Nature form part of a greater order which expresses itself in and through nature in the physical realm and man in the moral realm. Indeed, there are no two separate realms but a unified physically moral or morally physical realm.

The notion of ordered universe finds its later expression in *Dharma* which replaced *Ṛta*. *Dharma* is a much more sophisticated rational ethical order which included man-action-destiny in its fold. *Dharma* as the ethical order rationally explains man's condition — past, present and future — in terms of his own actions and character. Theories of *Karma* and transmigration constitute the ethical nucleus of *Dharma*. *Dharma* as the essential quality of a things refers to order in physical realm and as the duty of man or as object of human pursuit has moral ramifications. *Dharma* is the order of not only material but also social and ethical reality.

Though Indian systems differed as to the nature of action, its mode of fruition and process of transmigration, they accepted *Dharma* as an inviolable ethical order. *Dharma* is more comprehensive than *Ṛta* in its appeal and covers all the spheres — social, religious and spiritual — of human life.

What is common to both *Ṛta* and *Dharma* is their autonomy. In the case of *Ṛta*, it is not guided by gods, rather it guides them. *Ṛta* is not born of gods but gods are born of *Ṛta*. The gods are only guardians or functionaries of *Ṛta* which is an eternal autonomous order. If we substitute gods with natural phenomena (gods are only deified natural phenomena), or if we strip the natural phenomena off deification, we have a quite naturalistic autonomous order.

Again, *Dharma* too does not require a theistic agency for appropriation of results to actions. As *Mīmāmsakas* show, actions generate a new quality *(apūrva)* in the subject which leads to future consequences. Or as the samkhyas hold, every action brings about change in the three guṇas which give objective results at a later time. The Buddhist notion of every moment giving thrust to a new moment and the theory that the new moment contains all that is there in the past moment reject the need of any personal god for an action to accrue its consequences. Thus, even *Dharma* can be well conceived as an autonomous order without any need for external interference. In this sense *Dharma* is a secular universe of moral action.

The idea of an autonomous, rational and objective moral order which meaningfully explains human condition and destiny, is the strongest foundation of Indian ethics. At no point of time, Indian mind could conceive a chaotic or arbitrary moral realm. The ordered moral universe is the hallmark and surest foundation of Indian ethics.

Moral retribution or fitting consequences to every action is another ethical idea on which the Indian ethical theories build their systems. It constitutes the core of *Dharma*, the objective ethical order. The theory of *Karma* conceives a morally fitting consequence or atonement for every action. No action goes without consequence: this is the inviolable law of *Karma*.

There are certain older beliefs which contend the law of *Karma*. One of such is the belief that father's sin passes down to son. This older belief in heritage of sin or transfer of sin appears to be founded on equating sin with material liability or property. The belief that son is only extension of father also seems to support this view. However, this does not seriously hinder later theories based on *Karma*. This view is not supported by philosophical systems.

Another exception is expiatory rights. Certain expiatory rituals are prescribed to avoid the consequences of certain actions. This appears to be not in tune with *Karma*. However, as rites are also actions they can be viewed to counter balance the consequences of the original action. Again, repentance as suffering atones the suffering to be experienced as consequence of a sin. Repentance as suffering substitutes future suffering. The subjective intention or will always characterizes an action and thus repentance and expiation can said to be effective.

The third belief which goes against *Karma* is divine grace. The theistic understanding of God as merciful and benevolent leads to the notion of saving grace. However, the atheistic schools did not approve such notions and thus this belief is not universal.

The knowledge of *Brahman* is supposed to burn one's action and effect final release. This view also appears to swerve the law of *Karma*. However, given the role of intention in an action, one who identifies one's self with the universal self ceases to be the agent of action. Thus one is not bound by present and future actions. However, the past actions sanchita *Karma* have to get fruition and thus one has to experience the world till one's Sanchita *Karma* gets exhausted.

Two ways or paths of action are given: *Pravṛtti* and *Nivṛtti Mārga*. In *Pravṛtti Mārga* one involves oneself in all material actions and physical life and takes responsibility thereof. One strives for active life within the moral frame work. *Nivṛtti Mārga* is renouncing active life by avoiding *Kāmya Karmas* or desired actions. The *Bhagavad-Gīta* offers a middle path of disinterested actions. In this path, one undertakes or performs an action but only as a duty. One is not interested in the consequences and thus not bound by them. So he accrues neither merit nor sin. This leads to freedom or *Mōkṣa*.

As to the causal efficacy of an action and as to how an action leads to consequences in the future, being separated by time. To this question *Mīmāsakas* offer the theory of apurva, the potency which comes out of performing an action. This potency resides in self and attracts fitting result at a future time.

Sometimes, *adṛṣta* or unseen force is assumed (by some Naiyāyikas) to discharge results for an action in the future. Buddhists conceive that every moment thrusts another moment and the new moment carries all that is there in the previous moment. Hence, an action performed is not extinguished but is carried till its fruition. Actions also leave dispositions which go long way and determine one's character.

Sāmkhyas too have an explanation that an action brings change in the combination of *guṇas* according to the nature of the action. The disturbance or imbalance caused by an action continues till the consequences are accrued.

The theists interfere god's role as one who accords results according to the nature of action. But this divine interference is not accepted by many systems. *Dharma* is viewed as an autonomous moral order and action is independently efficacious.

Another foundational concept in Indian ethical tradition is an eternal moral agent. The individual self or soul is considered as agent and this agent is eternal. The self only changes bodies but continues to exist to reap the fruits of past actions.

Hence, the self as an eternal moral agent has eternal moral career with possibility of regeneration or degeneration or absolute freedom.

The self is conditioned by its own actions and takes up new bodies according the nature of its earlier actions. The self, though cannot transgress the law of *Karma,* however, has freedom to change dispositions through intentional efforts and can improve upon its moral career.

Soul's bondage to action and its results is due to its taking responsibility as the doer and enjoyer. This constitutes agency of action. *Mōkṣa* consists in soul realising its own nature and abandoning the responsibility as an agent. This is not moral irresponsibility but being relieved from egocentric activity. This is neither negative indifference but positive self-denial in action.

The philosophical systems differ as to nature of self but all of them accept role of self as an agent in action.

The repeated births and cycles of life is considered as the moral career of the soul. Thus retributive action and eternal soul lead to transmigratory life of the soul. This is called samsāra or bondage from which liberation is sought. In liberation the individual self ceases only in the sense of its undifferentiated identity or merger with the universal self.

Transmigratory moral career appears to be a vicious circle that each life invariably leads to another. In order to explain actions in a single life, an eternal series of lives is assumed both in the past and future. There appears to be no beginning for this transmigratory life or *Samsāra*. If there was a beginning, what caused that beginning? How the self came to be associated with bodies?.

As knowledge causes release from bondage, the cause of bondage should be its opposite. Of course, yes. Nescience or Avidya is the root cause of this bondage. Due to ignorance, the soul gets bound to body. This is accepted by almost all the systems of thought. Each school claims that knowledge of their own system releases the self from bondage. This claim exhibits the emancipatory zeal of Indian thought. Sometimes the ideal of *Mōkṣa* is grafted on systems whether it suits them or not.

Whether the eternality of soul and its transmigratory life can be metaphysically justified or not, they have immense significance in moral explanation and endorse ethical discipline. Their practical use is, beyond doubt, worthy of appreciation.

Even Buddhism accepts transmigration though it does not accept an enduring self. This fact lays bear the ethical significance of the concept in moral explanation.

What is more interesting is that the theory entails drastic social consequences. The *Upaniṣads* and *Smṛti* conceive that one's birth in a particular caste is due to one's actions in past life. Thus, transmigration has its social ramifications. *Smṛtis* enforce specific duties and restrictions for each caste. The institution of caste allows lesser social mobility and one has to endure throughout life the miseries entailed by one's accidental birth in a particular caste.

The theory of transmigration is thus used to justify the institution of caste morally. However, scope is given for moral regeneration. The exercise of free will and intentional development of faculties brought upliftment in caste hierarchy. At different places, different castes dominate the social structure.

The theory of transmigration does not preclude the exercise of free will and moral development. Though caste system was stringent, we find many movements against this institution. Right from Buddhism and Jainism to *Vīraśaivism* and *Brahmō Samāj*, the anti-caste element played a pivotal role.

Another foundation of Indian ethics is possibility of liberation or emancipation, whether it is called *Mōksa, Kaivalya* or *Nirvāṇa*. This idea of *Mōkṣa* has theosophical and mystical moorings but influenced the Indian ethical thought as the highest ideal.

The ultimate ideal of *Mōkṣa* is supposed to be achieved through *Vairāgya* and *Sanyāsa*. However, *Gīta* offers multitude of paths to this ultimate good of Hindu moral life. One can follow a method which is suitable to one. *Karma Mārga* — the path of action, *Bhakti Mārga* — the path of devotion and *Jñana Mārga* — the path of knowledge are the three main paths to reach the ultimate goal. The peculiarity of *Gīta* lies in its merging *Pravṛtti* and *Nivṛtti* marga and in its positively active view of life.

Despite its mystical leanings, *Mōkṣa* served as an ethical ideal which entails moral perfection as a prime prerequisite. The prescribed practical side of *Mōkṣa* includes *Vairāgya* (disinterest), *Śama* (equanimity), *Dama* (restraint), *Uparati* (rejection of formalism), *Titīkṣa* (endurance), *Śraddha* (faith) and *Samādhi* (concentration). One has to cultivate these qualities or attitudes through *Śravaṇa* (hearing) *Manana* (cogitation) and *Nidhidhyāsana* (contemplation) of the emancipatory message of scriptures and master.

One has to practice *Yamas* and *Niyamas* to make oneself fit for the end. *Yamas* include *Ahimsa* (non-injury), *Satya* (truth), *Astēya* (non-stealing), *Brahmacharya* (continence), *Aparigraha* (obstinence from avarice). *Niyamas* include *Śaucha* (cleanliness), *Santōṣa* (contentment), *Tapas* (penance), *Svādhyāya* (study) and *Īśvara Praṇidhāna* (devotion to God). Apart from this, *Āsana* (posture) *and Prāṇāyāma* (breath) are prescribed to gain control over mind and body.

Imagine what kind of a moral being is made if one strictly practices the requisite discipline of *Mōkṣa*. Such an individual can never act immorally and he is free from evil. What else need any ideal achieve than this? Thus, irrespective of its origin and development and its theoretical justification, *Mōkṣa* held sway over Indian conscience as the ideal the way to which is itself moral excellence. Even if one fails to achieve *Mōkṣa*, one would certainly achieve higher moral discipline by just making *Mōkṣa* as one's end.

Dharma, Artha, Kāma and *Mōkṣa* are universally accepted us four objects of human pursuit. Except Carvakas who accept only *Artha* and *Kāma* as human goals, the whole Indian ethical thought is unanimous about the fourfold objects of human endeavours.

These four *Puruṣārthas* make one's life an integrated whole and commendable. *Dharma* is the fundamental *Puruṣārtha* which should run throughout the other pursuits. Wealth and pleasures have to be achieved within the limits of morality and as we have seen *Dharma* is a prerequisite for *Mōkṣa*. If other pursuits are attained without *Dharma*, they fail to be acceptable.

For example, corruption political or economical is bad because wealth is pursued outside *Dharma*. Corruption is pursuit of a secondary goal without adhering to the primary goal of morality. It is transgression of bounds of duty.

Similarly, prostitution is bad because *Kāma* is pursued outside the legitimate social institution for sex i.e., family. *Dharma* thus includes the attitudes, institutions and actions to which conformity is sought in pursuit of the rest of human goals.

To those who criticise India ethics as pessimistic, it should be reminded that we have not only *Dharma* and *Mōkṣa Śāstras* but also *Artha* and *Kāma Śāstras*. The Indian aesthetics, architecture, sculpture, dance and other art forms show that sensuality is never undermined but is an integral part of Indian life. Even temples depict sensuous life and literature is abound with it. *Manu Smṛti* says that the four pursuits have to be accomplished for a meaningfully complete life. Reclusion is not common order but is limited to a small renounced group.

The *Sādhāraṇa Dharma* or universal moral principles form the basis of society and they are always regarded high. The discriminative caste duties have become redundant in modern India except their informal relics in the rural areas. Still, negative caste discrimination is being fought out by the liberal youth of India. The virtues of non-violence, truth, self-control, contentment, etc. are valued high even today.

Another hallmark of Indian thought is the fusion between metaphysics and ethics. This is true even from the ancient times. The metaphysical and ethical ideas are fused together to form a unified system of the universe. "Truth" is both metaphysical and ethical for Indian mind. Real, ethical and rational are always considered as one and any diversity is not acceptable. Nothing can be rational if it is not ethical. Similarly anything non-ethical cannot be "true". This unity of ethical, real and rational is a rare phenomenon in the west where ethical concerns are viewed apart.

Another major mark of Indian ethics is its association with religious practices. Many of the ethical insights are put to practice in the form of religious customs. However, some of them became superstitions when their original meaning is lost. Through universal literacy programmes and adult education, the superstitions are being fought.

It is more peculiar that instead of religions being advocates of conservatism and formalism, religions in India are vehicles of change. Buddhism and Jainism gained ground mainly due to their opposition to excessive ritualism, violence, caste and other forms of social oppression. Not only aristocrats but common men and women strengthened these religions.

Akbar's *Din-e-Lahi* is introduced with the fundamental objective of religious brotherhood and tolerance. The sufi saints and devotional poets used religion for propagation of humanistic ideals, love and sacrifice.

Vaiṣṇavism rejected ritualism and insisted on devotional self-denial and spread the message of love for all. *Vīraśaivism* fought against caste system and universalisation of religious privileges.

Brahmō-Samāj and *Ārya-Samāj* disseminated the ideals of overcoming superstitious beliefs and aberrations in Hindu system. New ideals of secularism and nationalism are promoted through these religious sects. Humanism is advocated in the place of ritualism and universal faith is sought to replace religious fanatism.

Gandhi further strengthened humanism as a religion with truth and non-violence as its foundations. The ancient values and true spirit of religion are resurrected into Indian society. Religious harmony, cooperative development of all, secular education and opportunities, equality.

Socio-economic freedom, popular welfare, etc., are the modern values which have their roots in the ethical tradition. Safe-guarding these democratic values is a fundamental ethical responsibility for everyone today. Everything that goes against these grand ethical and traditional virtues has to be opposed.

The study of Indian ethical thought offers us a proper understanding of our present and to formulate our future goals. The values and virtues cherished in our tradition give us an identity and the cultural heritage should not be lost at any cost.

The ethical categories and concepts, when understood in their origin and evolution provide us with better abilities to understand our present moral predicament. To understand and analyse our present form of life, these ethical categories should be creatively employed.

The *'Swaraj'* in ideas can be achieved if we try to understand our life in terms of our own concepts and ideas than borrowing intellectual frameworks from outside.

We can always critically evaluate our notions and concepts with a view to develop them to suit our times and purposes. One does not become conservative by using native concepts and categories nor does one become modern by borrowing foreign ideas. What matters most is how rational and critical we are in understanding our reality and how can we foster the quality of our thought and life without courting contradictions and paradoxes.

It is sincerely hoped that this humble effort to explicate the fundamental notions in Indian thought help, to whatever extent, further studies in the field and open up new debates for critical development of Indian ethical tradition.

Bibliography

Aiyer, P. Sivaswamy., *Evolution of Hindu Moral Ideals* - Calcutta, 1945.

Annambhatta, *Tarka-Sangraha* / edited by K C Mehendale. - Varanasi: Bharat-Bharati, 1980.

Bahadur, K.P., *The Wisdom of Mīmāmsa* - Sterling Publishers, New Delhi, 1983.

Banerjee, Nikunja Vihari. *Spirit of Indian Philosophy* - New Delhi: Arnold - Heinemann, 1974.

Basham, A.L., *The Wonder that was India* - New York. Grove Press, 1954.

Bharati, Agehananda, *Functional Analysis of Indian Thought and its Social Margins* - Varanasi: Chowkhamba Sanskrit Series Office, 1964.

Bhargava, Dayanand, *Jaina Ethics* - Delhi: Motilal Banarsidass, 1968.

Bishop, Donals H., (ed.), *Thinkers of the Indian Renaissance* - New Delhi: Wiley Eastern, 1982.

Broad, C.D., *Five Types of Ethical Theory* - Totowd: Littlefield, Adams, 1965.

Brunton, Paul. *Indian Philosophy and Modern Culture* - Delhi: Bharatiya Book Corporation, 1981.

Chattopadhyaya, Debiprasad, *Indian Atheism* - New Delhi: People's Publishing House, 1980.

Chattopadhyaya, Debiprasad, (ed.,), *Studies in the History of Indian Philosophy: An Anthology of Articles* / by scholars Eastern and Western, Calcutta: K.P. Bagchi, 1978.

Chattopadhyaya, S., *Traditional Values in Indian Life* - Delhi: Indian International Centre, 1961.

Chattopadhyaya, Debiprasad, *What is Living and What is Dead in Indian Philosophy* - New Delhi: People's Publishing House.

Crawford, Cromwell S., *Evolution of Hindu Ethical Ideals* - Hawaii: The University Press of Hawaii, 1982.

Creel, Austin B., *Dharma in Hindu Ethics* - Calcutta: Firma K.L., 1977.

Damodaran, K., *Man and Society in Indian Philosophy* - New Delhi: People's Publishing House, 1970.

Darmesteter, James, (Transl.) *The Zend Avesta* - (ed.) Max Muller, F., Sacred Books of East, Vol. 4, Delhi, 1980.

Das, B.G., *Hindu Ethics* - New Delhi: Oriental Publishers, 1976.

Dasgupta, Surama, *Development of Moral Philosophy in India* - New York: Frederick Ungar Pub., 1965. 170.954 D26D.

Dasgupta, Surama, 'The Individual in Indian Ethics', *The Indian Mind*/ed. Charles A. Moore, Honolulu, 1967.

Dasgupta, Surendranath, *History of Indian Philosophy* - Delhi: Motilal Banarsidass, 1975.

Datta, D.M., *The Six Ways of Knowing* - Calcutta University Press, Calcutta, 1960.

Daya Krishna, (ed.,) *India's Intellectual Tradition Attempts at Conceptual Reconstructions* - Delhi: Indian Council of Philosophical Research, 1987.

Devaraja, N.K., (ed.,) *Indian Philosophy Today* - Delhi: Macmillan Co. of India, 1975.

Gambhirananda, Swamy, (Transl.) *The Bhagavad-Gīta* -Advaita Asrama, Calcutta, 1984.

Gandhi, Mohandas Karamchand., *Hindu Dharma* - New Delhi: Orient Paperbacks, 1978.

Gangadhara Sastri, Tailanga, (ed.,) *Nyāyasūtras with Vātsāyana's Bhasya and Extracts from the Nyāya Vārttika and the Tātparyatīka.* - 2nd ed. - Delhi: Sri Satguru Pub., 1984.

Gangopadhyaya, Mrinalkanti, *Indian Atomism* - Calcutta: K.P. Bagchi & Co., 1980.

Gauchwal, Balbir Singh, 'The Metaphysical Foundations of Hindu Ethics and Religion', *Philosophical East and West,* Vol. 16, 1996, pp. 143-160.

Gaurinath, Sastri, *Corpus of Indian Studies* - Calcutta: Sanskrit Pustak Bhandar, 1980.

Ghose, J.C., *Character of Ancient Religion* - New Delhi: Brother Pub. House, 1982.

Gough, Edward, *Philosophy of the Upaniṣads* - Rediscovering India Series, Vol. 4, Cosmo Publications, Delhi, 1987.

Gough, A.E., and Cowell, E.B., (Transl.) *Sarva Darṣana Samgraha* - Rediscovering India Series, Cosmo Publications, Delhi, 1987.

Griffith, Ralph T.H., (Transl.) *The Hymns of the Atharva-vēda*- Chowkhamba Sanskrit Series Office, Varanasi, 1968.

Griffith, Ralph T.H., (Transl.) *The Hymns of the Ṛg-vēda* - Chowkhamba Sanskrit Series Office, Varanasi, 1971.

Hare, R.M., *Language of Morals* - New York: Oxford University Press, 1964.

Harmann, Arthur L., *Problem of Evil and Indian Thought* - Delhi: Motilal Banarsidass, 1976.

Haug, Martin, (Transl.) *Aitarēya Brāhmaṇa* - Bharatiya Publishing House, Delhi, 1977.

Haughton, G.C., (Transl.) *Mānav Dharma Śāstra* - Rediscovering India Series, Vol. 30. Cosmo Publications, Delhi, 1987.

Hiriyanna, M., *Essentials of Indian Philosophy* - Bombay: George Allen and Unwin, 1973.

Hiriyanna, M., *Indian Conception of Values* - Kavyalaya Publishers, Mysore, 1975.

Hiriyanna, M., *Outlines of Indian Philosophy* - Bombay: George Allen and Unwin, 1976.

Hudson, W.D. (ed.), *New Studies in Ethics,* London : Macmillan, 1974.

Humes, Robert Ernest., (Transl.) *The Thirteen Principal Upaniṣads* - Oxford University Press, Delhi, 1993.

Jauhari, Manorama., *Politics and Ethics in Ancient India* - Varanasi: Bharatiya Vidya Prakashan, 1968.

Jha, Ganganath, *The Nyāya Sūtras of Gautama* - Motilal Banarsidass, Delhi, 1984.

Jha, Ganganath, *The Prabhākara School of Pūrva Mīmāmsa* - Motilal Banarsidass, Delhi, 1978.

Jha, Ganganath, (Transl.) *Ślōkavārttika of Kumārila Bhatta* - Sri Satguru Pubs., Delhi, 1983.

Keith, A.B., *History of Sanskrit Literature* - Oxford University Press, Bombay, 1973.

Keith, A. Berriedale., *The Karma Mīmāmsa* -Oriental Books Reprint Corporation, New Delhi, 1978.

Keith, A.B., *The Ṛg-vēda Brahmaṇas* - Motilal Banarsidass, Delhi, 1981.

Keith, A.B., *Religion and Philosophy of the Vēda and Upaniṣads* - Motilal Banarsidass, Delhi, 1976.

Keith, A.B., *History of the Sāmkhya Philosophy* - Nag Publishers, Delhi, 1975.

Khan, Ehsanullah, *Evolution of the Religious and Social Life of Man* - New Delhi: Bail - At - Hikmat Trust, 1989.

Koller, John M., 'Dharma; An Expression of Universal Order', *Philosophy East and West,* Vol. 22, 1973, pp. 131-144.

Krishnananda, *Short History of Religious and Philosophic Thought in India* - Shivanandanagar: Divine Life Society, 1973.

Kunhanraja, C., *Some Fundamental Problems in Indian Philosophy* - Delhi: Motilal Banarsidass, 1974.

Lillie, William, *Introduction to Ethics* - New Delhi: Allied Publishers. 1986.

Macdonell, A. A., *History of Sanskrit Literature* - Motilal Banarsidass, Delhi, 1971.

Madan, T.N., *Non-Renunciation* - Oxford University Press, Delhi, 1987.

Madhava Acharya, *Sarva Darsana Samgraha or Review of the Different Systems of Hindu Philosophy* / translated by E B Cowell and A F Gough. - Varansai: Chowkhamba Sanskrit Series Office, 1978.

Mahadevan, T.M.P., *Contemporary Indian Philosophy* T.M.P. Mahadevan and G.V. Saroja - New Delhi: Sterling Publishers, 1981.

Maitra, Sushil Kumar, *Ethics of Hindus* - Delhi: Asian Publication Services, 1978.

Matilal, Bimal Krishna., *Logic, Language and Reality: An Introduction to Indian Philosophical Studies* - Delhi: Motilal Banarsidass, 1985.

Max Muller, Friedrich, *Six Systems of Indian Philosophy* - New Delhi: Associated Publishing House, 1980.

Max Muller, F., (ed.,) *Śatapatha Brāhmaṇa* - Sacred Books of East, Vol. 12, Motilal Banarsidass, Delhi, 1978.

Max Muller, F., (Transl.) *The Upaniṣads* - Sacred Books of East, Vol. 14 & 15, Motilal Banarsidass, Delhi, 1982.

Meckenzie, John, *Hindu Ethics: A Historical and Critical Essay* - London: Oxford University Press, 1971.

Meckenzie, John S., *Manual of Ethics* - Oxford: Oxford University Press, 1977.

Moore, George Edward, *Ethics* - London: Oxford University Press, 1975.

Moore, George Edward., *Principia Ethica* - London: Cambridge University Press, 1976.

Mohanty, Jitendranath, *Reason and Tradition in Indian Thought: An Essay on the Nature of Indian Philosophical Thinking* - Oxford: Clarendon Press, 1992.

Murti, T R V., *Studies in Indian Thought* - edited by Harold G Goward. Delhi: Motilal Banarsidass, 1983.

Murty, K. Satchidananda, *Quest for Peace* - Delhi: Ajanta Pub., 1986.

Oakeshott, Michael, *On Human Conduct* - London: Oxford University Press, 1975.

O'flaherty, Wendy Doniger, *Karma and Rebirth in Classical Indian Traditions* - Motilal Banarsidass, Delhi, 1983.

Pandey, R.R., *Man and the Universe* - Delhi: GDK Pubs., 1978.

Pansikar, Vasudeva Laxmana Sharma, (ed.,) *Yōgavāśiṣṭa* - Motilal Banarsidass, Delhi, 1984.

Potter, Karl, *Presuppositions of India's Philosophies* - Englewood Cliffs, Princeton Hall, 1963.

Potter, Karl, 'The Naturalistic Principle of Karma' *Philosophy East and West,* XIV.1, April 1964.

Prior, Arthur, *Logic and Basis of Ethics* - London: Oxford University Press, 1975.

Radhakrishnan, Sarvepalli, *Sourcebook in Indian Philosophy*/ edited by Sarvepalli Radhakrishnan and Charles A Moore. - Princeton: Princeton University Press, 1957.

Radhakrishnan, S., *Indian Philosophy* - London: George Allen, 1977.

Raju, P.T., *Philosophical Traditions of India* - London: George Allen and Unwin, 1971.

Raju, P.T., *Structural Depths of Indian Thought* - New Delhi: South Asian Pub., 1985.

Ramamurty, A., *The Central Philosophy of the Ṛg-vēda* -Ajanta Publications, Delhi, 1991.

Sandal, Mohan Lal, (Transl.) *Mīmāmsa Sūtras of Jaimini* - Motilal Banarsidass, Delhi, 1980.

Saral Jhingran, *Aspects of Hindu Morality* - Delhi: Motilal Banarsidass, 1989.

Satchidananda Murthy, K., *Philosophy in India: Tradition Teaching and Research*, Delhi: Motilal Banarsidass, 1985.

Satchidananda Murthy, K., (ed.) *Readings in Indian History, Politics and Philosophy,* Bombay: Allied Pubs., 1967.

Sen, Amartya, *On Ethics and Economics* -New York: Basil Blackwell, 1987.

Sharma, Chandradhar, *Critical Survey of Indian Philosophy* - Delhi: Motilal Banarsidass, 1983.

Sharma, Peri Sarvesvara, *The Anthology of Kumārila Bhatta's Works* - Motilal Banarsidass, Delhi, 1980.

Sidgwick, Henry, *Outlines of the History of Ethics* -New York: Macmillan, 1967.

Sinari, Ramakant A., *Structure of Indian Thought*. - Delhi: Oxford University Press, 1984.

Singh, Balbir, *Conceptual Framework of Indian Philosophy* - Delhi: Macmillan, 1976.

Sinha, Jadunath, *Indian Realism* - Delhi: Motilal Banarsidass, 1972.

Spencer, Herbert, *Principles of Ethics* -Indianapolis: Liberty Classic, 1978.

Sri Aurobindo, *The Foundations of Indian Culture* - Sri Aurobindo Asram, Pondicherry. 1985.

Tachibana, S., *Ethics of Buddhism* - Rediscovering India Series, Vol. 18, Cosmo Publications, Delhi, 1987.

Taylor, Paul W., *Principles of Ethics; An Introduction* - California: Wordsworth, 1975.

Telang, Kasinath Trimbak, (Transl.) *The Bhagavad-Gīta* - Sacred Books of East, Vol. 8., Motilal Banarsidass, Delhi, 1983.

Toulmin, Stephen, *An Examination of the Place of Reason in Ethics* - Cambridge University Press, 1961.

Uma Gupta, *Materialism in the Vedas* - New Delhi: Classical Pub. Company, 1987.

Verma, Prativa, *Social Philosophy of the Mahābhārāta and the Manu Smṛti* - Classical Publishing Company, New Delhi, 1988.

Walli, Koshelya, *Theory of Karman in Indian Thought* - Varanasi: Bharata Manisha, 1977.

Whitney, William Dwight, (Transl.) *Atharva Vēda Samhita* - Motilal Banarsidass, Delhi, 1984.

William, M.M., *Indian Wisdom* - Rediscovering India Series, Vol. 1, Cosmo Publications, Delhi, 1987.

Wilson, H.H., *Ṛg-Vēda Samhita,* Nag Publications, Delhi, 1977.

Winch, Peter, *Ethics and Action* - London: Routledge and Kegan Paul, 1972.

Index